# The Best
## of
# Robert Carrier

ROBERT CARRIER OBE is an undisputed star of the international gastronomic scene and one of the world's most well-known food writers and restaurateurs. He ran two award-winning restaurants, Carrier's in London and Hintlesham Hall in Suffolk. Former food editor of *The Sunday Times*, *Harper's Bazaar*, *Vogue*, and *Homes & Gardens*, he is the author of numerous cookery books, including the cornerstone publications *Great Dishes of the World*, *The Robert Carrier Cookbook* and *The Robert Carrier Cookery Course*. He has received many prestigious awards during his illustrious career, including prizes from France, Italy and Germany.

# Other books by Robert Carrier

*Great Dishes of the World (1963)*
*The Robert Carrier Cookbook (1965)*
*Cooking For You (1973)*
*The Robert Carrier Cookery Course (1974)*
*Entertaining (1977)*
*Great Dishes of the World – new edition (1982)*
*Quick Cook (1983)*
*A Million Menus (1984)*
*Food, Wine & Friends (1986)*
*Robert Carrier's Kitchen (1987)*
*Taste of Morocco (1987)*
*Feasts of Provence (1992)*
*The Vegetarian Gourmet (1994)*

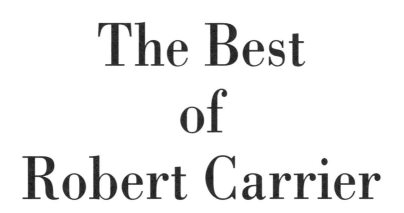

# The Best
# of
# Robert Carrier

*250 Favourite Recipes*

*from around the World*

BLOOMSBURY

First published in 1994 by
Bloomsbury Publishing Plc
2 Soho Square
London W1V 5DE
© by Robert Carrier 1994

The moral right of the author has been asserted
A copy of the CIP entry for this book is available from the British Library
ISBN 0 7475 1980 3
10 9 8 7 6 5 4 3 2 1

Edited, designed and typeset
by Book Creation Services, London
Illustrations by Sarah Maxey

Printed in Britain by Butler and Tanner, Frome and London

# Contents

Introduction                                    7
Soups                                          11
Starters and Light Luncheon
and Supper Dishes                              21
Pasta and Rice                                 49
Fish and Shellfish                             65
Beef and Veal                                  95
Lamb                                          139
Pork                                          153
Poultry and Game                              165
Vegetables                                     203
Salads                                         221
Sweets and Puddings                           231
Cakes and Pastries                            257
Acknowledgments                                281
Index                                         282

# Introduction

It has often been said that careless eating is as anti-social as careless cooking. And today, even a child should no more be encouraged to be indifferent to the flavour of food than to sing off tune. I must confess that I am sometimes surprised in France to see some tiny tot out with his family for a Sunday restaurant lunch, tucking into a sophisticated Artichoke à la Vinaigrette (or a Lobster Mousse) without a qualm. But why should it be so surprising? The subtleties of taste should be called to our attention early on in life.

Cooking can be a game in which you and the whole family can participate. I remember my own childhood in America during the early Thirties when the Depression suddenly took away those little luxuries which we once considered everyday necessities. My mother kept her family together with the wonderfully simple expedient of making her three sons as well as her husband join in to create family meals that were both inexpensive and pleasurable.

We all had our duties to perform. I was about six years old, and as the youngest in the family I had the simplest chores to do. I used to set the table for dinner – knives, forks, glasses, side plates, pepper and salt mills – and then wash and dry the lettuce, leaf by leaf, for the salad. My brother Jack, eight years older, prepared all the salad dressings, sliced the bread and then cleared the table after the meal was over. And brother Bud, the eldest of the three boys, used to help my mother in the kitchen during the week, while Sunday dinner was his full responsibility. Even my father was called into service every morning to make the breakfast coffee and beaten biscuits. He was justifiably proud of his batches of home-baked bread and rolls, a weekly ritual.

Ours was a family that revered its food. And every member of it was only too glad to contribute in some part to the effort and work involved to make such meals possible.

It was in those early years that I first discovered that cooking a new dish could

be an exciting adventure, one where intelligence, subtlety, a sense of poetry and friendship, could all play an important part. Few things in life give more real pleasure than sitting down with family and friends to a dish that one has cooked with care and attention. Such a dish demands to be tasted, talked about, compared with other dishes, other meals. It is, in fact, an experience to be shared. Just add a light first course before, a subtle sweet after, accompany it with a bottle of good wine and you have a meal to remember.

On a recent programme for Granada Television I prepared one of France's most famous recipes – one of the world's great culinary icons – and yet one of the simplest recipes to prepare that I know. It was a recipe that I have known and loved for years; one that has come down to us – unchanged, unspoiled – from ancient times: a simple vegetable soup made of French beans, white beans, carrots, leeks, courgettes and tomatoes – simmered (for minutes only) in vegetable stock. And yet this simple dish (half vegetable soup/half vegetable stew) achieves immediate greatness thanks to a simple homemade sauce that is stirred into it at the last minute.

The recipe? Provence's most famous soup, *Pistou* – a sort of French Minestrone. The sauce? A flavoursome blend of pounded garlic, fresh basil, pine nuts, Parmesan cheese and olive oil that we know as *Pesto*. The result? Well, if the delighted expressions on the faces of the camera crew and every one in the studio who clustered around the table to taste it were anything to go by – complete success.

And so the idea of this book was born – *The Best of Robert Carrier*: a compendium of my absolute favourite recipes. A book for you to dip into as you like, to enjoy through the years to come . . . to discover the delights I have enjoyed over my many self-indulgent years.

*The Best of Robert Carrier* is the result of years of travelling, tasting, testing and writing. The recipes in the book are chosen from thousands of cookery articles I have published in this country and abroad; from my many cookbooks (twelve, to date) that have sold in their millions around the world; and from my best-selling weekly part-work magazine, *Robert Carrier's Kitchen*.

I have included special star recipes from famous chef proprietors of restaurants around the world . . . as well as recipes for dishes that were firm favourites with diners at my two restaurants, Carrier's in Islington and Hintlesham Hall in Suffolk, and a selection of special dishes from my cookery school: The Carrier Seminar of Cookery.

Everyone concerned with food has

favourites – favourite ingredients, favourite recipes, favourite methods of cooking and favourite places to eat. So I am delighted to be able to share my absolute favourites with you – whether they include really simple dishes like a perfectly boiled egg (served with a wonderfully subtle green sauce from Tuscany) or an unbeatable dessert that combines the unusual flavours and textures of a hot dark chocolate soufflé with the icy excitement of coffee ice cream.

Some I have included in the book because of their happy associations: the truly Roman combination of paper thin rolls of veal wrapped around a strip of Parma ham and a fresh sage leaf and sautéed in butter and marsala, served in a famous Roman restaurant called Ranieri's one lazy Sunday afternoon brunch, to a suitably impressed Ava Gardner and Walter Chiari; and the thrill of first tasting turbot cooked in Champagne, one of the great specialities of René Lasserre at his restaurant Chez Lasserre in Paris, at that time one of Paris' most elegant restaurants. The occasion? The signing of my first French book contract. My host? My French publisher who, I later discovered, was the supremely elegant original of Françoise Sagan's story of a young girl's sophisticated love affair with an older man: *Bonjour Tristesse*.

Our likes and dislikes in food have changed greatly over the past few years. And so, I must admit, have mine. My tastes are for lighter fare these days, with shorter cooking times and a more healthy outlook in eating. So all these recipes – with a few deliciously wicked exceptions like the astounding *Daube de Mouton* (a leg of lamb cut into cubes and cooked in the lowest of ovens for four hours, so tender that you can almost eat it with a spoon) or the utterly delicious casserole of chicken cooked with twenty cloves of garlic – have been adapted for today's tastes, with the accent on flavour-filled recipes that minimise high-cholesterol ingredients and major on healthy, tasteful food combinations.

I hope you enjoy sampling my favourite recipes as much as I have enjoyed selecting them for you. Each and every one of them brings back so many warm memories of people and places and happy times around the table.

*Robert Carrier OBE*
*London, October 1994*

# Soups

*Soups – in the main – are not really my thing. The result, I suppose, of too many state dinners kicking off with a clear consommé of chicken or game, usually served lukewarm with a garnish of diced vegetables or thinly sliced egg roll. If only they had added zesty lemon dumplings or a spoonful of red caviar and a dollop of crème fraîche. But other soups turn me on: Spanish Gazpacho, Watercress Vichyssoise and creamy peasant combinations of leek and pumpkin or Italian white garlic and parsley and a sly drizzle of extra virgin olive oil. Or a poached combination of vegetables – marrow, tomato, onion, carrot and swede, cooked in a light stock, puréed separately into the soup terrine to preserve its rainbow colours and served with a pat of butter and freshly grated Parmesan for a final flavour fillip. These are the country-style offerings of the Mediterranean. All fast favourites in my country kitchen.*

# Gazpacho (Cold Spanish Vegetable Soup)

*Chilled Spanish soups on the Gazpacho theme – there are as many recipes for Gazpacho as there are cooks in Andaluz – come into their own as the first course of a sophisticated dinner.*

*Serves 4*

*6 large ripe tomatoes*
*½ Spanish onion, finely sliced*
*1 green pepper, seeded and thinly sliced*
*½ cucumber, peeled and thinly sliced*
*1 clove garlic, finely chopped*
*Salt and freshly ground pepper*
*Tabasco sauce*
*6 tablespoons olive oil*
*3 tablespoons wine vinegar*
*150–300 ml/5–10 fl oz chilled vegetable stock*
*1 tablespoon finely chopped parsley or chives*
*Garlic croutons*

Quarter and seed the tomatoes, dice the flesh coarsely, and combine in a salad bowl with the thinly sliced onion, pepper, cucumber and finely chopped garlic. Season to taste with salt and freshly ground pepper and a dash of Tabasco sauce. Add the olive oil and wine vinegar, stir to blend and leave to marinate for at least 30 minutes in the refrigerator.

Just before serving, add the chilled vegetable stock and finely chopped parsley and chives. Correct the seasoning and pour into a large soup bowl. Serve with garlic croutons.

*Robert Carrier Cookery Course*

# French Pea Soup with Vegetable Mosaic

*This is one of those 'show-off' recipes that is quite easy to do. The classic creamy purée of pea, potato and onion, enriched with beaten egg yolks and double cream, is garnished at the last minute with a colourful 'mosaic' of thinly sliced vegetable shapes.*

*Serves 4*

*350 g/12 oz packet frozen peas*
*2 medium potatoes, diced*
*1 large Spanish onion, chopped*

4 tablespoons butter
900 ml/1½ pints hot vegetable stock
(made with 2 cubes)
2 egg yolks, well beaten
150 ml/5 fl oz double cream
Salt and freshly ground pepper
Cayenne pepper

# Vegetable Mosaic Garnish

½ cucumber
1 large carrot
2 small turnips
1 slice canned pimento
1 tablespoon coarsely chopped parsley, or
chives

Combine frozen peas, diced potato and chopped onion in a small saucepan, or casserole, with a lid. Add butter and 150 ml (5 fl oz) of the vegetable stock. Stir; cover and allow vegetables to 'sweat' over a medium heat for 5 minutes; remove cover and continue to simmer, stirring, to ensure vegetables don't stick to bottom of pan, until onions and potatoes are soft, adding just enough stock, from time to time, if necessary, to keep vegetables moist.

Purée vegetables in electric blender or food processor.

Combine beaten egg yolks with double cream in the top of a double saucepan; add puréed vegetables and remaining hot stock (keeping 6 tablespoons stock for vegetable garnish) and cook over simmering water, stirring, until sauce is thick and smooth.

*Note:* do not let soup come to the boil, or eggs will curdle. Season with salt and freshly ground pepper and cayenne pepper to taste.

## *To prepare Vegetable Mosaic Garnish*

Peel and seed cucumber and cut into very thin matchstick-size strips. Cut carrot and turnips into very thin slices. Cut each slice into 'flower' or 'leaf' shapes with small aspic or cookie cutters.

Simmer prepared vegetables in reserved stock until cooked through, but still crisp. Keep warm. Cut 'flower' shapes from pimento and add to pan with other vegetables.

## *To serve Soup*

Just before serving, warm soup through, being careful not to let it come to the boil. Pour into individual bowls and add Vegetable Mosaic Garnish gently to each bowl with a spatula so that garnish stays on top. Sprinkle with a pinch of coarsely chopped herbs and serve immediately.

*Robert Carrier's Kitchen*

# Fresh Lettuce Soup

*Serves 6*

*2 heads of lettuce*
*4 tablespoons butter*
*2 shallots, finely chopped*
*100 g/4 oz frozen leaf spinach*
*750 ml/1¼ pints well-flavoured*
*vegetable stock*
*Salt and freshly ground pepper*
*Crushed dried chillies*
*2 tablespoons finely chopped parsley*
*2 tablespoons finely chopped chervil*

Wash the lettuces and dry well. Remove any discoloured leaves and hard stalks, and shred the remaining leaves.

Melt the butter in a saucepan and add the finely chopped shallots; cook over a medium heat for 5 to 7 minutes, or until just soft, stirring occasionally with a wooden spoon. Add the shredded lettuce and leaf spinach and simmer for 10 minutes, stirring frequently.

Add the vegetable stock and bring to the boil. Reduce the heat, cover and simmer gently for 15 minutes. Season with salt and freshly ground pepper to taste.

Purée the soup in a blender until smooth and return it to a clean saucepan. Stir in the finely chopped parsley and chervil and reheat. Correct the seasoning and serve immediately.

*The Robert Carrier Cookery Course*

# Chicken Consommé with Lemon Dumplings

*Serves 6*

*900 ml/1½ pints hot chicken consommé*
*4 sprigs of watercress*
*2 carrots, thinly sliced*
*2–4 celery stalks, thinly sliced*
*3–4 green spring onions, thinly sliced*
*Crushed dried chillies*
*2–3 tablespoons Madeira*
*Finely chopped parsley*

## Lemon Dumplings

*50 g/2 oz stale coarse breadcrumbs*
*¼ teaspoon grated lemon rind*
*Generous pinch of dried thyme*
*1 teaspoon finely chopped parsley*
*2 tablespoons softened butter*
*1 egg yolk*
*Salt and freshly ground pepper*
*Pinch of ground nutmeg*

### *To make Lemon Dumplings*

Knead first 6 ingredients to a smooth paste and season with salt and freshly ground pepper, to taste, and a pinch of ground nutmeg. Roll mixture into a sausage shape. Chill for at least 1 hour. Divide mixture into 36 portions, then roll into neat balls. Makes

36 dumplings. Poach dumplings in gently simmering salted water for 15 to 20 minutes, or until light and tender. Drain.

### To make Consommé

Remove watercress leaves from stems and reserve. Simmer thinly sliced carrots, celery and green spring onions in two-thirds of the hot chicken consommé for 8 to 10 minutes, or until vegetables are tender. Combine vegetables and their juices with remaining consommé and stir in reserved watercress leaves and Madeira. Serve consommé hot, each portion garnished with 6 Lemon Dumplings and a sprinkling of finely chopped parsley.

*Woman's Own*

# Zuppa di Fagioli

*Italian peasant fare at its optimum best: a purée of cooked white beans studded with whole cooked beans and dressed at the last moment with extra virgin oil, finely chopped garlic and parsley.*

*Serves 4 to 6*

*225 g/8 oz white beans*
*1.5 l/2½ pints water*
*Salt and freshly ground pepper*
*4 tablespoons olive oil*
*2 cloves garlic, chopped*
*5 tablespoons chopped parsley*

Soak beans overnight in cold water. Drain and put them into a stock-pot with 1.5 l (2½ pints) cold water. Bring to the boil, then lower heat and simmer beans as slowly as possible for 2 hours, or until they are tender. Remove half the beans, blend them to a smooth purée in an electric blender (or press them through a fine sieve) and add this purée to the soup. Add reserved beans to soup and season with salt and freshly ground pepper to taste, and heat through.

Heat olive oil in a small saucepan and simmer chopped garlic until just golden. Add chopped parsley and pour it into the soup. Serve very hot.

*The Sunday Times*

# Vernon Jarratt's Leek and Pumpkin Soup

*Vernon Jarratt, self-taught restaurateur, owner of one of the finest restaurants in Rome, was a dab hand at making elegant fare out of peasant ingredients. His delicious version of pumpkin and leek soup is a case in point.*

*Serves 4 to 6*

450 g/1 lb pumpkin
225 g/8 oz potatoes
1 Spanish onion
50 g/2 oz butter
100 g/4 oz fresh haricot or broad beans
600 ml/1 pint milk
Salt and cayenne pepper
50 g/2 oz leek, cut in strips
600 ml/1 pint hot chicken stock
150 ml/5 fl oz double cream
100 g/4 oz boiled rice
2 tablespoons chopped chervil or parsley

Peel and dice pumpkin and potatoes. Chop onion and simmer in half the butter until golden; add diced pumpkin and potatoes, beans and milk. Bring to the boil and simmer for 45 minutes, stirring from time to time, to prevent scorching. Strain through a fine sieve into a clean saucepan; add salt and cayenne pepper to taste.

Cut leeks into fine strips and 'melt' in the remaining butter. Add to the soup, along with hot chicken stock, and bring slowly to the boil. Just before serving, stir in cream, boiled rice and chopped chervil or parsley.

*Vogue*

# Argentinian Pumpkin Soup

*Many years ago, in New York, there was a restaurant devoted to the folk foods and arts of South America. This orange-tinted soup was one of the mainstays of La Fonda del Sol. I like to serve it when the first pumpkins come into the shops.*

*Serves 6*

1 kg/2½ lb
1 l/1¾ pints chicken stock
1 medium onion, chopped
6 spring onions, chopped
4 tomatoes, cut in quarters
300 ml/10 fl oz light cream
Salt and freshly ground pepper
Crushed dried chillies

### Garnish
150 ml/¼ pint crème fraîche
6 spring onion (green parts only) cut into
6 mm/¼ in segments
18 small fresh coriander leaves

Cut pumpkin in pieces. In a large saucepan, combine pumpkin pieces, chicken stock, chopped onion and spring onions and tomatoes and simmer over a low heat until vegetables are tender. Cool until warm.

In an electric food processor (or blender) process (or blend) until smooth. Add light cream and salt, freshly ground pepper and crushed dried chillies (be generous here, South American dishes are highly spiced) and process (or blend) again. Chill.

When ready to serve: pour chilled soup into pre-chilled soup bowls or cups. Just before serving, add a dollop of chilled crème fraîche to each serving; sprinkle with green onion top segments and fresh coriander leaves and serve immediately.

*The Sunday Times*

# La Soupe au Pistou

*Pistou is one of the great soups of France. A Provençal invention with ancient ties to Liguria on the Italian coast, this lovely green-tinted soup is a winter standby throughout all Mediterranean France.*

*Serves 4 to 6*

*450 g/1 lb dried haricot beans*
*450 g/1 lb French beans*
*2 courgettes, sliced*
*4 medium-sized carrots, sliced*
*2 leeks, sliced*
*2.5 l/4 pints boiling water*
*Salt and freshly ground pepper*
*Crushed dried chillies*
*Freshly grated Parmesan*

## For the Pistou Sauce

*8 large cloves garlic*
*8 sprigs fresh basil*
*Olive oil*
*8 tablespoons freshly grated Parmesan*

Soak the dried haricot beans overnight. Cut the French beans into 18mm (¾ in) slices and put them, with the haricot beans, sliced courgettes, carrots, potatoes and leeks into 2.5 l (4 pints) of boiling water. Season with salt, freshly ground pepper and crushed dried chilles, to taste, and let them cook fairly quickly. When the vegetables are cooked, add the Pistou Sauce and cook gently for 5 minutes more. Serve this hearty soup with grated Parmesan.

### *To make Pistou Sauce*

Mash the garlic cloves in a mortar; add the fresh basil and mash it with the garlic. Add a glass of olive oil, little by little, to this sauce and blend thoroughly. Then add the grated Parmesan and pound smooth.

*Great Dishes of the World*

# Watercress Vichyssoise

*Serves 6*

*6 large leeks (white parts only)*
*4 tablespoons butter*
*4 medium potatoes*
*1 l/1¾ pints chicken stock*
*Salt and freshly ground pepper*
*Finely grated nutmeg*
*150 ml/5 fl oz double cream*
*6 tablespoons finely chopped watercress leaves*

Cut the green tops from the leeks and cut the white parts into 2.5 cm (1 in) lengths. Sauté the white parts gently in butter until soft. Do not allow to brown. Peel and slice potatoes and add to leeks with chicken stock, and salt, freshly ground pepper and finely grated nutmeg, to taste, and simmer until vegetables are cooked. Force the vegetables and stock through a fine sieve; add double cream; cook and chill. When ready to serve, whisk in 4 tablespoons finely chopped watercress leaves; pour into individual soup bowls and sprinkle with finely chopped watercress leaves.

*Harper's Bazaar*

# Soupe de Poissons 'Fifine'

*Serves 6*

*1–1.5 kg/2½–3 lb fish (choose 3 or 4 varieties of exotic fish, now available in supermarkets and speciality fish shops: rouget, monkfish, sea bass, red snapper, grouper, emperor bream, perch and a slice or two of eel, if possible)*
*2–3 tablespoons olive oil per person*
*2–3 Spanish onions, sliced*
*2–3 cloves garlic, chopped*
*6 ripe tomatoes, seeded and coarsely chopped*
*1 bouquet garni (parsley, thyme, rosemary, dried fennel)*
*1 bay leaf*
*3 l/2½ quarts water*
*Salt and freshly ground pepper*
*½–¾ teaspoon saffron*
*1 small dried hot red pepper, chopped*
*Freshly grated Parmesan*
*Stale French bread, sliced and rubbed with garlic*

In a large, thick-bottomed casserole, heat olive oil. Add sliced onions and sauté, stirring, until onions are transparent. Add chopped garlic, seeded and chopped tomatoes, *bouquet garni* and bay leaf, and simmer, stirring

frequently, until lightly browned. Then add fish and continue to cook, stirring constantly, until the fish are tender.

Add water and season with salt, saffron and chopped hot red pepper and bring to the boil. Skim and cook over a fairly high heat for 20 minutes. Strain well, pressing all the fish and vegetable juices through a sieve. Reheat and serve the soup in a large bowl, accompanied by freshly grated cheese and rounds of stale French bread rubbed with garlic.

*The Robert Carrier Cookbook*

# Rich Lobster Soup

*Serves 4*

*50 g/2 oz raw lobster meat
(from the small claw)
300 ml/10 fl oz fish stock
½ lobster shell
175 ml/7 fl oz dry white wine
2 teaspoons lemon juice
1 teaspoon butter
1 shallot, finely chopped
450 ml/15 fl oz double cream
50 ml/2 fl oz Lobster Glaze
(for recipe, see below)
100 g/4 oz cold butter, diced
Freshly ground pepper
Cayenne pepper*

Poach the lobster meat in fish stock to cover for about 10 minutes, or until it flakes. Drain and reserve.

Meanwhile, in a separate saucepan, melt the butter and sauté the finely chopped shallot for 1 to 2 minutes, until transparent. Add the double cream and simmer for 5 minutes. Strain the juices from the cooked shell into the cream, discarding the shell, and stir in the Lobster Glaze (see below). Remove the pan from the heat and gradually whisk in the cold, diced butter, piece by piece.

Reheat gently, add the remaining lemon juice and season to taste with freshly ground pepper and cayenne pepper.

Cut the cooked lobster meat into four small slices, about 10 g (½ oz) each, and place them in 4 individual, heated soup bowls. Shred each slice gently with 2 forks. Spoon the hot soup over the lobster meat and serve immediately.

## Lobster Glaze

Put the lobster shell, dry white wine, fish stock and 1 teaspoon lemon juice in another large saucepan. Bring to the boil and boil for 10 minutes, or until reduced to 50 ml (2 fl oz).

*Robert Carrier's Kitchen*

# Spinach and Oyster Soup

*Wine-poached fresh oysters, little green spinach packets (in the form of oysters) and caviar make this one of the most glamorous recipes in the book. For a fresh-tasting soup when it is time to pull out all the stops – this is a world beater.*

*Serves 8*

*60 g/2½ oz butter*
*1 onion, finely chopped*
*1 stalk celery, finely chopped*
*1 small carrot, finely chopped*
*4 tablespoons chopped parsley*
*50 g/2 oz flour*
*900 ml/1½ pints fish stock*
*16 oysters*
*2 tablespoons dry white wine*
*75 g/3 oz spinach*
*300 ml/12 fl oz double cream*
*Lemon juice*
*Salt and fresh ground pepper*
*Pinch crushed dried chillies*
*2–4 teaspoons caviar*

In a saucepan melt 50 g (2 oz) butter. Add the chopped onion, celery, carrot and parsley, cover and simmer for 5 minutes, until soft. Add the flour and cook, stirring, over a low heat for 1 to 2 minutes, without allowing it to colour. Gradually stir in the fish stock and simmer, stirring occasionally, for 5 minutes, until thickened and no longer tasting of flour.

Meanwhile, open the oysters over a shallow bowl to catch the juices. Using an oyster knife or a heavy, short-bladed knife, insert the blade into the hinge of each one and sever it. Reserve the oyster meats in a saucepan; strain oyster juices into a small bowl.

Add the white wine to the oysters, cover and simmer for 1 minute. Remove from the heat and keep warm. Wash the spinach leaves and remove the stalks. Heat the remaining butter in a saucepan and add the spinach. Sauté for 1 minute, then allow to cool slightly.

In a small bowl, whip 50 ml (2 fl oz) double cream until stiff. Stir in the lemon juice, to taste, and season with salt and freshly ground pepper. Spoon 1 teaspoon of this cream into each of 8 shallow, heated soup plates. Garnish with ¼ teaspoon caviar. Add the remaining cream to the soup. Bring to the boil, add the oyster liquid and season to taste with salt, freshly ground pepper and crushed dried chillies. Pass the soup through a fine wire sieve.

Place 2 poached oysters on top of the cream in each soup bowl and gently pour in the soup. From the warm sautéed spinach, make 8 small packages the size of an oyster. Place one spinach 'oyster' in each soup plate. Serve immediately.

*Taste*

# Starters and Light Luncheon and Supper Dishes

*Often, when dining out, I find I stick to the starters section on the menu to choose an original-sounding appetiser for both my first and my main course. I've included some of my all-time favourites in this chapter: Artichoke Hearts en Salade, topped with a surprise slice of foie gras, Brochettes of Bread-Crumbed Mussels, deep-fried and served with a golden Sauce Béarnaise, Rillettes of Smoked Trout with Diced Vegetables (one of the most elegant and popular first courses served at Carrier's), Fruits de Mer in Aspic, with a delicious Green Herb Sauce . . . and the richest pâté in the world – Fondant de Volailles as served in Restaurant Père Bise on the shores of Lake Annecy.*

# Danish Cucumber Salad

*Serves 6*

*2 cucumbers*
*1 tablespoon salt*
*White wine vinegar*
*2 tablespoons sugar*
*White pepper*
*2 tablespoons finely chopped parsley*

Peel and slice cucumbers very finely. Sprinkle with salt and place in a glass bowl under a weighted plate for at least 1 hour. Wash well; drain. In a small bowl, combine wine vinegar, sugar and white pepper, to taste, and pour over cucumber slices. Let stand for 1 hour in refrigerator. Just before serving, pour off excess juices, sprinkle with finely chopped parsley and serve with poached salmon, gravadlax or grilled meat, fish or chicken.

*The Sunday Times*

# Greek Orange and Black Olive Salad

*Sliced fresh oranges and red onion and fat black olives make an appetising starter that is easy to put together. Set this colourful salad in a circle of salad leaves (cos, radicchio, arugula, little gem) for maximum effect.*

*Serves 4*

*3–4 ripe navel oranges*
*10–12 large black olives*
*1 small red onion*
*150 ml/5 fl oz well-flavoured vinaigrette dressing*
*Salt and freshly ground pepper*
*Pinch crushed dried chillies*

Peel and slice oranges crosswise. Peel and slice red onion. Pit and slice olives. Combine in a salad bowl with red onion rings and vinaigrette dressing. Correct seasoning, adding in a little more salt, freshly ground pepper and crushed dried chillies, and toss before serving.

*Vogue*

# Raw Mushroom Salad

*Raw button mushrooms, thinly sliced and tossed in lemon juice and olive oil, make a wonderfully fresh-tasting starter when chopped green herbs are added to the lemony dressing*

*Serves 6*

*450 g / 1 lb button mushrooms*
*Juice of 2 lemons*
*8 tablespoons olive oil*
*Salt and freshly ground pepper*
*1 tablespoon finely chopped chives*
*1 tablespoon finely chopped flat-leafed parsley*

Remove stems from mushrooms; wash and dry caps but do not peel. Slice caps thinly and arrange them in a salad bowl and pour well-flavoured lemon and olive oil dressing over them. Toss carefully and chill in the refrigerator for 2 hours before serving. Sprinkle with chopped chives and parsley.

*The Sunday Times*

# Fresh Asparagus Hollandaise

*Hollandaise sauce – one of the three classic emulsion sauces of French cuisine – is very easy to make at home. Just combine lemon juice and cold water; add egg yolks and butter and whisk over heat until smooth and thick, adding a little more butter from time to time as you go. If – heaven forbid – your sauce curdles, just swirl in an ice cube until sauce reforms or, more traditionally, beat in a little iced water.*

*Serves 4*

*24–32 fresh asparagus spears*

## Hollandaise Sauce

*1 teaspoon lemon juice*
*1 tablespoon cold water*
*Salt and white pepper*
*100 g / 4 oz softened butter*
*4 egg yolks*
*Lemon juice*

Wash stalks under the cold tap, scrubbing them with a small brush if they are sandy. Remove stray leaf points from stem below the head. Trim stalks; scrape the lower ends with the back of a knife. If stalks are 'woody', break the woody part off – you will find that the stalk snaps off right at the point where the tender part begins. Trim broken edge of stalk with a knife. Put stalks into cold water.

### To prepare Hollandaise Sauce

Combine lemon juice, cold water, and salt and white pepper to taste, in the top of a double saucepan or *bain marie*.

Divide butter into 4 equal pieces. Add egg yolks and a quarter of the butter to the liquid in the saucepan, and stir the mixture rapidly and constantly with a wire whisk over hot, but not boiling, water until the butter is melted and the mixture begins to thicken. Add the second piece of butter, stirring from the bottom of the pan until it is melted. Be careful not to allow the water over which the sauce is cooking to boil at any time. Add rest of butter, beating until it melts and is incorporated in the sauce.

Remove top part of saucepan from heat and continue to beat for 2 to 3 minutes. Replace saucepan over hot, but not boiling, water for 2 minutes more, beating constantly. By this time the emulsion should have formed and the sauce will be rich and creamy.

Finish the sauce with a few drops of lemon juice. Strain and keep warm over warm water until ready to serve.

*Note:* if at any time in the operation the mixture should curdle, beat in 1 or 2 tablespoons cold water to rebind the emulsion, or use an ice cube (see page 23).

### To cook Asparagus

Grade stalks into bundles of even thickness. Stand bundles upright in a tall saucepan and pour in boiling water to come just under the tips. Salt the water. Bring to the boil; cover tips loosely with a cap of crumpled foil and simmer gently until tender, 10 to 15 minutes from the time the water comes to the boil again. In this way, the stalks cook in water, while the more tender tips are steamed. Drain as soon as stems feel tender when pierced with the tip of a sharp knife.

Serve 6 to 8 asparagus spears per person. Accompany with Hollandaise Sauce.

*Great Dishes of the World*

# Persillade of Green Beans

*Serves 4 to 6*

*700g / 1½ lb green beans*
*Salted water*
*6–8 tablespoons olive oil*
*2–3 tablespoons wine vinegar*
*Salt and freshly ground pepper*
*Crushed dried chillies*

### Garnish
*½ bunch flat-leafed parsley*
*2 cloves garlic, finely chopped*

Top and tail young green beans (*haricots verts*) and cook them in boiling salted water until they are barely tender. Drain and toss them, while still warm, in a well-flavoured vinaigrette dressing (olive oil and wine vinegar seasoned with salt, freshly ground pepper and crushed dried chillies). Chill.

When ready to serve: transfer green beans and dressing to a clean serving bowl; add chopped parsley and garlic; correct seasoning and serve immediately.

*Great Dishes of the World*

# Salade de Tomates à la Crème

*Serves 4 to 6*

*8 ripe tomatoes*
*1 large onion, finely chopped*
*6 tablespoons olive oil*
*2 tablespoons wine vinegar*
*Salt and freshly ground pepper*
*6 tablespoons mayonnaise*
*4 tablespoons double cream*
*5 tablespoons chopped basil or flat-leafed parsley*

Cut the tomatoes in slices crosswise and arrange in overlapping circles on a serving dish; sprinkle with finely chopped onion and

spoon over with vinaigrette sauce. Chill.

When ready to serve: combine mayonnaise and cream and spoon over chilled tomatoes and onion. Sprinkle with basil or parsley.

*The Sunday Times*

# Haricots Blancs en Salade

*Serves 4 to 6*

*350 g/12 oz dry white beans*
*1 Spanish onion, finely chopped*
*2 tablespoons olive oil*
*1 clove garlic*
*1 bay leaf*
*1 teaspoon salt*
*1 small green pepper*
*4–6 tablespoons olive oil*
*Wine vinegar*
*Salt and freshly ground pepper*

## Dressing

*½ Spanish onion, finely chopped*
*4 tablespoons parsley, finely chopped*
*1 teaspoon prepared mustard*
*1 clove garlic, finely chopped*
*Salt and freshly ground pepper*
*Olive oil*
*Juice of ½ lemon*

## Garnish

*Lettuce leaves*
*Finely chopped parsley*
*Rolled anchovy fillets*
*Black olives*

Soak beans overnight in water to cover. Drain. Sauté finely chopped onion in olive oil until golden brown. Add garlic, bay leaf, salt, 1.5 l (2 ½ pints) of water and simmer beans in this stock for about 2 hours, or until beans are tender. Drain.

Seed and dice green pepper and add to beans along with 4 tablespoons olive oil and vinegar, salt and freshly ground pepper, to taste.

Combine finely chopped onion, parsley, mustard, garlic, salt and freshly ground pepper in a bowl. Mix well and then pour in olive oil, drop by drop as if you were making a mayonnaise, beating the mixture all the time, until sauce thickens. Flavour with lemon juice.

### *To Garnish*

Arrange beans in a lettuce-lined salad bowl; mound salad dressing in centre and garnish with finely chopped parsley, rolled anchovy fillets and black olives.

*Vogue*

# Fonds d'Artichauts au Foie Gras

*Serves 4*

*8 large artichokes*
*Lemon juice*
*Boiling water, salted*
*150 ml/5 fl oz vinaigrette dressing*
*1 tablespoon chopped tarragon*
*Salt and freshly ground pepper*
*Green salad*
*8 thin rounds pâté de foie gras*

### *To prepare Artichokes*

Cut off stalks and tough outer leaves; slice through leafy part down to two last rows of leaves nearest stalk. Then pare off remaining leaves until only heart and 'choke' of each artichoke are left. Remove 'choke' with the sharp edge of a knife (or sharp-edged teaspoon) and place artichoke hearts immediately in cold water with the juice of a lemon added to preserve colour.

Poach artichoke hearts in boiling salted water for about 30 minutes. Cool; drain and dry.

Marinate artichoke hearts in a well-flavoured vinaigrette dressing for at least 45 minutes.

### To serve

Remove each artichoke heart plus dressing with a slotted spoon and arrange on a bed of seasoned salad leaves and sprinkle with chopped tarragon. Place 1 slice of pâté de foie gras on each artichoke. Moisten with 1 teaspoonful of vinaigrette and serve immediately.

*The Sunday Times*

Place artichokes in a saucepan just large enough to hold them and pour mixture over them. Season with salt, freshly ground pepper and crushed dried chillies, to taste; cover saucepan tightly and simmer gently over a low heat for 30 minutes, or until artichokes are tender, adding a little more wine and olive oil, if necessary. When tender, remove pan from heat and serve artichokes hot (or cold) with the sauce poured over them.

*Great Dishes of the World*

# Artichokes in White Wine with Coriander

*Serves 6*

*4 medium artichokes*
*2 tablespoons olive oil*
*150 ml/5 fl oz dry white wine*
*2 cloves garlic, finely chopped*
*1 small onion, finely chopped*
*2 tablespoons finely chopped parsley*
*12 coriander seeds*
*Salt and freshly ground pepper*
*Crushed dried chillies*

Cut off tops of the artichokes and remove chokes. In a small bowl combine olive oil, dry white wine, finely chopped garlic, onion and parsley, and coriander seeds.

# Carciofi alla Romana

*Serves 6*

*6 artichokes*
*Lemon juice*
*2 tablespoons finely chopped parsley*
*2–4 cloves garlic, mashed*
*2 tablespoons chopped fresh mint*
*2–4 fillets anchovies, mashed*
*4 tablespoons fresh breadcrumbs*
*Salt and freshly ground pepper*
*150 ml/5 fl oz olive oil*
*100 ml/10 fl oz dry white wine*

Trim tough outer leaves and stems. Open leaves of artichokes by pressing on the corner of kitchen table. Sprinkle with lemon juice to prevent them from turning colour. Then mix parsley, garlic, mint, anchovies, breadcrumbs, salt, freshly ground pepper and a little olive oil or dry white wine. Stuff artichokes with this mixture and place them, face up, in a shallow casserole just large enough to hold them.

Preheat oven to 170°C (325°F, Gas Mark 3). Pour over remaining oil and dry white wine and cover with a piece of oiled paper or foil. Bake in the preheated oven for about 45 minutes, or until tender. Serve cold in their own juices as an hors d'oeuvre, or hot as a vegetable Roman style.

*Vogue*

# Gazpacho Salad

*Serves 6*

*1 Spanish onion, thinly sliced*
*1 large cucumber, thinly sliced*
*12 ripe medium tomatoes, thinly sliced*
*4–6 tablespoons dry French bread crumbs*
*Salt and freshly ground pepper*

## French Dressing

*9 tablespoons olive oil*
*3 tablespoons wine vinegar*
*2 fat cloves garlic, finely chopped*
*Coarse salt and freshly ground pepper*

Put the thinly sliced onions in a bowl of iced water and leave to soak for 1 hour. Drain well.

Meanwhile, make the French dressing: in a bowl combine the olive oil, wine vinegar and finely chopped garlic, and coarse salt and freshly ground pepper to taste. Beat with a fork until the mixture emulsifies.

### *To prepare the Salad*

In a tall glass bowl, layer up the thinly sliced cucumber and tomatoes with the drained onions, sprinkling some dry breadcrumbs over each layer and seasoning each layer with a little salt and freshly ground pepper to taste. Repeat until all ingredients are used. Beat the dressing again and pour over the Gazpacho Salad. Serve immediately.

*Entertaining*

# Provençal Pepper Salad

*Serves 6*

*2 large green peppers*
*2 large sweet red peppers*
*6 firm ripe tomatoes*
*6 hard-boiled eggs*
*24 anchovy fillets*
*24 ripe olives*

# Herb Dressing

*2 cloves garlic, finely chopped*
*1 tablespoon each: finely chopped parsley,*
*tarragon, chervil and chives*
*6–8 tablespoons olive oil*
*3 tablespoons wine vinegar*
*Salt and freshly ground pepper*

## *To prepare the Dressing*

Prepare herb dressing by combining finely chopped garlic and fresh herbs with oil, vinegar, salt and freshly ground pepper, to taste.

## *To prepare the Peppers*

Wash and dry whole; place under grill, as close to flames as possible. Cook, turning peppers from time to time, until skin on all sides has charred. Remove charred skin under cold water. Cut peppers in lengths – 4 to 6 to each pepper – and wash off seeds and excess fibre; drain on absorbent paper and pat dry.

## *To prepare the Salad*

Slice raw tomatoes thickly and cover bottom of a large flat serving dish with slices. Sprinkle with three-quarters of the salad dressing; add a layer of prepared red pepper slices; sprinkle

with salad dressing; add a layer of pepper slices and sprinkle with dressing.

Shell eggs and slice into rings; cover red pepper with a layer of sliced eggs and pour over the rest of the dressing. Arrange anchovy fillets in a latticework on top and place a ripe olive in the centre of each latticework square. Chill in refrigerator for at least 30 minutes before serving.

*The Sunday Times*

# Italian Stuffed Pepper Appetiser

*Serves 4 to 6*

*2–3 green peppers*
*2–3 red peppers*
*6 tomatoes, peeled, seeded and diced*
*2 cloves garlic, finely chopped*
*1 can anchovy fillets, drained and finely chopped*
*4–6 tablespoons dry breadcrumbs*
*Olive oil*
*Salt and freshly ground pepper*
*2–3 tablespoons butter*

Cut peppers in half lengthwise, and scoop out seeds and fibres. Combine diced tomatoes, finely chopped garlic and anchovies, breadcrumbs and 4 to 6 tablespoons olive oil.

Stuff pepper halves with this mixture and arrange them in a well-oiled heatproof baking dish. Dot with butter and bake in a slow oven (180°C, 350° F, Gas Mark 4) for 30 to 40 minutes, or until tender. Serve cold.

*The Robert Carrier Cookbook*

# Artichoke Hearts
# à la Grecque

*Only the hearts of the artichokes are used in this dish. Boil the leaves separately in salted, acidulated (see below) water until tender, and serve them with a bowl of melted butter or vinaigrette to dip into. They are far too good to waste.*

*Serves 6*

*6 tender artichokes*
*Juice of 1–2 lemons*
*150 g/6 oz onions, minced or grated*
*12 button onions*
*Salt*
*6–8 tablespoons olive oil*
*Freshly ground pepper*

Lay each artichoke on its side and slice off the leaves level with the choke. Then, holding the artichoke firmly, peel round with a sharp knife from the base to remove remaining leaves right down to the heart. Have ready a bowl of cold water heavily acidulated with lemon juice and immerse the artichoke in it as soon as you have cut down to the heart. Otherwise it quickly goes black when exposed to the air.

Now scrape out all the fibres or 'choke' growing on the heart, dipping it into the bowl of lemon water occasionally to keep it white.

Prepare remaining artichoke hearts in the same way. Arrange artichoke hearts side by side in one layer in a wide, shallow pan. Spoon some of the minced or grated onion over each one. Slip button onions in between hearts and barely cover with salted water.

Bring to the boil; cover pan and simmer gently until artichoke hearts and onions are tender, about 20 minutes. Then remove lid; pour in olive oil and raise heat under the pan. Boil hard for about 10 minutes, or until water has evaporated, leaving the oil behind.

Transfer artichoke hearts and button onions to a shallow serving dish, spooning pan juices over them. Season to taste with freshly ground pepper and more salt if necessary. Sprinkle with a little lemon juice and chill until ready to serve.

*Note:* if you feel the dish is too dry, you can spoon over a little more raw olive oil just before serving.

*The Robert Carrier Cookery Course*

# Potted Shrimps or Prawns

*Serves 4*

*350 g/12 oz cooked peeled shrimps or
prawns
Juice of 1 lemon
Generous pinch of cayenne
Salt and freshly ground pepper
100 g/4 oz butter
2 pinches each salt, crushed dried chillies,
paprika, powdered cumin and ginger*

Preheat oven to moderate 180°C (350°F, Gas Mark 4). Toss shrimps or prawns with lemon juice, cayenne, salt and freshly ground pepper, to taste. Draw shrimps or prawns and pack them tightly into 4 individual ovenproof ramekins 6 cm (2½ in) in diameter, and dot each ramekin with 1 level tablespoon butter. Bake ramekins for 10 minutes.

Remove ramekins from the oven and pour in enough seasoned clarified butter to cover shrimps generously (about 2 tablespoons per ramekin). Cool and chill.

*Note:* to make seasoned clarified butter, combine butter in a small, heavy pan with crushed dried chillies, paprika, powdered cumin and ginger and melt over a medium heat without allowing it to sizzle. Then strain through fine muslin. You will be surprised at the amount of curdled sediment this removes from the butter.

*The Robert Carrier Cookery Course*

# Rillettes of Smoked Trout with Diced Vegetables

*Serves 4 to 6*

*450 g/1 lb fresh smoked eel
1 fresh smoked trout
Salt and freshly ground pepper
Cayenne pepper
150 ml/5 fl oz double cream
Lemon juice*

## Garnish

*4 small radishes, washed
2 thin slices cooked beetroot
1 medium carrot, cooked until just firm
Tiny sprigs curly endive
or corn (mâche) salad
1 tablespoon finely chopped tarragon
1 tablespoon chopped flat-leafed parsley*

## Mustard Vinaigrette

*6–8 tablespoons olive oil*
*2 tablespoons vinegar or lemon juice*
*¼ teaspoon Dijon mustard*
*Salt and freshly ground pepper*

Skin and fillet eel and trout. Combine the trout and one-third of the eel in a blender or food processor. Season with salt, ground pepper and cayenne, to taste. Add half the double cream and the juice of a quarter lemon and process until smooth. Add remaining double cream and season with lemon juice and more salt and freshly ground pepper, if desired. Continue to process until well mixed. Transfer mixture to a bowl. Cut remaining eel into thin strips about the size of matchsticks and fold gently into eel and trout mixture. Set aside.

### *To prepare Mustard Vinaigrette*

Mix together wine vinegar or lemon juice with Dijon mustard and season to taste with salt and freshly ground pepper. Add olive oil and beat with a fork until mixture emulsifies.

### *To prepare Garnish*

Cut radish, beetroot and blanched carrot into fine dice. Soak each vegetable in a little vinaigrette dressing until needed.

### *To serve*

Shape 'rillettes' mixture into 4 to 6 oval shapes using 2 tablespoons dipped in hot water (*note:* shapes should resemble eggs), and serve in individual plates. Garnish each plate with tiny sprigs of curly endive or corn salad (mâche), and spoon out small heaps of the diced carrot, beetroot and radish around the rillette.

Dribble remaining vinaigrette dressing over salad greens and vegetables, and sprinkle each rillette 'egg' with finely chopped tarragon and parsley.

*Note:* on no account should frozen eel or trout be used, as they produce too much moisture.

*Carrier's*

## Smoked Fish Platter

*Serves 12*

*12 thin slices smoked sturgeon*
*12 thin slices smoked salmon*
*12 thin slices smoked haddock or tuna*
*12 smoked trout fillets*
*12 smoked sprats*
*Watercress sprigs*
*Tomato wedges*
*Lemon wedges*
*Freshly ground pepper*

## Horseradish Chantilly

*4 tablespoons grated horseradish*
*2 tablespoons lemon juice*
*Salt*
*150 ml/5fl oz double cream*
*1–2 tablespoons finely chopped chives*

Arrange thin slices of smoked fish and fillets of smoked trout in concentric circles on a very large serving platter or serving tray. Or, if you do not have a platter or tray large enough, use two.

Garnish with sprigs of watercress, tomato wedges and lemon wedges. Cover with clingfilm and chill until ready to serve.

Meanwhile make the Horseradish Chantilly. In a small bowl, combine the horseradish with the lemon juice and salt, to taste. Whip the double cream with chopped chives until thick then fold in the grated horseradish and lemon juice.

Serve fish with Horseradish Chantilly on the side.

*Hintlesham Hall*

## Pickled Smoked Salmon à la Russe

*Serves 4*

*4 thick slices smoked salmon*
*½ Spanish onion, thinly sliced*
*5 tablespoons olive oil*
*2 tablespoons wine vinegar*
*1 small clove garlic, crushed*
*½ bay leaf*
*Salt and freshly ground pepper*
*4 slices buttered rye bread*

Select a 9 cm (3½ in)-deep china dish just large enough to take a slice of smoked salmon flat. It should preferably have a tight-fitting lid, but you can use foil instead. Separate onion slices into rings. Arrange alternate layers of smoked salmon and onion rings in china dish. Combine next 3 ingredients in a bowl and beat with a fork to make a dressing. Add bay leaf and season generously with salt and freshly ground pepper. Pour dressing over salmon and onions. Cover dish tightly and leave to marinate at the bottom of your refrigerator for a week to 10 days.

Serve a slice of salmon per person garnished with a few of the onion rings and accompanied by thinly sliced buttered rye bread.

*Carrier's*

# Dressed Crab

*Serves 4*

*1–1.25 kg/2–2½ lb freshly cooked crab, in
the shell
Olive oil
Mayonnaise
Lemon juice
Salt and freshly ground pepper
1 egg, hard-boiled
1 tablespoon finely chopped parsley*

Shell the crab and extract the meat, keeping
the white and dark meats separate. Wash and
scrub the shell. On the underside of the shell
you will see a distinct line round the border.
Trim the shell to this line, using flat-nosed
pliers or breaking off the rough edges with a
hammer. Brush the shell with olive oil to
make it shine. Season the mayonnaise well
with lemon juice and mix mayonnaise into
the white meat in the proportion
3 tablespoons mayonnaise to 100 g (4 oz)
meat. Season with salt and freshly ground
pepper to taste.

Strain any excess juice from the dark meat
into the lemony mayonnaise and mix
mayonnaise with the dark meat in the
proportion 2 tablespoons to 100 g (4 oz)
meat. Season with salt and freshly ground
pepper to taste.

## To Serve

Arrange the meat in the oiled shell, with the
dark meat in the centre, and the white meat
in two panels either side.

Press the egg yolk and white separately
through a sieve. Using a knife as a guide,
cover the dividing lines between the dark and
white meats with a line each of egg yolk, egg
white and chopped parsley.

*The Robert Carrier Cookery Course*

# Salade de Moules

*Serves 4*

*1 kg/2 lb mussels (1.2 1/2 pints
medium size)
2 tablespoons finely chopped shallots
2 sprigs thyme
2 sprigs parsley
1 bay leaf
150 ml/5 fl oz dry white wine
6 tablespoons olive oil
2 tablespoons wine vinegar
Salt and freshly ground pepper
4 tablespoons finely chopped parsley*

Scrub the mussels thoroughly in several
changes of cold water and trim off the hairy
'beards'. Discard any cracked mussels or any

that remain open after this operation. Place the prepared mussels in a saucepan with the finely chopped shallots, sprigs of thyme and parsley, bay leaf and the white wine. Cover and simmer for 5 minutes or until the mussels open. Discard any mussels that have not opened. Remove the remaining mussels from their shells. Cool.

### Prepare the Dressing

Strain 100 ml (3 fl oz) of the mussel liquor into a bowl. Add the olive oil and wine vinegar; season the dressing with salt and freshly ground pepper to taste and beat with a fork until the mixture emulsifies.

Transfer the mussels to a serving dish and pour over the dressing. Sprinkle with finely chopped parsley. The mussels should be moist, but without excess dressing. Serve cold.

*The Sunday Times*

# Fruits de Mer in Aspic, Sauce Verte

*Serves 6*

*1 cooked lobster or king crab,
shelled and sliced*
*225 g/8 oz halibut or sole, poached*
*1 salmon steak, poached*
*100 g/4 oz frozen shrimps, defrosted*

## Fish Aspic

*Fish bones and trimmings*
*1 chicken stock cube*
*4 tablespoons dry white wine*
*1 Spanish onion, sliced*
*2 carrots, sliced*
*1 large tomato, chopped*
*2 stalks parsley*
*Salt and freshly ground pepper*
*10 g/ ½ oz powdered gelatine*
*½ leek, thinly sliced*
*50 g/2 oz minced lean beef*
*2 egg shells, crushed*
*2 egg whites*

## Garnish

*Fresh tarragon leaves*
*½ small head lettuce*
*Quartered tomatoes*

# Sauce Verte

*25 g/1 oz each fresh watercress,*
*parsley and chervil*
*300 ml/10 fl oz mayonnaise*
*(use egg yolks left over from clarifying fish*
*aspic to make mayonnaise)*
*1 level tablespoon each finely chopped*
*watercress, parsley, chervil and fresh*
*tarragon*
*1 tablespoon lemon juice*
*Salt*
*Freshly ground pepper*

Ask your fishmonger for a selection of fish heads, bones and trimmings. Put them in a large pan with the stock cube, dry white wine, onion, carrots, tomato, parsley stalks, and salt and freshly ground pepper to taste. Cover with 600 ml (1 pint) water; bring to the boil and simmer for 20 minutes.

Meanwhile, sprinkle gelatine over 2 tablespoons cold water in a cup and leave to soften.

To clarify aspic, strain stock through a fine sieve. Rinse pan and return stock to it. Add sliced leek, minced beef, crushed egg shells and softened gelatine. Whisk egg whites until foamy and add to the pan. Heat gently until stock foams up to the top of the pan. Quickly draw pan off heat and allow foam to subside. Repeat this process three times in all, then strain stock through a sieve lined with muslin. It should be crystal clear.

Decorate the base of 6 individual moulds or soufflé dishes with a few tarragon leaves and a piece of lobster or king crab. Arrange halibut or sole, pieces of salmon and a few shrimps in each dish. Spoon over liquid aspic to cover and chill in the refrigerator until firm. Pour remaining aspic into a wide, shallow dish and allow this to set as well.

## To make Sauce Verte

Wash sprigs of watercress, parsley and chervil carefully, and plunge them into a small pan of boiling salted water. Bring back to the boil and simmer for 5 to 6 minutes. Drain well and press dry between the folds of a cloth or absorbent paper. Pound blanched herbs to a paste in a mortar (or purée in an electric blender). Add to mayonnaise and mix well.

Stir in finely chopped herbs and lemon juice, and season to taste with salt and freshly ground pepper.

## To serve

Wrap a cloth wrung out of hot water around each mould (one at a time) for 2 to 3 seconds only, to loosen it without melting aspic too much, and turn out on to individual dishes garnished with lettuce leaves and quartered tomatoes. Chop remaining aspic and arrange a little around each mould. Serve with Sauce Verte.

*The Robert Carrier Cookery Course*

## Cold Parsleyed Ham

*Serves 6 to 8*

*1 kg/2 lb cooked ham (cut in 1 slice)*
*600 ml/1 pint well-flavoured chicken or*
*veal stock*
*150 ml/5 fl oz dry white wine*
*Freshly ground pepper and nutmeg*
*6–8 tablespoons finely chopped fresh*
*parsley*
*2 tablespoons gelatine*
*1 tablespoon tarragon vinegar*

Dice ham; simmer gently for 5 minutes in chicken (or veal) stock and white wine with freshly ground pepper and nutmeg, to taste. Drain, reserving stock, and place diced ham in a wet glass bowl which you have lightly dusted with a little finely chopped parsley. Soften gelatine in a little water. Stir into hot stock; add remaining parsley and tarragon vinegar. Allow to cool until syrupy and pour over diced ham, which should be covered. Allow to set for 12 hours before unmoulding.

*Vogue*

## Minute Provençal Tarts

*Serves 4*

*4 10 cm/4 in tart cases, baked blind*
*4 large tomatoes, skinned*
*8 anchovy fillets*
*3 tablespoons olive oil*
*Salt and freshly ground pepper*
*2 tablespoons freshly grated Parmesan*
*½ teaspoon dried oregano*
*18 black olives, halved and pitted*

Preheat oven to slow, 170°C (325°F, Gas Mark 3). Slice tomatoes thickly. Cut anchovy fillets into fine strips. Heat olive oil in a large frying pan and sauté tomato slices for 1 ½ to 2 minutes on each side, or until lightly browned, turning with a fish slice. Season with salt and freshly ground pepper, to taste. Transfer to a plate and allow to cool.

With a palette knife place cooked tomato slices in pastry shells, allowing 1 tomato per shell. Sprinkle with freshly grated Parmesan cheese and dried oregano. Make a lattice from anchovy strips and place a half olive between each lattice.

Cook tarts in preheated oven for 15 minutes, or until golden brown.

*The Robert Carrier Cookery Course*

# Curried Chicken Liver Crescents

*My mother was of German descent and loved to make pastries and tortes. This super-rich pastry recipe which combines butter, flour and cream cheese is one of my favourites. I use it often.*

*Makes 12 chicken liver crescents*

## Pastry

*75 g/3 oz butter*
*75 g/3oz Philadelphia cream cheese*
*75 g/3 oz flour*

## Filling

*100 g/4 oz chicken livers*
*2 tablespoons butter*
*1 tablespoon lemon juice*
*½–1 teaspoon curry powder*
*Salt and freshly ground pepper*
*1 hard-boiled egg, finely chopped*
*1 tablespoon finely chopped parsley*

### *To prepare Pastry*

Combine butter and cream cheese and stir until the mixture is well blended. Sieve flour into the mixture and blend in with a fork. Knead dough and form into a ball before chilling. Refrigerate for 1 hour.

### *To prepare Filling*

Sauté chicken livers in butter. Cool and chop finely. In a mixing bowl, combine finely chopped chicken livers with lemon juice, curry powder and salt and freshly ground pepper, to taste. Add finely chopped egg and parsley, and mix well.

### *To assemble Pastry Crescents*

Roll dough on floured surface into a rectangle 30 x 21 cm (12 x 8 in), and about 1.5 mm (⅟₁₆ in) thick. Cut into six 10 cm (4 in) squares. Cut squares in half to form triangles. Place one teaspoon of filling in centre of each triangle. Roll from wide edge towards point, twisting ends to seal. Turn ends to form a crescent. Place on baking sheet; cover with foil and chill in refrigerator until ready to bake.

Preheat oven to 230°C (450°F, Gas Mark 8). Bake in preheated oven for 10 minutes, or until golden brown. Serve hot.

*The Robert Carrier Cookery Course*

# Chopped Chicken Livers with Chicken Fat

*Serves 4*

*350 g / 12 oz chicken livers*
*Chicken fat*
*½ Spanish onion, finely chopped*
*2 hard-boiled eggs*
*1 stalk celery, finely chopped*
*¼–½ small green pepper, finely chopped*
*Salt and freshly ground pepper*

Sauté chicken livers in a little chicken fat until they are firm, but not cooked through. Sauté finely chopped onion in chicken fat until transparent. Chop hard-boiled eggs coarsely and put through the finest blade of your mincer with chicken livers and onion.

Combine in a large bowl with celery, green pepper, and enough additional chicken fat to make mixture smooth. Season to taste with salt and freshly ground pepper.

*Great Dishes of the World*

# Egg and Anchovy Barrels

*Serves 4*

*4 hard-boiled eggs*
*8 anchovy fillets*
*2–4 tablespoons mayonnaise*
*1–2 pinches paprika*
*Salt and freshly ground pepper*
*Watercress*
*Capers*

Shell eggs and cut tops and bottoms off with a sharp knife dipped in cold water. Carefully remove yolks from broad end of eggs, being careful not to split whites. Mash yolks to a smooth paste with 4 anchovy fillets, paprika, and enough mayonnaise to bind mixture. Season with salt and freshly ground pepper and stuff eggs with this mixture.

### *To serve*

Place eggs, broad end up, on a bed of watercress sprigs. Split remaining anchovy fillets and wrap around centre of each egg. Top each barrel with capers.

*The Robert Carrier Cookbook*

# Fredy Girardet's Charlottes d'Aubergines et de Courgettes aux Foies de Volaille

*Old-style chefs would create a recipe and then present it year after year with no variation. Not so Fredy Girardet. His dishes change all the time, all part of his 'cuisine spontanée'; that is, responding to whatever is freshest in the market. Other chefs marvel at his creativity. Paul Bocuse said of him: 'He is the only chef who ever surprises me.' Girardet has transformed his father's modest bistro in Crissier near Lausanne into one of the finest restaurants in the world. This appetiser – or vegetable accompaniment to roast lamb or veal – looks complicated. In fact, it is beautifully simple.*

*Serves 4*

*2 large aubergines*
*3 tablespoons olive oil*
*1 tablespoon butter*
*2 medium-sized courgettes*
*4 small onions, finely chopped*
*4 garlic cloves, finely chopped*
*Salt and freshly ground pepper*
*3 chicken livers, coarsely chopped*
*2 teaspoons finely chopped parsley*

Preheat oven to cool (120°C, 250°F, Gas Mark ½.) Using a sharp knife, remove purple skins of aubergines and cut into long thin strips, about 2.5cm (1 in) wide. Blanch strips in boiling water for 30 seconds; drain and sauté quickly in 1 tablespoon each olive oil and butter. Brush 4 soufflé moulds, approximately 8 cm (3 in) in diameter and 4 cm (1 ½ in) high, with melted butter. Line each mould with blanched aubergine strips, making sure purple sides of skins are facing sides of mould (each strip to be placed from centre of mould so strips extend easily over edge of mould). Cover bottom of each mould with a small square of aubergine skin. If desired, line moulds with long thin strips of courgette skin prepared in the same manner. In this case you will need extra courgettes.

Cut courgette and aubergine flesh into small dice. In a thick-bottomed frying pan, heat remaining olive oil and sauté finely chopped onions and garlic cloves until soft. Add equal quantities of diced courgette and aubergine flesh (you'll find you have extra aubergine flesh for another use); season with salt and pepper to taste, and continue to sauté for a further 3 minutes. Using a slotted spoon, transfer diced vegetables to a bowl.

Season chicken livers generously with salt and pepper and sauté for a few minutes in remaining pan juices. Using a slotted spoon, transfer to bowl of cooked vegetables together with finely chopped parsley and mix well. Fill lined moulds with stuffing, pressing down with a wooden spoon. Fold over aubergine strips, pressing down with the palm of your hand. Place in a roasting tin and pour in boiling water to come one-third of the way up sides of moulds (a *bain marie*). Set tin over a high heat until water comes to the boil again, then cook in pre-heated oven for 20 minutes.

Serve immediately.

*Sunday Express Magazine*

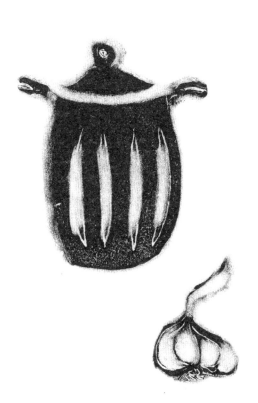

# Délices au Gruyère

*This hot first course — crisp-coated little puffs of melting Gruyère cheese spiked with freshly grated Parmesan — is wonderfully easy to make. In fact, it is only a thickened version of cheese sauce, chilled, cut into squares, coated in breadcrumbs and deep fried. Delicious.*

*Serves 4*

*300 ml / 10 fl oz milk*
*4 tablespoons butter*
*5 tablespoons flour*
*60 g / 2½ oz Gruyère cheese, grated*
*2 egg yolks*
*Salt and freshly ground pepper*
*Freshly grated nutmeg*
*2 tablespoons Parmesan*
*Oil for deep-frying*
*Flour for coating*
*2 eggs, beaten*
*Fresh white breadcrumbs*

In a saucepan bring the milk to the boil. Set aside. In a heavy-based saucepan, melt the butter and stir in the flour. Cook over a low heat for 2 to 3 minutes to make a pale roux, stirring constantly. Pour in the milk gradually and whisk vigorously to prevent lumps forming. Bring to the boil and simmer for 3 minutes or until the sauce is very thick and no longer tastes of flour, stirring constantly.

Remove from the heat and beat in the freshly grated Gruyère cheese. Beat in the egg yolks one at a time and season with salt and freshly ground pepper to taste, and a little nutmeg. Stir in the Parmesan.

Line a rectangular baking tin with clingfilm and spread the delicate mixture in it. Allow to cool. Cover with clingfilm and chill in the refrigerator for 2 hours or until required.

Just before serving, heat the oil in a deep fat fryer to 190°C (375°F). With a floured knife, cut the délice mixture into 14 rectangles. At this stage the mixture is on the soft side.

Sprinkle flour on to a plate and beat the egg in a shallow dish; spread the breadcrumbs in a separate shallow dish. Toss the délice rectangles in flour to coat, shaking off the excess, and reshape into rectangles carefully. Dip in the egg mixture to coat; drain and gently toss in breadcrumbs. Lay the coated délices on a flat tray.

Fry the délices in batches in the preheated oil for 1½ minutes or until golden, turning once during cooking. Drain them on absorbent paper and arrange in a serving dish. Serve immediately.

*The Robert Carrier Seminar of Cooking*

# Brochette de Moules

*Serves 4*

*2.5 l/2 quarts mussels*
*2 tablespoons finely chopped shallots*
*2 sprigs thyme*
*2 sprigs parsley*
*1 bay leaf*
*Salt*
*150 ml/5 fl oz dry white wine*
*225 g/8 oz green bacon (1 thick piece)*
*Freshly ground pepper*
*Melted butter*

## Béarnaise Sauce

*3 sprigs tarragon, coarsely chopped*
*3 sprigs chervil, coarsely chopped*
*1 tablespoon chopped shallot*
*2 black peppercorns, crushed*
*2 tablespoons tarragon vinegar*
*150 ml/5 fl oz dry white wine*
*3 egg yolks*
*225 g/8 oz softened butter, diced*
*Salt*
*Lemon juice*
*Cayenne pepper*

## To prepare Mussels

Scrape, beard and wash mussels and place in a saucepan with finely chopped shallots, thyme, parsley and bay leaf. Season lightly with salt and moisten with dry white wine. Cover saucepan and steam, 3 to 5 minutes, or until shells are well opened.

Remove mussels from their shells; cut green bacon into mussel-sized pieces and place mussels on small skewers with pieces of bacon between them. Season to taste with freshly ground pepper.

Brush mussels and bacon with a little melted butter and cook under grill until bacon is golden, turning skewers from time to time. Serve with Béarnaise Sauce.

## To make Béarnaise Sauce

Combine coarsely chopped herbs, chopped shallot, crushed black peppercorns, tarragon vinegar and dry white wine in the top of a double saucepan. Bring to the boil and cook over a high heat until liquid is reduced to about 2 tablespoons in the bottom of the pan. Remove from heat. Beat egg yolks with 1 tablespoon of water and combine with reduced liquid in the top of the double saucepan. Stir briskly with a wire whisk over hot but not boiling water until light and fluffy. To egg mixture add a piece of butter at a time, whisking briskly until completely incorporated. As sauce begins to thicken, increase the butter to several pieces at a time, whisking it in thoroughly as before until sauce is thick. Season to taste with salt, lemon juice and cayenne pepper. Strain sauce through a fine sieve and serve.

*Great Dishes of the World*

# Pissaladière

*Pissaladière is a French Provençal 'twist' on that old Italian favourite: Pizza. It is a more sophisticated version. Quite delicious. Try it, too, topped with roasted red and green pepper strips - Pepper Pissaladière.*

*Serves 6*

*4 tablespoons olive oil*
*6 large ripe tomatoes*
*2 tablespoons tomato concentrate*
*Salt and freshly ground pepper*
*2 Spanish onions*
*2 tablespoons butter*
*Rosemary or tarragon*
*2 tablespoons grated Parmesan*
*1 tin anchovy fillets*
*Black olives*

## Dough

*Bread, brioche or rich pastry*
*dough – for the case*
*Butter or egg yolk*
*Extra oil for anchovies and olives*

Use bread dough, brioche dough or rich pastry for this savoury tomato and onion tart. If you use bread or brioche dough, roll it out 6 mm (¼ in) thick and line a 23 cm (9 in) pie tin. Brush with butter and put in a warm place to rise slightly while you prepare the filling. If you use pastry, roll it out 6 mm (¼ in) thick, line the pan, fluting the edges, and chill. Then brush with a little lightly beaten egg yolk and bake in a hot oven (230°C, 450°F, Gas Mark 8) just long enough to set the crust, but not brown. Allow to cool.

Heat olive oil in a pan; add ripe tomatoes, peeled, seeded and chopped, and 2 tablespoons tomato concentrate. Cook over a low heat until excess moisture is cooked away, mashing occasionally with a wooden spoon to form a purée. Season to taste with salt and freshly ground pepper.

Slice Spanish onions and simmer in butter with a little freshly chopped rosemary or tarragon until soft and golden, but not brown. Season with salt and freshly ground pepper.

Sprinkle bottom of pastry or dough case with Parmesan; add onions and then cover with the tomato purée. Arrange anchovies in a latticework on top and place a black olive in the centre of each square. Brush olives and anchovies lightly with oil and bake in a moderate oven (190°C, 375°F, Gas Mark 4) for about 30 minutes.

*The Sunday Times*

# Cheese and Spring Onion Quiche

*Serves 6 to 8*

*225g/8 oz plain flour, sifted*
*1 tablespoon icing sugar*
*½ teaspoon salt*
*100 g/4 oz cold butter*
*3 tablespoons freshly grated Parmesan*
*cheese*
*2 tablespoons iced water*
*1 tablespoon lemon juice*
*1 egg yolk, beaten*

## Filling

*4 egg yolks*
*300 ml/10 fl oz single cream*
*150 ml/5 fl oz vegetable stock cube,*
*crumbled*
*4 tablespoons white wine*
*4 tablespoons freshly grated Gruyère*
*Salt and freshly ground pepper*
*Freshly grated nutmeg*
*Cayenne pepper*
*6 tablespoons spring onion, finely sliced*

### To prepare Pastry Case

Sift flour, icing sugar and salt into a large bowl. Cut cold butter into 6 mm (¼ in) dice and add to the bowl with freshly grated Parmesan cheese. Using a pastry blender, or two knives held scissor-fashion in each hand, cut diced butter and Parmesan cheese into flour mixture until it resembles coarse breadcrumbs.

Discard pastry blender or knives. Scoop up some of the mixture in the palms of both hands and let it shower back lightly through your fingers, gently rubbing out the crumbs of fat between your fingertips. You should only need to do this six or seven times for the mixture to be reduced to fine breadcrumbs.

Sprinkle flour mixture with iced water and lemon juice, and toss and mix pastry with a fork until about three-quarters of the pastry is holding together. Then, using your hand, cupped, press the pastry lightly into one piece.

Shape pastry into a round. Wrap in a sheet of greaseproof paper, followed by a dampened tea towel, and chill for at least 1 hour before using.

### To bake Pastry Case

Roll out pastry and line a 23 cm (9 in) pastry tin with removable bottom, and prick bottom of pastry with a fork.

Preheat oven to moderately hot (200°C, 400°F, Gas Mark 6).

Line pastry case with greaseproof paper or foil and weight it down with raw dried beans or rice and bake in preheated oven for 10 minutes. Remove from the oven and carefully lift out paper (or foil), and beans or rice. Turn heat down to 180°C (350° F, Gas Mark 4) and return Pastry Case for just 5 to 8 minutes longer, or until bottom crust is cooked. Cool. Brush with beaten egg yolk to seal crust.

### To prepare Filling

Beat egg yolks in a bowl with single cream until well mixed. Add crumbled vegetable stock cube, dry white wine, freshly grated Gruyère and season with salt, ground pepper, freshly grated nutmeg and cayenne pepper, to taste. Stir in finely sliced spring onion. Pour mixture into prepared Pastry Case and bake in a preheated 180°C (350°F, Gas Mark 4) oven for 30 to 35 minutes. Serve immediately.

*Cooking with Carrier*

# Smoked Salmon Quiche

*Serves 8*

*8 individual pastry cases (10–12 cm/ 4–5 in in diameter)*
*4 eggs*
*150 ml/5 fl oz double cream*
*150 ml/5 fl oz fish stock or canned clam juice*
*Salt and freshly ground pepper*
*Freshly grated nutmeg*
*Thinly sliced smoked salmon*
*Butter*

Whisk eggs together with cream, milk and fish stock or canned clam juice. When well mixed, season with salt, freshly ground pepper and grated nutmeg, to taste.

Fill baked pastry cases (see method for baking pastry cases in preceding recipe) with egg mixture; cover with thin strips of smoked salmon; dot with butter and bake in a slow oven (160°C, 325°F/Gas Mark 3) for 30 to 40 minutes. Serve immediately.

*The Robert Carrier Cookbook*

# Fondant de Volailles

*I remember the excitement which greeted my Sunday Times articles on the three-star restaurants of France when I first started to write in that august newspaper. Each week I would publish 3 or 4 recipes from one of the greatest restaurants in France. This gloriously extravagant recipe for Fondant de Volailles was one of the best of the series.*

*Serves 11 to 12*

1 large capon (about 1.5 kg/3½ lb)
300 ml/10 fl oz dry sherry
2 tablespoons cognac
6–8 tablespoons Noilly Prat
2 tablespoons port
4 sprigs thyme
1 bay leaf
4 sprigs parsley
4 shallots
2 carrots
½ Spanish onion
6–8 peppercorns
225 g/8 oz pork fat
450 g/1 lb lean pork
2 tablespoons coarse salt
Freshly ground pepper
225 g/8 oz foie gras
25 g/1 oz pistachio nuts
Thin strips pork fat (about 450 g/1 lb)
Diced foie gras (optional)

Dough (flour, water and salt)
2 cloves garlic

Skin chicken and remove meat from bones, leaving breasts whole. Combine sherry, cognac, Noilly Prat and herbs, port, shallots, carrots and onion, all finely chopped with garlic and peppercorns in a large porcelain bowl. Add chicken pieces and marinate in this mixture for at least 12 hours.

Dice pork fat and 225 g (8 oz) lean pork and combine with coarse salt and freshly ground pepper, to taste. Leave in the refrigerator for 6 hours so that meat does not change colour during cooking. Pass through the finest blade of your mincer.

Place chicken pieces in a roasting pan with remaining pork, diced, and roast in a hot oven (230°C, 450°F, Gas Mark 8) for 5 minutes, or until meat has coloured slightly. Then strain marinade juices over meat and continue to cook for 5 minutes more.

Remove chicken breasts and pass the remaining chicken pieces and pork juices through the finest blade of your mincer, blending in foie gras at the same time. (I use a *roulade de foie d'oie truffée*.) Combine minced pork and pork fat with chicken mixture; stir in pistachio nuts and remaining marinade juices and place pâté mixture in refrigerator to 'relax' for 2 to 3 hours.

When ready to cook pâté line a large terrine or pâté mould with paper-thin strips of pork fat; fill one-quarter full with pâté mixture; scatter diced foie gras over this for a really luxurious terrine as served at Père Bise; cover with a layer of pâté mixture and place marinated chicken breasts on this. Repeat alternate layers of pâté mixture and diced foie gras, ending with pâté mixture. Top with thin strips of pork fat; cover terrine and seal edges with a dough made of flour, water and salt so that no moisture escapes. Place terrine in a pan of boiling water and bake in a preheated slow oven (170°C, 325°F, Gas Mark 3) for 1 hour.

Keep pâté in refrigerator for 2 days before serving.

*The Sunday Times*

# Pasta and Rice

Ever since I lived in Italy I have been mad about pasta dishes and Italian
risottos as an elegant and yet easy way to begin a dinner with friends.
And I often choose a creamy Risotto Milanese or a comforting bowl of
Pasta e Fagioli when dining out. Both of these recipes are wonderfully easy to
create at home. Try, too, Polenta as a first course, with an Italian Mushroom
Sauce or Gnocchi alla Romana. Easy Saffron Rice or Saffron Rice with
Avocado (the same recipe with diced avocado added) make excellent
accompaniments to grilled or sauced meats . . . as does Riz à la Basquaise.

# Spaghetti with Oil and Garlic

*Serves 4*

*225 g/8 oz spaghetti*
*Salt*
*3 tablespoons butter*
*2 tablespoons olive oil*
*2 cloves garlic, finely chopped*
*2 tablespoons finely chopped parsley*
*Freshly ground pepper*
*Crushed dried chillies*
*4–6 tablespoons freshly*
*grated Parmesan cheese*

Cook the spaghetti in boiling salted water for 12 minutes or until tender, but not soft. Drain and keep warm. In a large saucepan heat 2 tablespoons butter and the olive oil and simmer the finely chopped garlic and parsley until hot.

Add the drained spaghetti to the oil and garlic mixture and stir until thoroughly moistened, adding a little more warm oil if necessary. Season to taste with salt, freshly ground pepper and crushed dried chillies.

Turn the spaghetti into a heated serving dish, sprinkle with freshly grated Parmesan cheese, dot with the remaining butter and serve immediately.

*Great Dishes of the World*

# Spaghetti with Meat Balls (New York Style)

*This is Sunday night supper food at its best. More American than Italian, perhaps, but one of the favourite standbys of my youth. It was perhaps the very first time that I realised just how much flavour finely chopped onion and garlic, chopped mushrooms and tomatoes and tomato concentrate could give to a humble dish of spaghetti and meat balls.*

*Serves 4*

*350 g/12 oz spaghetti*
*Salt*
*Freshly grated Parmesan cheese*

## Sauce

*2–3 tablespoons olive oil*
*1 Spanish onion, finely chopped*
*1 clove garlic, finely chopped*
*100 g/4 oz mushrooms, sliced*
*350 g/14 oz can Italian peeled tomatoes*
*3 tablespoons tomato purée*
*1 bay leaf*
*1 small strip lemon peel*
*150 ml/5 fl oz beef stock*
*Salt and freshly ground pepper*
*1 tablespoon Worcestershire sauce*

# Meat Balls

*350 g/12 oz minced beef*
*350 g/12 oz minced pork*
*2 slices bread, crusts removed,*
*soaked in milk*
*2 cloves garlic, finely chopped*
*2 tablespoons finely chopped parsley*
*Salt and freshly ground pepper*
*Crushed dried chillies*
*1 egg, beaten*
*3 tablespoons flour*
*2 tablespoons olive oil*

## *To prepare Sauce*

Heat the olive oil in a large frying pan. Sauté the finely chopped onion and garlic for 5 to 7 minutes or until soft, stirring occasionally with a wooden spoon.

Add the sliced mushrooms and sauté for a further 3 to 4 minutes or until lightly browned. Add the canned tomatoes, tomato purée, bay leaf, lemon peel and beef stock. Season to taste with salt and freshly ground pepper, cover and simmer gently for 30 minutes, stirring occasionally. Stir in the Worcestershire sauce and correct the seasoning.

## *To prepare Meat Balls*

Meanwhile, in a bowl combine the minced beef, minced pork, bread, finely chopped garlic and parsley. Season with salt, freshly ground pepper and crushed dried chillies, to taste, and stir in the beaten egg to bind the mixture. Shape into 16 small meat balls.

Sprinkle the flour on to a plate and coat each meat ball in flour, shaking off the excess.

Heat the oil in a frying pan large enough to take the meat balls in one layer. Place the meat balls side by side and cook for 1 to 2 minutes each side or until browned, turning them with a spatula. Transfer the meat balls to the saucepan with the tomato sauce, using a slotted spoon. Simmer gently for 20 minutes, turning the meat balls once or twice with a slotted spoon.

## *To prepare Spaghetti*

Bring a large saucepan of salted water to the boil, add the spaghetti and cook for 12 to 13 minutes or until *al dente* – tender but still firm. Drain and rinse in hot water.

Arrange the spaghetti in a large heated serving dish. Spoon the meat balls on top, with the tomato sauce. Serve immediately with a bowl of Parmesan cheese to pass separately.

*Homes and Gardens*

# Fettucine alla Capricciosa

*When I first lived in Rome, I used to enjoy lunching on the open-air terraces of the little restaurants in Trastevere. This light dish of pasta garnished with peas, ham and mushrooms was one of my favourites from this period. It is still a favourite today.*

*Serves 4*

*100 g/4 oz stewing veal, finely chopped*
*50 g/2 oz butter*
*Salt and freshly ground pepper*
*5 tablespoons red wine*
*300 ml/10 fl oz tomato sauce★*
*50 g/2 oz mushrooms, finely sliced*
*1 slice Parma ham, cut in strips*
*100 g/4 oz frozen peas, defrosted*
*225 g/8 oz fettucine*

## To prepare Sauce

Heat half the butter in a small frying pan and sauté the finely chopped veal over a high heat for 2 minutes or until golden. Season with salt and freshly ground pepper to taste. Pour in the red wine and simmer for 5 minutes.

In a saucepan combine the tomato sauce with the veal and wine mixture, and simmer gently for 20 minutes. In a medium-sized frying pan heat the remaining butter. Add the finely sliced mushrooms and the Parma ham and sauté for 5 minutes or until golden, tossing with a spatula.

Add the mushrooms, peas and ham to the tomato sauce mixture and cook for a further 10 minutes. Correct the seasoning, and keep warm.

## To cook Pasta

Meanwhile bring a saucepan of salted water to the boil and boil the fettucine until *al dente* (tender but still firm). Drain and transfer to a serving dish. Pour over the tomato sauce and serve immediately.

★Available fresh from most supermarkets.

*Harper's Bazaar*

# Trenette col Pesto (Noodles with Italian Basil Sauce)

*Serves 4*

*2 cloves garlic*
*4 small bunches fresh basil*
*2 level teaspoons toasted pine nuts*
*Coarse sea salt*
*2 tablespoons freshly grated Parmesan*
*2 tablespoons freshly grated Pecorino*
*185 ml/6 fl oz olive oil*
*Freshly ground pepper*
*3 medium-sized potatoes, peeled and diced*
*225 g/8 oz trenette or thin ribbon noodles*
*Freshly grated Parmesan or Pecorino, to serve*

Pound first three ingredients to a paste in a mortar, adding coarse salt, to taste. Beat in grated cheeses gradually, and when paste is smooth again, add olive oil a little at a time, as for mayonnaise. Season to taste with freshly ground pepper, and more salt if necessary. (If you have an electric blender, add all the ingredients at the same time and blend at top speed for 1 minute.)

Bring a large pan of salted water to the boil. Add diced potatoes and noodles, bring to the boil again and cook briskly for 10 minutes, or until both are tender but not disintegrating. Drain potatoes and noodles, and place them in a deep, heated serving dish.

Pour over sauce; toss quickly and serve immediately, accompanied by a large bowl of more grated Parmesan or Pecorino to sprinkle over the top.

*The Robert Carrier Cookery Course*

# Penne alla Carbonara

*A rustic pasta dish with a highly flavoured creamy sauce.*

*Serves 6*

*450 g/1 lb penne*
*Salt*
*6 tablespoons butter*
*2 tablespoons olive oil*
*3 tablespoons finely chopped onion*
*150 g/6 oz streaky bacon,*
*cut into thin strips*
*3 egg yolks*
*6 tablespoons single cream*
*Freshly grated Parmesan cheese*
*Freshly ground pepper*

Bring a large pan of salted water to the boil and cook penne until tender but not mushy.

Meanwhile, heat butter and olive oil together in a heavy, medium-sized pan. Add finely chopped onion and simmer until soft and golden but not brown. Add bacon strips and continue to sauté gently for about 5 minutes.

In a bowl, blend egg yolks with cream and 6 tablespoons freshly grated Parmesan cheese. As soon as penne is cooked, drain thoroughly in a colander. Return penne to dry pan. Pour eggs and cream mixture over hot penne and toss vigorously with a large fork and spoon so that heat of penne 'cooks' the sauce into a creamy dressing. *Note:* do not overcook or sauce will curdle or scramble.

Add bacon and onion mixture and season to taste with salt and freshly ground pepper. Serve immediately, piled in a well-heated serving dish, with more freshly grated Parmesan cheese to sprinkle over each portion.

*The Robert Carrier Cookery Course*

# Lasagne Bolognese

*Serves 8 to 10*

*450 g/1 lb lasagne*
*Butter*
*100 g/4 oz freshly grated Parmesan cheese*

## Bolognese Meat Sauce

*4 tablespoons olive oil*
*Butter*
*1½ Spanish onions, finely chopped*
*2 carrots, finely chopped*
*2 stalks celery, finely chopped*
*100 g/4 oz bacon, finely chopped*
*225 g/8 oz lean pork, minced*
*225/8 oz lean beef, minced*
*100 g/4 oz sausage meat*
*300 ml/10 fl oz dry white wine*
*Freshly ground pepper*
*Crushed dried chillies*
*6 tablespoons tomato concentrate*
*450 ml/15 fl oz beef stock*
*225 g/8 oz button mushrooms, sliced*
*1–2 cloves garlic, crushed*
*2 tablespoons finely chopped parsley*

## Italian Mushroom Cream Sauce

*Butter*
*8 tablespoons plain flour*
*1 vegetable stock cube, crumbled*

*1.5 l/2¼ pints milk*
*Salt and freshly ground pepper*
*Freshly grated nutmeg*
*1 clove garlic, lightly crushed*
*8 porcini mushrooms*
*2 tablespoons finely chopped parsley*

Heat 2 tablespoons olive oil with 4 table-spoons butter in a large, shallow casserole and sauté finely chopped onions, carrots and celery stalks over a moderate heat until soft and golden brown.

Combine 2 tablespoons olive oil and 2 tablespoons butter in a large deep-frying pan; add finely chopped bacon, minced pork and beef and sausage meat, and sauté gently until meats brown, crumbling them with a fork. Add to vegetables in casserole. Moisten with dry white wine and simmer until wine evaporates (15 to 20 minutes). Season with freshly ground pepper and crushed dried chillies, to taste.

Dilute tomato concentrate with a little of the beef stock and stir into meat and vegetable mixture. Cover casserole and simmer very gently for 1½ hours, stirring occasionally and adding remaining stock gradually as sauce evaporates.

## To prepare Cream Sauce

Melt 6 tablespoons butter in a heavy pan and stir in flour to form a roux. Add crumbled vegetable stock cube and continue to stir over a low heat for a minute or two, taking care not to let the roux brown: then gradually add 1 l (1¾ pints) of the milk, stirring constantly, and bring to the boil slowly; boil for 3 to 5 minutes, stirring occasionally. Season Cream Sauce to taste, with salt, freshly ground pepper and freshly grated nutmeg, and put aside, with a piece of dampened greaseproof paper covering the surface to prevent a skin forming on top.

Melt 2 tablespoons butter and lightly sauté crushed garlic for 2 to 3 minutes until golden brown. Remove garlic with a slotted spoon and discard. Pour soaked dried mushrooms into a small pan with their soaking water. Bring to the boil and simmer gently for a few minutes until mushrooms have softened.

Strain, and reserve liquid; then chop mushrooms very finely and add to the pan with garlic-flavoured butter. Toss for 2 to 3 minutes over a low heat and add remaining mushroom liquor, finely chopped parsley and remaining 300 ml (10 fl oz) milk. Simmer gently for 15 to 20 minutes. Combine with Cream Sauce and mix well. Correct seasoning.

## To assemble Lasagne

Melt 2 tablespoons butter in a sauté pan and sauté sliced button mushrooms, crushed garlic cloves and finely chopped parsley for 4 to 5

minutes, or until mushrooms are tender. Fold into Bolognese Sauce.

Preheat oven to moderate (190°C, 375°F, Gas Mark 5). Pour boiling water over lasagne and leave to soak for five minutes.

Butter a deep, 23 x 30 cm (9 x 12 in) or 35 cm (14 in) heatproof oven dish, or use two smaller ones. Cover the base of dish (or dishes) with a layer of prepared lasagne (saving most attractive pieces for top); spread one-third of the Bolognese Meat Sauce over the lasagne and then cover with one-third of the Cream Sauce. Sprinkle with a little freshly grated Parmesan cheese; cover with a layer of lasagne; spread remaining Bolognese Meat Sauce on top; and then cover with one-third of the Cream Sauce; sprinkle with a little grated Parmesan cheese. Top with lasagne and then spread remaining Cream Sauce on lasagne. Sprinkle with freshly grated Parmesan cheese; dot dish (or dishes) generously with diced butter.

Bake lasagne for 30 to 40 minutes, or until sauce is bubbling and a golden crust has formed on top. Serve straight from the oven dish (or dishes), with a large bowl of additional freshly grated Parmesan cheese at hand so that each guest can sprinkle more over his dish.

*Great Dishes of the World*

# Pasta e Fagioli

*When I was young boy in America, I used to stay over for dinner with two of my little Italian friends, Raimundo and Umberto. Their family was not rich, but one of the dishes we often enjoyed there was Pasta e Fagiole, absolute ambrosia to my steak-and-chop-fed American palate. It wasn't until years later when I arrived in Italy, that I realised this simple dish of pasta and beans from my youth was one of the great dishes of the Veneto.*

*Serves 6*

*225 g/8 oz dried red kidney beans, soaked overnight*
*1 beef marrow bone, 10 cm/4 in long*
*2 vegetable stock cubes, crumbled*
*4 tablespoons tomato purée*
*2–3 tablespoons olive oil*
*1 Spanish onion, finely chopped*
*1 clove garlic, finely chopped*
*2 tablespoons finely chopped parsley*
*¼ teaspoon cayenne pepper*
*2 teaspoons dried oregano*
*150 g/6 oz short-cut macaroni*
*Salt and freshly ground pepper*
*Freshly grated Parmesan cheese*

Drain the kidney beans and combine in a large heavy-based saucepan with the marrow

bone, crumbled vegetable stock cubes and tomato purée. Pour over 1.2 l (2 pints) cold water and bring to the boil. Boil for 10 minutes then reduce the heat, cover and simmer gently for 1 ½ to 2 hours, or until tender.

Heat the olive oil in a small saucepan. Add the chopped onion and garlic and cook over a moderate heat for about 7 minutes or until just tender, stirring with a wooden spoon occasionally. Add the onion and garlic to the kidney beans with the finely chopped parsley, the cayenne pepper, the dried oregano and the macaroni. Season with salt, freshly ground pepper and crushed dried chillies, to taste.

Cook for a further 10 to 15 minutes, or until the macaroni is tender, stirring frequently with a wooden spoon and adding more hot water if necessary. Correct the seasoning and transfer the pasta and beans to a heated serving dish. Sprinkle generously with Parmesan cheese and serve immediately with an accompanying bowl of extra Parmesan cheese.

*The Sunday Times*

# Polenta with Italian Mushroom Sauce

*Serves 4 to 6*

*350 g/12 oz yellow cornmeal*
*1.2–1.5 l/2–2½ pints salted water*
*Softened butter*
*Freshly grated Parmesan*
*Olive oil*

## Italian Mushroom Sauce

*3 level tablespoons butter*
*3 tablespoons olive oil*
*225 g/8 oz button mushrooms, sliced*
*1 slice bacon, about 3 mm/¼ in thick, diced*
*½ Spanish onion, finely chopped*
*300 ml/10 fl oz chicken stock*
*¼ teaspoon dried sage or oregano*
*Salt and freshly ground pepper*
*Italian tomato sauce*

### *To make Polenta*

Bring water to a boil. Dribble the cornmeal in slowly through your fingers, stirring constantly with a wooden spoon. Continue cooking for 30 minutes, stirring frequently, until the polenta is thick and soft and leaves sides of pan easily; add a little more water

from time to time, if necessary. Stir in 4 level tablespoons softened butter and 6 to 8 level tablespoons freshly grated Parmesan.

Oil a large rectangular baking dish. Pour in polenta and allow to set. Polenta should be about 4 cm (1½ in) thick.

### To make Italian Mushroom Sauce

Heat butter and olive oil in a saucepan; add sliced mushrooms, diced bacon and finely chopped onion; sauté, stirring constantly, until brown. Add chicken stock and dried sage or oregano, and season to taste with salt and freshly ground pepper; simmer gently until tender – about 15 minutes. Add Italian tomato sauce (choose a fresh sauce from your supermarket) and keep warm.

### To assemble dish

Slice polenta into even slices about 12 mm (½ in) thick. Brush each slice with softened butter and grill until polenta is hot and starts to turn a light gold. Turn polenta slices and cook as above on other side.

Arrange grilled polenta slices in a large serving dish; pour over Italian Mushroom Suace and serve immediately with additional grated Parmesan.

*Homes and Gardens*

# Gnocchi alla Romana

*Serves 4*

*225 g/8 oz cottage cheese*
*12 tablespoons butter*
*8 tablespoons freshly grated Parmesan*
*3 egg yolks*
*4 tablespoons flour*
*Salt and freshly ground pepper*
*Crushed dried chillies*
*Freshly grated nutmeg*

Press the cottage cheese through a sieve into a mixing bowl.

In another mixing bowl, with a wooden spoon, beat 4 tablespoons softened butter, 4 tablespoons freshly grated Parmesan cheese and the egg yolks together. Stir in the sieved cottage cheese alternately with the flour and season with salt, freshly ground pepper, crushed dried chillies and freshly grated nutmeg, to taste.

Preheat the grill to high. Bring a large saucepan of salted water to the boil.

Spoon the cheese mixture into a pastry bag fitted with a 12 mm (½ in) nozzle and hold over saucepan. Force the mixture through the nozzle, cutting it into 2.5 cm (1 in) pieces with scissors. Poach the gnocchi at a gentle simmer for 6 to 7 minutes, or until cooked through. Remove with a slotted spoon and drain on absorbent paper.

Grease a *gratin* dish large enough to take the gnocchi in 1 layer with a little softened butter. Arrange the gnocchi in the dish; melt 4 tablespoons butter and spoon over the dish. Sprinkle with the remaining freshly grated Parmesan cheese and grill under the preheated grill for 10 minutes, or until the butter is bubbling and gnocchi are golden brown.

*Robert Carrier's Kitchen Cookbook*

# Saffron Rice

*Serves 4*

*350 g / 12 oz long-grain rice*
*½ teaspoon saffron*
*½ teaspoon turmeric powder*
*6 tablespoons dry white wine*
*900 ml / 1½ pints hot chicken stock*
*Salt and freshly ground pepper*
*Crushed dried chillies*

In a medium-sized saucepan, combine saffron, turmeric, dry white wine and hot chicken stock. Bring to the boil; add long-grain rice; season with salt, freshly ground pepper and crushed dried chillies, to taste. Cover pan and simmer until all the liquid is absorbed and the rice is tender, but still moist.

*Great Dishes of the World*

# Saffron Rice with Avocado

*Serves 4*

*1 recipe for Saffron Rice*
*(see left)*
*1 ripe avocado pear*
*Lemon juice*
*Olive oil*
*Salt*

Make saffron rice. Peel avocado and cut flesh into 6 mm (¼ in) dice. Place diced avocado into a small bowl with equal quantities of lemon juice and olive oil, to cover. Add salt to taste, and toss gently.

### To serve

Pile saffron rice in a bowl (or serving dish). Remove avocado dice from lemon and olive oil marinade with a slotted spoon and sprinkle the bright-coloured cubes over the rice. Serve immediately.

*The Robert Carrier Seminar of Cooking*

# Italian Green Rice

*Serves 4*

*225 g/8 oz long-grain rice*
*600 ml/1 pint water*
*Salt*
*4 celery stalks, finely sliced*
*2 bunches flat-leafed parsley, finely chopped*
*8 tablespoons finely chopped spring onions,*
*green parts only*
*4 tablespoons butter*
*Freshly ground pepper*
*Crushed dried chillies*

In a medium-sized saucepan, boil water with 1 teaspoon salt. Wash and drain rice. Add drained rice to boiling salted water; reduce heat and cook, covered, for 12 to 15 minutes until water is almost completely absorbed.

Stir in finely chopped vegetables, cover and continue cooking over low heat until liquid is completely absorbed, about 5 minutes. (Rice should be firm and separate, vegetables crisp to tender.)

Add butter, and season with salt, freshly ground pepper and crushed dried chillies, to taste. Toss lightly and serve immediately.

*The Robert Carrier Cookbook*

# Risotto Milanese

*Serves 4 to 6*

*350g/12 oz arborio rice*
*½ Spanish onion, finely chopped*
*Butter*
*4–6 tablespoons dry white wine*
*900 ml–1.2 l/1½–2 pints hot beef stock*
*½ teaspoon saffron*
*Salt and freshly ground pepper*
*Crushed dried chillies*
*Freshly grated Parmesan*

Place chopped onion in a deep saucepan with 4 tablespoons butter. Cook gently for 2 to 4 minutes, stirring constantly with a wooden spoon, taking care that the onion does not become brown. Add the rice and cook over a medium heat, stirring constantly. After a minute or so, stir in the dry white wine and continue to cook, stirring, until wine has evaporated. Then add a cup of hot beef stock in which you have infused the saffron.

Continue cooking, adding stock and stirring as needed, until the rice is cooked – 15 to 18 minutes – or until all the stock in the pan is absorbed and the rice is tender but still moist. Correct seasoning, adding salt, freshly ground pepper and crushed dried chillies, to taste. Serve immediately with extra butter and freshly grated Parmesan.

*The Robert Carrier Cookbook*

# Chicken Liver and Pea Risotto

*Serves 4*

*225 g/8 oz chicken livers*
*4 tablespoons vegetable oil*
*1 large onion, finely chopped*
*1 small red pepper, deseeded and diced*
*225 g/8 oz basmati rice*
*¼–½ teaspoon saffron*
*600 ml/1 pint vegetable stock*
*Salt and freshly ground pepper*
*50 g/2 oz mushrooms, finely sliced*
*Crushed dried chillies*
*100 g/4 oz frozen peas*
*Tomato slices, to garnish*

Heat half the oil in a saucepan, add the freshly chopped onion and diced red pepper and cook, stirring for 5 minutes until the onion is translucent. Add the rice and saffron and fry for a further minute, stirring all the time.

Add the stock and season carefully with salt, ground pepper and crushed dried chillies. Bring to the boil, then lower the heat. Cover pan and simmer gently for 15 to 20 minutes or until the rice is tender and all the liquid has been absorbed.

Meanwhile, heat the remaining oil in a frying pan, add the chicken livers and cook over gentle heat for 5 minutes, turning them from time to time. Take care not to overcook the chicken livers as they will go hard if left in the frying pan for too long. They should still be slightly pink in the middle when chopped. Season livers with salt, freshly ground pepper and crushed dried chillies, to taste.

Remove the chicken livers with a slotted spoon and allow to cool slightly. Chop the livers fairly coarsely and stir them into the cooked rice mixture. In the same pan, sauté the sliced mushrooms in the remaining oil until golden. Add the frozen peas and continue to cook, stirring constantly; when the peas are cooked thoroughly stir into the rice. Cover the pan and leave to stand in a warm place for 5 minutes. Taste and adjust seasoning, then turn into a warmed serving dish. Garnish with the tomato and serve at once.

*Harper's Bazaar*

# Chinese Fried Rice with Prawns and Peppers

*Serves 4*

*2 tablespoons olive oil*
*1 small onion, coarsely chopped*
*225 g/8 oz frozen prawns, defrosted*
*½ green pepper, seeded and sliced*
*½ red pepper, seeded and chopped*
*225 g/8 oz day-old cooked rice*
*Salt and freshly ground pepper*
*Crushed dried chillies*
*2 eggs*
*1 tablespoon soy sauce*

In a large frying pan, heat olive oil and sauté coarsely chopped onion for 5 to 6 minutes, or until golden brown, stirring with a wooden spoon. Add prawns, sliced peppers and cook for a further 2 to 3 minutes. Add day-old cooked rice to pan; season with a little salt and freshly ground pepper and sauté gently, stirring continuously for 3 to 4 minutes until the mixture becomes hot. In a small bowl beat eggs with a fork. Season with salt, freshly ground pepper and crushed dried chillies, to taste. Add soy sauce to rice mixture, then eggs, and continue to sauté – tossing rice, prawns, peppers and egg mixture – for 1 minute, or until egg has cooked. Correct seasoning. Serve immediately.

*Robert Carrier's Kitchen*

# Singapore Rice Noodles

*Serves 4*

*100 g/4 oz thin rice noodles★*
*3 tablespoons peanut oil*
*1 Spanish onion, thinly sliced*
*1 tablespoon dried Chinese prawns,*
*soaked in water to cover for 30 minutes*
*and drained*
*1 garlic clove, thinly sliced*
*100 g/4 oz raw chicken, diced*
*100 g/4 oz cooked pork, diced*
*100 g/4 oz frozen prawns, thawed*
*100 g/4 oz broccoli florets, thinly sliced*
*2 stalks celery, thinly sliced*
*6 tablespoons peeled, diced tomatoes*
*2 tablespoons soy sauce*
*½ teaspoon curry powder*
*⅛ teaspoon cayenne pepper*
*Salt and freshly ground pepper*

Put the rice noodles in a 3.6 l (3 quart) bowl and cover with tap-hot water. Leave to soak for 15 minutes, stirring occasionally. Drain well. (*Note:* do not use boiling water; the rice noodles become waterlogged.)

Heat the peanut oil in a wok or a large frying pan over a moderately high heat and fry the sliced onions, drained dried prawns and the sliced garlic for 1 minute or until golden, stirring constantly. Add the diced

*Pasta and Rice*

chicken, diced cooked pork and prawns and stir-fry for 2 minutes. Add the thinly sliced broccoli, celery and drained noodles and stir-fry for a further 2 minutes. Finally add the peeled and diced tomato, soy sauce, curry powder and cayenne pepper and season to taste with salt and freshly ground pepper. Cook, stirring, for 2 minutes.

Transfer to a heated serving dish and serve immediately.

*Available in Oriental stores.

*Robert Carrier's Kitchen*

# Riz à la Basquaise

*Serves 4 to 6*

*350 g / 12 oz long grain rice*
*1 Spanish onion, finely chopped*
*6–8 tablespoons olive oil*
*6–8 tablespoons tomato concentrate*
*150 ml / 5 fl oz dry white wine*
*Salt and freshly ground pepper*
*Crushed dried chillies*
*1 chorizo sausage, sliced*
*12 pitted black olives*
*Butter*
*1 small can pimentos*

In a medium-sized heatproof casserole, sauté finely chopped onion in olive oil until it just begins to turn golden in colour. Add washed rice and stir until the oil has been absorbed by the rice. Stir in the tomato concentrate which you have diluted in the dry white wine, and add enough hot water to cover rice. Season with salt, freshly ground pepper and crushed dried chillies, to taste. Arrange the sliced sausage and the pitted black olives on top of the rice and fit a piece of well-buttered foil over the casserole; cover casserole and cook over a low heat until water has evaporated and the rice is tender but not mushy. Add canned pimentos, drained and cut into strips. Correct seasoning and toss rice well just before serving.

*The Robert Carrier Cookbook*

# Arancini
# (Little Rice Balls)

*Serves 4 to 6*

*350 g/12 oz rice*
*100 g/4 oz chicken livers, chopped*
*1 Spanish onion, finely chopped*
*1 clove garlic, finely chopped*
*4 tablespoons olive oil*
*Salt and freshly ground pepper*
*Crushed dried chillies*
*4–6 tablespoons tomato concentrate*
*150 ml/5 fl oz dry white wine*
*Butter*
*4–6 tablespoons freshly grated Parmesan*
*2 egg yolks, well beaten*
*2 eggs, well beaten*
*Breadcrumbs*
*Fat, for deep-frying*

Sauté chopped chicken livers and finely chopped onion and garlic in olive oil until vegetables are transparent. Season with salt, freshly ground pepper and crushed dried chillies, to taste. Add tomato concentrate which you have diluted with dry white wine. Add enough water to make a creamy sauce; cover saucepan and simmer gently for 30 minutes, adding a little more water, if necessary, during cooking time.

Boil or steam the rice in the usual way until tender but not mushy. Drain well. Then add 4 to 6 tablespoons butter and season rice with freshly grated Parmesan and salt, freshly ground pepper and crushed dried chillies, to taste. Then add well-beaten egg yolks and toss lightly to ensure that butter, egg yolks, grated cheese and seasonings are well distributed in the cooked rice.

Strain sauce from the chicken livers into the rice and mix again. Form small balls (the size of golf balls) with the seasoned rice mixture; then, with your forefinger, dig a hole in the centre of each ball and put 1 teaspoon of liver mixture into each; pinch shut and reroll ball. Chill.

When ready to deep-fry: dip the Arancini in beaten eggs and then into breadcrumbs, and deep-fry in deep fat until golden brown.

*Robert Carrier's Kitchen*

# Fish and Shellfish

*Thank God we are all so health-minded today . . . it allows me to choose fish, fish and more fish for entertaining whether at home or out on the town. I like fish for its lightness, but also for the speed and ease with which it can be cooked: just four or five minutes in a teflon pan for a fillet or thin medaillon of fresh fish. Add a splash of the best olive oil, a squeeze of lemon, a grind of pepper, a hint of crushed dried chillies and sea salt from Guérandes, and the game is played. Moroccan Grilled Fish was a revelation to me when I first tasted it in the open-air fish restaurant in the port at Essouira. As was the fabulous sauce by John Stais at London's White Tower restaurant. But perhaps the most unusual (and the most fun to prepare) is Georgette Descats' Tortillons (Little Twists) of Sole with cut-out balls of cucumber, tomato and carrot. A triumph of presentation and flavour.*

# Moroccan Grilled Fish with Chermoula

*'Chermoula' is the Moroccan word for a highly flavoured 'dry' marinade absolutely guaranteed to give flavour and excitement to grilled fish, lamb or poultry. Use it, too, to flavour casseroles of lamb, chicken and pulse vegetables. Rub it into a whole fish, or fish fillets, before roasting or grilling.*
*It is magic.*

*Serves 4 to 6*

*1 sea bream (about 1.25 kg/2½ lb)*
*or 2 sea bass*
*Salt*
*Flour, sifted*
*Oil for frying*
*Lemon quarters*

## Chermoula

*½ bunch fresh green coriander, finely chopped*
*3 cloves garlic, peeled and crushed*
*2 teaspoons coarse salt*
*½ teaspoon each powdered cumin and sweet red pepper*
*¼ teaspoon hot red pepper*
*½ teaspoon powdered saffron*
*4–6 tablespoons olive oil*
*3 tablespoons lemon juice*

To prepare Chermoula, combine all the ingredients.

Scale, clean and wash the fish carefully in salted water, inside and out, then pat dry. Cut fish into steaks 4 cm (1½ in) thick, and rub well with Chermoula. Allow fish to marinate in this mixture for at least 2 hours, or overnight.

When ready to cook, pat fish dry with paper towels and dredge well with sifted flour. Heat oil in a large frying pan (skillet) or shallow flameproof casserole large enough to hold fish comfortably. Fry in hot oil (190°C, 375°F) until golden brown. Serve with lemon quarters.

*Taste of Morocco*

# Fingers of Turbot Amandine

*Serves 6*

*700 g/1½ lb fillets of halibut or turbot (4 fillets, cut into 6 pieces each)*
*50 g/2 oz breadcrumbs*
*6 tablespoons chopped almonds*
*Salt and cayenne pepper*
*5 tablespoons flour*
*1 egg, beaten with 3 tablespoons milk*
*6 tablespoons olive oil*
*6 tablespoons butter*

## Marinade

*3 tablespoons dry white wine*
*3 tablespoons olive oil*
*¼ clove garlic, finely chopped*
*1 tablespoon finely chopped parsley*
*1 bay leaf, crumbled*
*Salt and freshly ground pepper*

### To prepare Marinade

Combine dry white wine, olive oil, finely chopped garlic, parsley, crumbled bay leaf, salt and freshly ground pepper, to taste. Marinate the fish pieces in this mixture for at least 2 hours, turning the pieces from time to time to allow flavours of marinade to permeate fish.

### To prepare Fish

Mix the breadcrumbs and chopped almonds together and season with salt and cayenne pepper, to taste. Strain the fish, coat with flour, dip in the beaten egg mixture and coat well with the chopped almond and breadcrumb mixture. Sauté the fish in the olive oil and butter and serve immediately with Sour Cream Tartare Sauce or Quick Tartare Sauce.

*Robert Carrier's Kitchen*

## Sour Cream Tartare Sauce

*150–300 ml/5–10 fl oz sour cream*
*(or Greek yoghurt)*
*1–3 teaspoons each chopped flat-leafed parsley, tarragon, chervil, capers and gherkins*
*Salt*
*Crushed dried chillies*

In a bowl, combine sour cream (or Greek yoghurt) and stir in chopped herbs, capers and gherkins. Season with salt and crushed dried chillies, to taste.

*Robert Carrier Cookery Course*

## Quick Tartare Sauce

*Serves 4*

*300 ml/10 fl oz mayonnaise*
*1 tablespoon each chopped parsley, tarragon, chervil, capers*
*2 tablespoons chopped gherkins*
*Lemon juice*
*Crushed dried chillies*

In a bowl, combine first 6 ingredients. Mix well and add lemon juice and crushed dried chillies, to taste.

*Robert Carrier Cookery Course*

# New England Cod Chowder

*Serves 4 to 6*

*450 g / 1 lb cod fillet*
*300 ml / 10 fl oz milk*
*3 tablespoons butter*
*50 g / 2 oz salt pork, diced*
*1 Spanish onion, sliced*
*4 celery stalks, finely chopped*
*1 tablespoon flour*
*2 medium potatoes, sliced*
*Bay leaf*
*Salt and white pepper*
*100 ml / 3 fl oz double cream*
*3 tablespoons finely chopped parsley*
*Paprika*

Skin the cod and place in a medium saucepan (cut into pieces if necessary). Pour over the milk, cover and bring to a simmer. Simmer gently for 10 minutes or until it flakes easily with a fork.

Drain the milk into a measuring jug and make up to 750 ml (1¼ pints) with water. Reserve. Flake the cod and remove any bones.

In a saucepan melt 3 tablespoons butter, add the diced salt pork and sauté for 5 minutes or until golden brown. Remove with a slotted spoon and add the sliced onion and the finely chopped celery. Sauté over a moderate heat, stirring occasionally with a wooden spoon, for about 5 minutes or until vegetables are just *al dente* (tender crisp).

Meanwhile, melt the remaining butter in a large saucepan and blend in the flour. Cook over a low heat, stirring, for 2 to 3 minutes to make a pale roux. Gradually pour in the reserved liquor and stir vigorously with a wire whisk to prevent lumps forming; bring to the boil to thicken slightly.

Add the sliced potatoes, softened vegetables and the bay leaf to the soup. Season with salt and white pepper to taste, then simmer gently for 15 to 20 minutes or until the potatoes are tender. Stir in the flaked cod and the cream, correct the seasoning and reheat. Ladle the soup into individual heated soup bowls and sprinkle with the diced pork, finely chopped parsley and paprika.

*The Sunday Times*

# Cod in Beer Batter with Chips

*Cod is one of my favourite fishes. I like to simmer it with bacon and potato bits in milk and cream in New England fish chowders, serve it lightly salted (or lightly smoked) and then simply poached. Or, perhaps one of my favourites, dipped in a light beer batter and deep-fried in oil (or lard for extra flavour) until crisp and golden. Serve with fat golden chips and homemade tomato ketchup for a top-selling combination in the new-style eating houses of Britain.*

*Serves 4*

*700 g/1½ lb cod fillets, skinned*
*Oil or lard, for deep-frying*

## Beer Batter

*125 g/5 oz plain flour*
*Salt*
*3 tablespoons olive oil*
*200 ml/7 fl oz beer, preferably lager*
*1 egg white*

### To prepare Beer Batter

Sift flour and salt into a mixing bowl and make a well in the centre. Pour in olive oil and gradually add beer, stirring with a wooden spoon to incorporate flour from sides of well. Batter should be completely smooth and slightly thicker than a crêpe batter. Leave to rest for 2 hours.

### To prepare Fish

Preheat oil or lard in a deep-fryer to 190°C (375°F), until a 2.5 cm (1 in) cube of day-old bread takes 60 seconds to turn crisp and golden brown. Pat fillets dry with absorbent paper or clean cloth and cut into strips 3.75 x 7.5 cm (1¼ x 3 in).

In a bowl whisk egg white until stiff but not dry and fold lightly but thoroughly into Beer Batter using a large metal spoon. Just before cooking dip half the fish strips into the Beer Batter, shaking off excess batter, and deep-fry in preheated oil or lard for 4 to 5 minutes, or until a rich golden colour. Drain strips on absorbent paper. Transfer to a heated serving platter and keep warm. Skim oil or lard and reheat to 190°C (375°F) before frying remaining strips in the same way.

Serve Cod in Beer Batter immediately with chips and tomato sauce.

*Robert Carrier's Kitchen*

# Variation on Cod in Beer Batter

Cod fillets can be pan-fried using the same method as above then: leave fillets whole if small; if large, cut into 4 strips. Fold egg whites into batter, as above. Just before cooking dip fillets into batter, one at a time, shaking off excess.

In a large frying pan heat 3 tablespoons butter with 3 tablespoons olive oil. Sauté fillets, 2 at a time, for 3 minutes on each side, or until a light golden colour, turning with a fish slice. Drain fillets on absorbent paper. Transfer to a heated serving platter and keep warm.

*Robert Carrier's Kitchen*

# Cod Steaks with Potato Balls

*Serves 6*

*6 slices fresh cod, about 2.5 cm/1 in thick*
*6 peeled potatoes*
*Salt*
*1 Spanish onion, thinly sliced*
*150 ml/5 fl oz tinned clam juice*
*(or well-flavoured fish stock)*
*Freshly ground pepper*

## Marinade

*6 tablespoons olive oil*
*6 tablespoons dry white wine*
*1 clove garlic, finely chopped*
*1 bay leaf, crumbled*
*3 tablespoons finely chopped parsley*
*Salt and freshly ground pepper*

## Garnish

*12 heart-shaped croutons*
*6 slices grilled bacon*
*3 tablespoons finely chopped parsley*

## Sauce

*1 tablespoon butter*
*1 tablespoon flour*
*150 ml/5 fl oz tinned clam juice,*
*or well-flavoured fish stock*
*Salt and cayenne pepper*
*1 egg yolk*
*150 ml/5 fl oz double cream*
*Juice of ¼ lemon*

Combine marinade ingredients in a large shallow bowl and marinate cod slices for at least 4 hours. Scoop balls from potatoes with a potato or melon scoop; boil them in salted water for 15 minutes.

Drain and reserve.

Place marinated cod steaks in a large shallow heatproof casserole on a bed of sliced

onion; add clam juice or well-flavoured fish stock, the marinade juices and just enough water to cover fish; season to taste with salt and freshly ground pepper and bring to boil.

Lower heat; cover casserole and simmer gently for 15 to 20 minutes, or until fish flakes easily with a fork. Pour fish juices into a small saucepan and reduce to half original quantity. Keep fish warm in a low oven.

Heat butter in the top of a double saucepan; add flour and cook over water, stirring, until sauce is smooth and thick. Add canned clam juice or well-flavoured fish stock; season to taste with salt and cayenne pepper, and simmer until smooth. Stir in egg yolk, cream and lemon juice and enough of the reduced fish juices to flavour sauce. Simmer until thickened, being careful not to let sauce come to a boil. Strain through a fine sieve into a clean saucepan. Add potato balls to sauce and heat for 3 minutes, stirring from time to time.

Place fish on a heated serving dish; garnish with croutons, grilled bacon and finely chopped parsley, and serve accompanied by sauce.

*Vogue*

# Fish Souvlakia

*The late John Stais, proprietor of The White Tower restaurant, and his Irish wife Eileen, were great friends of mine. I used to join them often for dinner and I always chose Souvlakia of Halibut or Turbot.*

*Serves 4 to 6*

*1 kg/2 lb halibut*
*6 tablespoons dry white wine*
*6 tablespoons olive oil*
*Lemon juice*
*Salt and freshly ground pepper*
*2 bay leaves, crumbled*
*1 clove garlic, finely chopped*
*1 slice onion, finely chopped*
*4–6 small onions*
*4 tomatoes*

Cut halibut into 2.5 cm (1 in) squares and combine in a bowl with dry white wine, olive oil and lemon juice, salt and freshly ground pepper, to taste. Add crumbled bay leaves and finely chopped garlic and onion. Peel small onions and blanch in salted water for 5 minutes. Slice blanched onions; slice tomatoes; cover fish with these slices and let marinate for at least 1 hour. When ready to grill, thread alternate slices of fish, onion and tomato onto skewers. Preheat grill and cook until tender, turning brochettes occasionally.

*Vogue*

# Poached Salmon with Cucumber 'Scales'

*Bruce Bolton, who used to work for me years ago, became one of New York's most noted caterers. One day, when I was staying with him in his Upper East Side apartment, I found him in despair. He had overcooked four salmon for a great presentation buffet party for millionaire hostess Mary Lazar. It was a moment for creation: I asked him for aspic powder, homemade mayonnaise, a cucumber and canned pimento. We had to mask the fish to make them suitable to be the centrepiece of the buffet. I set aside the heads and tails of the four fish; spiked Bruce's mayonnaise with tiny bottled capers and chopped red onion; folded the overcooked salmon pieces in the dressing; placed the reserved heads and tails of the salmon on great platters and 'reformed' each fish with the now delicious salmon salad. To poach the salmon, you'll need a fish poacher with a removable rack. Measure your poacher first to make sure the salmon will fit.*

*Serves 12*

1 small whole salmon (about 2 kg/4½ lb),
cleaned but with the head still on
450 ml/12 fl oz mayonnaise

## Court Bouillon

1 bottle dry white wine
1 large Spanish onion, sliced
4 carrots, sliced
3 mushrooms
2 bay leaves
10 white peppercorns
Salt
Bouquet garni
4 stalks celery, sliced

## Fish Aspic

Fish bones and trimmings
1 chicken stock cube
4 tablespoons dry white wine
1 Spanish onion, sliced
2 carrots, sliced
1 large tomato, chopped
2 stalks parsley
Salt and freshly ground pepper
10 g/½ oz powdered gelatine
½ leek, thinly sliced
50 g/2 oz minced lean beef
2 egg shells, crushed
2 egg whites

## Decoration

1 large cucumber
1 can pimento, drained

## To prepare Court Bouillon

Put the Court Bouillon ingredients and 2.4 l (4 pints) cold water in the fish kettle. Bring to the boil and skim off any scum that rises. Lower the heat and simmer for 20 minutes. Remove the kettle from the heat and let the Court Bouillon cool slightly.

## To cook Salmon

Lay the salmon carefully on the removable rack and lower it gently into the Court Bouillon. Bring the Court Bouillon to the boil again (about 3 minutes), reduce the heat, cover and simmer for 25 to 45 minutes, or until you can pull out the dorsal fin. Remove from the heat and leave the salmon in the Court Bouillon.

When the salmon is cool enough to handle, lift it carefully out of the Court Bouillon on the rack and drain it thoroughly.

## To prepare Salmon

Transfer salmon to a board and, with a sharp knife, remove the skin, leaving the head and tail intact. Handling the salmon very carefully, place it best side up on the dish on which you are going to serve it, and place in the refrigerator to chill.

## To prepare Fish Aspic

Strain off 1.2 l (2 pints) of the Court Bouillon and use it to make the aspic.

Ask your fishmonger for a selection of fish heads, bones and trimmings. Put them in a large pan with the stock cube, dry white wine, onion, carrots, tomato, parsley stalks, and salt and freshly ground pepper to taste. Cover with 600 ml (1 pint) water; bring to the boil and simmer for 20 minutes.

Meanwhile, sprinkle gelatine over 2 tablespoons cold water in a cup and leave to soften.

To clarify aspic strain stock through a fine sieve. Rinse pan and return stock to it. Add sliced leek, minced beef, crushed egg shells and softened gelatine. Whisk egg whites until foamy and add to the pan. Heat gently until stock foams up to the top of the pan. Quickly draw pan off heat and allow foam to subside. Repeat this process three times in all, then strain stock through a sieve lined with muslin. It should be crystal clear.

## To decorate

Peel the cucumber and cut into paper thin slices, preferably using a food processor or mandolin cutter. Halve the slices, cut the pimento into strips.

Put about 150 ml (5 fl oz) liquid aspic in a bowl and chill it until it is the syrupy

consistency of unbeaten egg whites. Remove the fish from the refrigerator and brush the cold fish with the chilled aspic until it is evenly coated. Chill more aspic as you need it, and return the fish to the refrigerator as well if it starts to warm up. Don't worry too much about keeping the serving dish clean as you can clean it up afterwards. When the fish is well coated, chill for 20 to 30 minutes to set the coating. Chill a little more aspic.

Remove the coated fish and the chilled decorations from the refrigerator. Using the tip of a pointed knife, or a skewer, and your fingers, carefully dip each halved cucumber slice in turn in the syrupy aspic and arrange them carefully on the glazed fish as overlapping 'scales'. Hold them in place with small wooden toothpicks. Make 'fins' from the strips of canned pimento. When the decoration is complete, return the fish to the refrigerator for 20 to 30 minutes until the fresh aspic is set.

Chill the remaining aspic. When it is syrupy, very carefully spoon a layer of aspic over the whole fish, to complete the glaze. Chill again until set. When the aspic is firm, remove the toothpicks. Clean up the serving dish, scraping off the spilt aspic with a knife, then wiping the dish with a cloth wrung out in very hot water. Keep the fish chilled until 20 to 30 minutes before serving. Serve with mayonnaise.

*Food, Wine & Friends*

# Peppered Salmon Steaks

*Serves 4*

*4 salmon steaks, 2 cm/¾ in thick
(about 75–100 g/3–4 oz each)
2–3 tablespoons coarsely crushed black
peppercorns
Salt
6 tablespoons melted butter
Juice of ½ lemon
3 tablespoons finely chopped parsley*

Press coarsely chopped black peppercorns into the flesh of the salmon steaks with the heel of your hand and sprinkle with salt to taste. Brush steaks with melted butter and sprinkle with lemon juice.

Grill steaks about 10 cm (4 in) from the heat for 8 to 10 minutes on each side, brushing with melted butter when you turn them over. When steaks are done, place them on a heated serving dish and garnish with finely chopped parsley.

*Food, Wine & Friends*

# Sole Soufflés with Asparagus

*Serves 6*

*6 fillets of sole*
*Butter*
*Salt and freshly ground pepper*
*450 g / 1 lb fish fillets*
*1 egg white*
*Cayenne pepper*
*150 ml / 5 fl oz double cream*
*Sprigs of parsley*

## Sauce

*1 small packet frozen asparagus*
*Salt*
*150 ml / 5 fl oz double cream*
*1 egg*
*Freshly ground pepper*

### To prepare Soufflés

Lightly butter six individual soufflé dishes. Line each one with a sole fillet which you have seasoned generously with salt and freshly ground pepper. Put fish fillets through a mincer.

Add egg white, season to taste with salt, freshly ground pepper and cayenne, and blend until smooth in an electric blender or press through a fine sieve. Beat in cream and continue beating over ice until mixture is smooth and fluffy. Correct seasoning. Fill the centre of each dish with the fish mousse.

Preset oven to 160°C (325°F, Gas Mark 3). Place soufflé dishes in an ovenproof dish containing 2.5 cm (1 in) of boiling water. Bake in preheated oven for 25 minutes, or until mousse tests firm and sole flakes easily with a fork.

### To make Sauce

Cook asparagus in lightly salted boiling water until just tender. Drain and blend in an electric blender with double cream and egg. Season to taste with salt and freshly ground pepper. Serve the soufflés in their dishes (or, if desired, turned out), garnished with sauce and a sprig of parsley.

*Robert Carrier's Kitchen*

75

# Tortillons of Sole

*This is a set piece recipe from a great French chef, Georgette Descats, which she used to serve in her Paris restaurant Lou Landes. The tortillons (twists) of sole were simmered in a wine court bouillon (2 tortillons for each service) and served with tiny balls of ripe tomato, cucumber and lightly poached carrot (Georgette used a melon ball cutter) and topped with thread-thin strips of cucumber, carrot and chives.*

*Serves 4*

## Vegetables

*5 carrots, peeled*
*3 turnips, peeled*
*½ cucumber, peeled*
*1–2 tomatoes, skinned, seeded and cut into dice*
*Salt*

## Sole

*8 fillets of lemon sole*
*6 tablespoons butter*
*6 tablespoons finely chopped onion*
*8 basil leaves*
*Leaves from 6 sprigs tarragon*
*450 ml/15 fl oz fish stock*
*1 chicken stock cube, crumbled*
*Freshly ground pepper*

*Crushed dried chillies*
*Juice of ½ lemon*
*Salt and ground pepper*

Poach 4 carrots and 2 turnips in boiling salted water until *al dente* (tender but firm). With a small melon ball cutter, cut eight small balls from the carrots and turnips. Cut balls the same size from raw cucumber. Cut eight 6 mm (¼ in) batons, 5 cm (2 in) long from raw carrot, turnip and cucumber.

### *To prepare Sole*

Roll each sole fillet around your finger corkscrew fashion. Secure with cocktail sticks and set aside. Melt 2 tablespoons butter in a saucepan and sauté the chopped onion until transparent. Add basil and tarragon leaves, fish stock and chicken stock cube. Bring to the boil and reduce to a simmer; simmer for 5 minutes. Season with freshly ground pepper and crushed dried chillies.

Place Tortillons of Sole in the stock and cover. Cook for approximately 2 to 3 minutes. When the sole is cooked, remove from stock with a slotted spoon and keep warm.

Add remaining butter to the stock and add lemon juice to taste. Adjust seasoning if necessary. Strain the sauce through a sieve over the sole and garnish with the prepared vegetables. Serve immediately.

*The Robert Carrier Seminar of Cooking*

# Trout with Almonds (*Truite Amandine*)

*Serves 4*

*4 225g/8 oz trout, cleaned*
*Salt and freshly ground pepper*
*150 ml/5 fl oz milk*
*6 tablespoons flour*
*100 g/4 oz butter*
*1–2 tablespoons olive oil*
*6 tablespoons flaked almonds*
*1–2 tablespoons lemon juice*
*3 tablespoons finely chopped parsley*

Cut fins from fish and neaten tail fin with scissors. Pat fish dry with absorbent paper or clean cloth. Season inside of each cavity with salt and freshly ground pepper. Pour milk into a shallow dish. Put flour in a separate shallow dish and season with salt and freshly ground pepper. Just before cooking dip fish in milk and then in seasoned flour, shaking off excess.

In a frying pan, large enough to take fish in 1 layer, melt half the butter with the olive oil. Sauté fish until golden brown on both sides and flesh flakes easily with a fork, turning once with a fish slice. (This takes 4 to 5 minutes on each side.) Drain fish on absorbent paper. Transfer to a heated serving platter and keep warm.

Drain fat from pan; add remaining butter and when it begins to foam add flaked almonds and sauté over a medium heat, shaking pan continuously, until almonds are golden brown. Sprinkle with lemon juice and finely chopped parsley, tossing lightly.

Carefully spoon almonds over trout and serve immediately.

*Robert Carrier's Kitchen*

# Trout 'Père Louis'

*Serves 4*

*4 fresh trout*
*3 tablespoons butter*
*Salt and freshly ground pepper*
*6 tablespoons fresh double cream*
*3 tablespoons Grand Marnier*
*3 tablespoons cognac*
*2–4 tablespoons sliced toasted almonds*

Melt butter in a thick-bottomed frying pan and sauté trout until tender. Season trout with salt and freshly ground pepper. Heat cream, without letting it come to the boil, in a saucepan. Add Grand Marnier and cognac. Correct seasoning, adding strained juices of trout. Place trout on a heated serving dish; pour over the sauce, and sprinkle with sliced toasted almonds. Serve immediately.

*Vogue*

# Baked English Trout with Bacon

*Serves 4*

*4 fresh trout*
*8 slices trimmed bacon*
*2 tablespoons finely chopped parsley*
*Salt and freshly ground pepper*
*Crushed dried chillies*
*2–4 tablespoons melted butter*

Clean trout; split them open and remove backbones. Cover the bottom of a heatproof gratin dish or shallow baking dish with bacon slices. Lay the split fish on the bacon, cut sides down, and sprinkle the fish with chopped parsley and salt, freshly ground pepper and crushed chillies, to taste. Drizzle with melted butter and bake in a moderate oven (190°C/375°F/Gas Mark 5) for 20 minutes, or until fish flakes easily with a fork. Serve from baking dish.

*The Robert Carrier Cookbook*

# Truite Fourrée au Fumet de Meursault

*Georges Garin was one of the old school French chefs whose restaurant Chez Garin was famous in Paris in the early Sixties. The restaurant no longer exists, but I still make Truite Fourrée au Fumet de Meursault and think fondly of Georges.*

*Serves 6*

*7 fresh trout (225g/8 oz each)*
*6 large mushrooms, finely chopped*
*1 finely chopped black truffle (optional)*
*3 tablespoons butter*
*1 egg white*
*Salt and freshly ground pepper*
*150–300 ml/5–10 fl oz double cream*
*300 ml/10 fl oz fish stock*
*300 ml/10 fl oz Meursault, or other dry white wine*
*6 shallots, finely chopped*
*Truffle slices (optional)*

## Sauce

*150 ml/5 fl oz Fish Velouté*
*(see page 182)*
*300 ml/10 fl oz double cream*
*1 egg yolk*
*Few drops lemon juice*
*1 tablespoon butter*
*Beurre Manié* *

Slit 6 trout carefully down the back and bone and empty them. Fillet seventh. Sauté finely chopped mushrooms and truffle in 3 tablespoons butter. Pound meat of filleted trout to a smooth paste in a mortar; pass through a fine sieve and pound in mortar again with raw egg white. Season to taste with salt and freshly ground pepper. Place mixture in a bowl, over ice, for 1 hour, gradually working in cream by mixing with a spatula from time to time. Add sautéed mushrooms and truffles to this mixture and stuff fish.

Just before serving, poach stuffed trout in fish stock and Meursault with shallots and salt and pepper, to taste.

When trout are cooked, place on a heated serving dish; garnish with a few truffle slices and pour over sauce.

## To make Sauce

Reduce cooking liquid over a high flame to one-quarter of the original quantity; add Fish Velouté mixed with double cream and egg yolk. Whisk in a few drops of lemon juice and butter.

*If sauce seems too thin, thicken with a little *beurre manié* made by mashing equal quantities of flour and butter to a smooth paste.

Heat until sauce is smooth and thick, stirring constantly. Strain over fish and serve immediately.

*The Sunday Times*

# Turbot en Brochettes

*Serves 6*

*1.5 kg/3 lb turbot*
*190 ml/7 fl oz olive oil*
*½ teaspoon each chopped fresh thyme,*
*rosemary and fennel*
*Salt and freshly ground pepper*
*3 green or red peppers*
*6 tomatoes, quartered and seeded*
*Oil for greasing*

## Lemon Butter

*150 g/6 oz butter, softened*
*Juice of 1 large lemon*
*Generous pinch of cayenne*

Cut the turbot into twenty-four 2.5 cm (1 in) cubes, removing the bones and skin. In a bowl combine the olive oil and the freshly chopped thyme, rosemary and fennel. Season with salt and freshly ground pepper to taste.

Halve the peppers, core and seed them. Cut each pepper into 8 squares. Add to the marinade with the cubes of turbot and quartered and seeded tomatoes. Toss to coat with the marinade. Leave to marinate for a few minutes.

Preheat the grill to high.

### *To prepare Lemon Butter*

In a bowl, cream the softened butter until almost runny. Beat in a drop of lemon juice and continue adding it gradually until all the lemon juice is incorporated. Season with cayenne pepper to taste. Transfer to a sauce boat.

### *To prepare Brochettes*

Thread six 21 cm (8 in) skewers, starting with a piece of tomato followed by a cube of turbot and then a piece of pepper. Use 4 of each ingredient for each skewer. Brush the grid of the grill pan with a little olive oil. Lay the turbot brochettes side by side on the grid and grill for 6 minutes, turning the brochettes once during cooking and basting with the marinade.

Transfer to a heated serving platter and serve immediately with the sauce boat of Lemon Butter.

*Robert Carrier's Kitchen*

# Turbot with Green Butter

*Serves 4*

*1 medium Spanish onion*
*2 carrots*
*3 tablespoons butter*
*1 bouquet garni (leek, bay leaf, parsley stalks, juniper berries and peppercorns)*
*175 ml/6 fl oz dry white wine*
*175 ml/6 fl oz fish or chicken stock*
*Pinch of cinnamon*
*Pinch of crushed dried chillies*
*4 100 g/4 oz fillets of turbot*
*Salt and freshly ground pepper*

## Green Butter

*3 spinach leaves*
*3 lettuce leaves*
*3 sprigs watercress*
*3 sprigs parsley*
*1 shallot, chopped*
*1 hard-boiled egg*
*100 g/4 oz softened butter*
*1 clove garlic*
*1 tablespoon capers, roughly chopped*
*¼ teaspoon French mustard*
*Lemon juice*
*Salt and freshly ground pepper*

Roughly chop onion and carrots and sauté in butter until onion is soft; add *bouquet garni*, white wine, stock and a pinch of cinnamon and crushed dried chillies. Bring to the boil. Reduce over a high heat to a quarter of original quantity.

Place turbot fillets on top of reduced white wine, stock and vegetables; season with salt and freshly ground pepper, bring to the boil over a high heat, cover with lid or aluminium foil and place in a moderate oven – 190°C (375°F, Gas Mark 5) – for 15 to 20 minutes.

Bring a large pan of water to the boil, dip in spinach leaves, lettuce leaves, watercress sprigs, parsley sprigs and shallots for seconds only, remove and drain.

Place blanched vegetables in a liquidiser or food processor with hard-boiled egg, softened butter and clove of garlic and process until mixture is fairly smooth; spoon into a bowl. Mix capers, mustard, lemon juice, salt and freshly ground pepper with butter mixture; form into a roll, wrap in greaseproof paper and chill.

## *To serve*

Place fillets on serving dish and spoon a little of the strained cooking liquid over each fillet. Slice butter into wheel shapes and place on each fillet.

*Carrier Seminar of Cooking*

# Turbot au Champagne

*René Lasserre was one of the great entrepreneurial restaurateurs of Paris. His three-star restaurant Chez Lasserre, now run by his son, is still one of the great gastronomic delights of the French capital. I usually use half of a quarter bottle of champagne for this recipe and polish off the rest while cooking this delicious dish. I suggest you do the same.*

*Serves 4*

*4 pieces turbot fillets, skinned (weighing 5–6 oz each)*
*100 g/4 oz butter*
*2 shallots, finely chopped*
*100 g/4 oz button mushrooms, sliced*
*6 tablespoons fish stock, made from fish trimmings*
*½–1 quarter-bottle champagne (90 ml/3 fl oz)*
*Salt and white pepper*
*150 ml/10 fl oz double cream*
*1 tablespoon cornflour*

Melt half the butter in a large shallow saucepan; sauté finely chopped shallots until transparent; add sliced mushrooms and continue cooking until tender. Remove from pan with a slotted spoon and keep warm. Add remaining butter to pan and sauté turbot fillets until lightly coloured. Returned sautéed mushrooms and shallots and add fish stock and half the champagne, adding more if necessary barely to cover the turbot fillets. Season with salt and white pepper, to taste, and simmer very slowly for 5 minutes until tender. Remove turbot fillets to a serving dish and keep warm.

Add double cream to liquid in pan and simmer without boiling until cream is warm. Mix cornflour with a small amount of water to a smooth paste; add to sauce and cook, stirring constantly, over a very low heat until sauce is smooth and rich.

When ready to serve: pour in remaining champagne; stir and mix with sauce until warm.

*Note:* if you prefer a thicker sauce, use less champagne. Pour sauce over turbot fillets and serve immediately.

*Great Dishes of the World*

# Turbot Baked in Cream

*Serves 4*

*4 thick slices turbot*
*Butter*
*Salt and freshly ground pepper*

*600 ml/1 pint double cream*
*Lemon juice*
*Dijon mustard*
*Worcestershire sauce*

Place turbot slices in a well-buttered heat-proof baking dish, or shallow casserole, and season fish generously with salt and freshly ground pepper.

In a small saucepan, bring double cream to the boil. Remove from heat and season to taste with lemon juice, Dijon mustard, a few drops of Worcestershire sauce and salt, freshly ground pepper and crushed dried chillies. Pour hot seasoned sauce over fish; cover fish with buttered paper, or a piece of buttered foil, and place baking dish in a pan of boiling water in a preheated oven (190°C, 375°F, Gas Mark 5) for 15 to 20 minutes, or until fish flakes easily with a fork.

Transfer turbot slices to a heated serving dish; correct seasoning of sauce and strain over fish. Serve immediately.

*The Robert Carrier Cookbook*

# Baked Fish Spanish Style

*Serves 4 to 6*

*1.25–1.5 kg/2½–3 lb cod, hake or halibut*
*Butter or oil, for baking dish*

## Tomato Sauce

*1 Spanish onion, chopped*
*3 tablespoons olive oil*
*1 350 g/14 oz can peeled tomatoes*
*150 ml/5 fl oz dry white wine*
*2 cloves*
*½ level teaspoon sugar*
*Salt and freshly ground pepper*
*1 level tablespoon cornflour*
*12 green olives, pitted and cut into pieces*
*1 level tablespoon chopped parsley*
*2 level tablespoons capers*

Preheat oven to moderate – 200°C (400°F, Gas Mark 6).

Sauté chopped onion in olive oil until soft, about 10 minutes. Add peeled tomatoes, dry white wine, cloves, sugar and salt and freshly ground pepper, to taste; cover pan and simmer for 20 minutes.

Blend cornflour to a smooth paste with a tablespoon of cold water. Stir into tomato mixture and simmer for 5 minutes longer. Add olives, chopped parsley and capers.

Grease a baking dish with butter or oil. Wash and dry fish, and place in baking dish. Pour the tomato sauce over it. Bake fish for 35 to 40 minutes, or until it flakes easily with a fork, with its own sauce. Serve hot with sauce.

*Note:* this is also very good served chilled.

*Robert Carrier's Kitchen*

# Aïoli Fifine

*Anyone who has ever read my articles or books knows all about the St Tropez restaurateur called Fifine who once had one of the best restaurants on the coast. Her versions of Bouillabaisse, Bourride and Chapon Farci were legendary. As was her Aïoli. Make it the raison d'être of a super summer lunch party. Double the recipe so you can invite all your garlic-loving friends. And don't serve anything before the great platters of salt fish, fresh fish and colourful cooked and raw fresh vegetables: you won't have room. Follow with Chilled Lemon Tartlets (pages 275–6).*

*Serves 6*

*450 g/1 lb salt cod fillets*
*Salt*
*6 potatoes in their jackets*
*12 tiny new potatoes*
*6 small courgettes, topped and tailed*
*450 g/1 lb small carrots, peeled*
*450 g/1 lb French beans,*
*topped and tailed*
*1 lettuce, washed and dried*
*6 hard-boiled eggs, in their shells*
*6 ripe tomatoes*
*Fresh herbs (parsley, basil, etc.)*

## Aïoli Sauce

*6 cloves garlic*
*2 egg yolks*
*300 ml/10 fl oz olive oil*
*Salt and freshly ground pepper*
*1–3 tablespoons lemon juice*

Soak cod fillets overnight in a bowl, changing water now and again.

### To make Aïoli Sauce

Crush garlic cloves in a large bowl; add egg yolks and whisk to a smooth light mixture. Dribble in olive oil as for mayonnaise. The Aïoli will thicken gradually. Once oil has been incorporated season with salt and freshly ground pepper, to taste, and lemon juice. Chill.

Drain cod fillets. Put fillets in a saucepan; cover with cold water and bring to the boil. Drain and return to saucepan; cover with cold water and bring to the boil again. Turn off heat and allow to steep in hot water for 10 minutes. Do not overcook or fish will toughen.

In separate saucepans of boiling salted water cook jacket potatoes for 10 to 12 minutes, peeled tiny new potatoes for 5 to 6 minutes, prepared courgettes for 7 minutes, peeled carrots for 10 minutes and prepared French beans for 4 minutes, or until each vegetable is tender.

### To serve

Arrange a bed of lettuce leaves on a large serving platter; group vegetables, hard-boiled eggs and tomatoes for best colour effect. Place diced cod in centre and decorate with fresh herbs. Serve immediately with chilled Aïoli Sauce.

*Harper's Bazaar*

# Pot-au-Feu de Poissons

*Serves 4 to 6*

*4 sticks celery,*
*cut into 5 cm (2 in) segments*
*4 carrots, cut into 5 cm (2 in) segments*
*4 leeks, cut into 5 cm (2 in) segments*
*Butter*
*Salt and freshly ground pepper*
*600 ml/1 pint chicken stock*
*Bones and trimmings from fish*
*700 g/1½ lb turbot fillets*
*700 g/1½ lb sole fillets*
*4–6 scallops, sliced*
*100 g/4 oz tiny Norwegian prawns*
*3 tablespoons flour*
*300 ml/10 fl oz double cream*
*3 tablespoons finely chopped parsley*
*3 tablespoons finely chopped chives*

Cut celery, carrot and leek segments into thin 'matchstick' strips. Sauté vegetables in 3 tablespoons butter in a shallow heatproof casserole for a few minutes, season with salt and freshly ground pepper. Add half the chicken stock and simmer until vegetables are just tender. Remove vegetables from casserole with a slotted spoon. Keep warm.

Add remaining chicken stock to casserole with bones and trimmings from fish, season well with salt and freshly ground pepper and bring to the boil. Skim; simmer for 10 minutes and then remove fish bones and trimmings. Poach turbot fillets for a few minutes in stock until fish flakes easily with a fork. Remove and keep warm. Add sole fillets to stock and poach for a few minutes until fish flakes with a fork. Remove and keep warm.

Add scallops and prawns to the casserole and poach for a few minutes, until scallops are cooked. Remove scallops and prawns and keep warm.

Reduce cooking liquids over a high heat to one-third of the original quantity.

In the meantime, melt 3 tablespoons butter in the top of a double saucepan over direct heat. Add flour and cook, stirring constantly, until the roux is well blended. Then stir in reduced fish stock and double cream and cook over simmering water, stirring from time to time, until sauce is smooth and thick. Correct seasoning.

To assemble pot-au-feu: divide the hot seafood between 4 to 6 shallow bowls, arrange poached vegetables decoratively among the servings, and pour sauce over seafood and vegetables. Sprinkle each bowl with a little finely chopped parsley and chives.

*Robert Carrier's Kitchen*

# Waterzoi of Seafood with the Zest and Juice of an Orange

*Waterzoi is unquestionably the national dish of Belgium. It may be made entirely of fish or shellfish, of chicken, of vegetables, or a mixture of them all. It's immensely buttery and satisfying and, we're now told, not good for our health. But Belgian chefs are gently reducing its richness and my favourite version brings this noble dish up to date with the zest and juice of a fresh orange.*

*Serves 4*

*2 tablespoons olive oil*
*2 garlic cloves, sliced*
*2 bay leaves*
*½ teaspoon dried rosemary*
*1 small carrot, cut into 1 cm (½ in) pieces*
*4 celery stalks with leaves,*
*cut into 1 cm (½ in) pieces*
*1 medium-sized leek, white part only,*
*cut into 1 cm (½ in) pieces*
*1 Spanish onion, quartered*
*4 medium-sized new potatoes, scrubbed*
*Salt*
*1 live lobster 700 g (1½ lb), optional*
*8 jumbo prawns, washed but left in their shells*
*16–20 mussels, cleaned but left in their shells*
*4 sea scallops, washed and muscle removed*
*2 frozen Alaskan king crab legs, defrosted and cut into 10 cm (4 in) pieces*
*2 tablespoons butter*
*2 tablespoons flour*
*2 large egg yolks*
*4 tablespoons double cream*
*4 tablespoons fresh orange juice*
*Paprika*
*Cayenne pepper*
*1 tablespoon finely grated orange zest*

In a saucepan, bring to the boil over a moderate heat 900 ml (1½ pints) water, olive oil, garlic, bay leaves and rosemary. Lower heat; cover and simmer 1 hour. Add carrot, celery and leek pieces and quartered onion to pan. Stir once, cover and continue to simmer for a further 15 minutes, or until vegetables are tender. Pass through a fine sieve into a clean pan, pressing down on vegetables to extract juices.

In an electric blender or food processor, purée vegetables until smooth. Cook potatoes in simmering salted water until tender. Drain. Keep warm.

## To cook the Shellfish

Bring vegetable liquid to the boil over a high heat. If used, add lobster, head first, bending it so that it fits into the pan. Cover and begin timing. After 8 minutes, add prawns and when liquid returns to the boil, cover and cook for a further 3 minutes. Add mussels and when liquid returns to the boil, cover and cook for a further 2 minutes. Add scallops and when liquid returns to the boil, cover and cook for a further minute. Transfer shellfish to a heated platter. Drop crab pieces into pan and heat through. Transfer to platter; cover loosely with foil and keep warm.

## To prepare Sauce

Strain stock through several layers of wet cheesecloth into a clean pan. Over a high heat, reduce stock to 300 ml (10 fl oz). In a thick-bottomed saucepan, melt butter over a low heat. Add flour and cook for 2 to 3 minutes, stirring constantly, until flour is cooked through. Gradually add three-quarters of the stock, stirring constantly. When sauce is smooth, whisk in vegetable purée. Remove pan from heat.

Whisk together egg yolks and double cream. Whisking briskly, gradually add egg yolk mixture to sauce. Return pan to heat and cook, stirring constantly, until sauce thickens slightly, taking care that it never reaches simmering point. If sauce becomes too thick, stir in remaining reduced stock, 1 tablespoon at a time. Stir in orange juice and season with paprika, cayenne pepper and salt, to taste.

## To serve

Remove lobster claws. With a cleaver, cut lobster tail crosswise into 2.5 cm (1 in) pieces through shell. Have ready 4 heated soup plates. Ladle about 5 tablespoons sauce into each. Arrange shellfish on sauce and sprinkle with a little finely grated orange zest. Top each dish with a potato. Serve remaining sauce separately.

*Sunday Express Magazine*

# Mussels Cooked like Snails

*I first tasted this great recipe at the old-fashioned Walsdorf Victoria Hotel in Cannes, a hangover from the days when Britain's Queen wintered on the French Riviera. The Walsdorf is long gone now, but the recipe for mussels grilled with Snail Butter lives happily on.*

*Serves 4*

*24 mussels
3 tablespoons butter
¼ Spanish onion, finely chopped
1 stalk celery, finely chopped
Freshly ground pepper
2 teaspoons lemon juice
150 ml/5 fl oz dry white wine*

## Snail Butter

*225 g/8 oz butter, softened
2 cloves garlic, finely chopped
3 tablespoons finely chopped parsley
3 tablespoons finely chopped chives
Freshly ground pepper*

## To prepare Mussels

Scrape mussel shells with a sharp knife to remove all traces of mud, seaweed and barnacles. Scrub them carefully in several changes of cold water and pull away the black 'hairy beards', discarding any cracked mussels or any that remain open.

In a large heavy saucepan, melt the butter and cook the finely chopped onion and celery over moderate heat for about 10 minutes or until softened, stirring occasionally with a wooden spoon. Add the mussels. Season with freshly ground pepper to taste and sprinkle with lemon juice. Add the dry white wine. Cover the pan tightly and cook over a high heat, shaking the pan, for about 5 minutes, or until the shells open. Then simmer over a low heat for a further 5 minutes. Make Snail Butter by mixing ingredients to a paste. Remove mussels from the heat and serve immediately with the Snail Butter.

*The Sunday Times*

# Chinese Steamed Scallops

*Chinese oyster sauce, fermented black beans and finely chopped ginger and spring onion combine to make this seafood starter especially delicious. One of truly great dishes of the Chinese repertoire.*

*Serves 4*

*8 scallops, with half-shells*

## Sauce

*1 teaspoon cornflour*
*3 tablespoons oyster sauce*
*3 tablespoons dry sherry*
*3 tablespoons oil*
*3 tablespoons canned fermented black beans, drained*
*1.5 cm/½ in fresh root ginger, peeled and very finely chopped*
*2 spring onions, finely chopped*

## Garnish

*Thin strips (bâtons) of cucumber*

Place the scallops, on their shells, in a steamer, cover and steam for 6 to 8 minutes.

Meanwhile, make the sauce in a small bowl or cup: mix together the cornflour, oyster sauce and sherry to form a smooth paste. Reserve. Heat the oil in a frying pan or wok, add the black beans, ginger and spring onions and stir-fry for 1 minute. Stir in the cornflour paste and cook for 1 minute. Pour the sauce over the scallops, and garnish with cucumber batons.

*Cooking with Carrier*

# Coquilles St Jacques aux Herbes de Provence

*Serves 4*

*20 fresh scallops*
*6 tablespoons olive oil*
*1 teaspoon chopped fresh thyme or*
*¼ teaspoon dried thyme*
*1 teaspoon chopped fresh sage or*
*¼ teaspoon dried sage*
*1 teaspoon chopped fresh basil or*
*¼ teaspoon dried basil*
*1 bay leaf*
*Salt and freshly ground pepper*
*2 green peppers*
*Oil for greasing*
*Lemon juice*

Rinse the scallops and slip a short knife between the shells, near the hinge. Cut through the hinge and prise the shells apart. Remove the scallops from the shells and trim off the valves. Rinse the scallops to remove all traces of sand.

In a bowl mix the olive oil and chopped herbs and bay leaf. Season with salt and freshly ground pepper and add the scallops. Leave them to marinate for 2 hours.

Cut the green peppers into 16 pieces about the same size as the scallops. Blanch the peppers in boiling water for 2 to 3 minutes until slightly softened, then drain and refresh under cold running water. Drain again. Thread 5 scallops alternately with pieces of blanched green pepper on to each of four 20 cm (8 in) skewers.

Heat the grill to high. Brush the grill grid with olive oil. Place the brochettes on the grid and cook, 8 cm (3 in) from the heat, for 5 minutes or until scallops are tender. To serve, arrange the brochettes on a heated serving platter, squeeze over a little lemon juice and serve immediately.

*The Robert Carrier Cookery Course*

# Batter-fried Scallops, Prawns and Vegetables

*Serves 4*

*24 raw prawns*
*4 scallops*
*8 thin slices aubergine*
*8 thin slices courgette*
*8 sprigs parsley (or basil)*
*Vegetable oil for deep-frying*

## Japanese Tempura Batter

*1 egg*
*300 ml/10 fl oz water*
*1 tablespoon soy sauce*
*100 g/4 oz plain flour*

In a small bowl, combine ingredients for Japanese Tempura Batter. Whisk until just blended.

Shell prawns, leaving tail fins attached. Remove black veins. Wash and drain. Wash and trim scallops and cut into thin slices. Drain.

Make sure that all vegetables and seafood are thoroughly dry.

When ready to cook: pour about 10 cm (4 in) of vegetable oil into a wok or deep-fryer. Heat to 180–190°C (350–375°F).

Dip prawns, sliced scallops and then vegetables, one by one into the batter (holding each for a moment against the sides of the bowl so that all excess batter drips off) then lower ingredients, as you cover them with batter, to deep-fry in the hot oil. When batter is golden brown (about 2 to 3 minutes) remove from oil with a slotted spoon and keep warm on a tray (lined with kitchen paper to absorb excess fat) while you deep-fry remaining ingredients.

*The Robert Carrier Cookery Course*

# Medallions of Lobster with Chive Sauce

*Serves 4*

*100 g/4 oz cold unsalted butter, diced*
*8 slices raw lobster meat from the tail*
*8 slices raw lobster meat from the large claw*
*1 shallot, finely chopped*
*28 small button mushrooms,*
*stalks removed*
*Lemon juice*
*Salt and crushed dried chillies*
*3 tablespoons dry white wine*
*1 tablespoon finely chopped chives*
*Freshly ground pepper*

In a frying pan, melt 25 g (1 oz) of the butter and sauté the sliced lobster very gently for about 30 seconds on each side. Remove the lobster with a slotted spoon and arrange 2 slices of tail meat and 2 slices of claw meat on each of 4 warmed serving plates; keep warm.

Add the finely chopped shallot, the mushroom caps and ¼ teaspoon lemon juice to the pan and simmer for 2 minutes, until the shallots are transparent but not coloured. Season with salt and crushed dried chillies to taste. Remove the mushrooms and shallots from the pan with a slotted spoon, and divide them between the 4 serving plates, placing them in the centre of the plate with the lobster slices round them.

## To prepare Sauce

Add the dry white wine to the juices remaining in the frying pan and boil until reduced to half the original quantity.

Remove the pan from the heat and add the remaining butter, whisking it in gradually piece by piece, until the sauce thickens and emulsifies. Add the chives and season with salt, freshly ground pepper and lemon juice to taste. Spoon a little of the sauce over each piece of lobster and serve immediately.

*Robert Carrier's Kitchen*

# Quick Lobster Newburg

*Lobster Newburg is one of the classic dishes of nineteenth-century American restaurants such as Delmonico's in New York where I believe it was created. This quick version uses pre-cooked lobsters to great effect.*

*Serves 4*

*4 small cooked lobsters (350 g / 12 oz each)*
*4 tablespoons butter*
*4 tablespoons heated cognac*
*2 egg yolks, beaten*
*300 ml / 10 fl oz double cream*
*Salt and freshly ground pepper*
*Cayenne pepper and paprika*
*Boiled rice*

Cut lobsters in half lengthwise. Crack claws. Remove lobster meat from the shells and cut into large cubes or thin slices. Sauté lobster pieces in butter for a few minutes. Add heated cognac and flame.

Combine beaten egg yolks and cream in the top of a double saucepan and cook over water, stirring continuously, until the mixture coats the back of a spoon. Add lobster meat and pan juices, and heat through, being careful not to allow the sauce to curdle. Season with salt, freshly ground pepper, cayenne and paprika, to taste. Serve on a bed of boiled rice.

*The Robert Carrier Cookbook*

# Lobster à l'Américaine

*This recipe (also known as Lobster à l'Armoricaine) is not a recipe for everyday eating. First of all, you will require 2 live lobsters. This, plus half a pint of dry white wine and 4 tablespoons top-quality cognac, make it a dish for special occasions only. And homemade fish stock adds greatly to the flavour as well. But this collection of my favourite recipes, The Best of Robert Carrier, wouldn't be complete without it.*

*Serves 4*

*2 live lobsters (1 kg / 2 lb each)*
*50 g / 2 oz butter*
*3 tablespoons olive oil*
*1 carrot, finely chopped*
*1 small onion, finely chopped*
*2 shallots, finely chopped*
*2 cloves garlic, finely chopped*
*300 ml / 10 fl oz dry white wine*
*6 tablespoons cognac*
*225 g / 8 oz tomatoes, skinned,*
*seeded and chopped*
*½ teaspoon tomato purée*
*1 bay leaf*
*150 ml / 5 fl oz fish stock*
*(or dry white wine)*
*Salt and freshly ground pepper*
*1 tablespoon flour*
*Lemon juice*

*Pinch of cayenne pepper*
*Finely chopped fresh parsley, chives and*
*tarragon*

Kill the lobsters with a knife, blanch them and separate the shells from the meat. Working over a shallow bowl to catch any juices, crack the claws. Cut each lobster tail into thick slices.

Heat 40 g (1½ oz) butter and 3 tablespoons olive oil in a thick-bottomed frying pan; add the lobster meat and sauté for 5 minutes, stirring occasionally. Remove with a slotted spoon and reserve.

Add the finely chopped carrot, onion, shallots and garlic and sauté until the onion is transparent. Place the lobster pieces on the bed of vegetables; pour over the white wine and simmer for 3 minutes.

Add the warmed brandy and ignite it. When the flames die down, add the tomatoes, tomato purée, bay leaf, any juice that came out of the lobsters, the fish stock and salt and freshly ground pepper, to taste. Cover the pan tightly and simmer for 15 minutes.

Remove the lobster meat with a slotted spoon; keep warm. Simmer the tomato sauce, uncovered, until slightly reduced (3 to 5 minutes). Sieve the lobster coral and cream it with 1 tablespoon flour and the remaining butter; blend it into the sauce and simmer until thickened: strain the sauce into a sauté pan and correct the seasoning with lemon

juice, salt, pepper and cayenne. Add the lobster pieces and heat through.

Spoon into a heated serving dish, sprinkle with finely chopped parsley, chives and tarragon. Serve immediately with boiled rice or rice pilaff.

*Great Dishes of the World*

# Beef and Veal

*Grilled Sirloin Strip Steaks, served crisply chargrilled on the outside and rare, moist and tender on the inside, with Roquefort or Green Butter, was an everyday regular at both my restaurants, and proved to be one of the most popular dishes on the menu. I give the recipe here, as well as my 'show-off' spectacular: 'No-Roast' Roast Beef, which cooks a two or three rib of beef for only 5 minutes per pound at a high temperature and then leaves it in a turned-off oven for two hours. And try, too, my Minute Sauté of Beef with Burgundy Garnish next time you give a kitchen party and want to show what elegant fare you can dish up in what seems like only minutes away from the table. The secret? You've prepared the garnish before the guests arrive (even the day before) and only have to sauté the cubed beef while your guests are helping themselves to another glass of Burgundy.*

# Grilled Steaks with Roquefort Butter

*At both my London restaurant, Carrier's, and Hintlesham Hall in Suffolk, we used to serve a trimmed, aged Sirloin Strip Steak with Roquefort Butter. And every day – for over eighteen years – it was the most popular item on the menu. There must be a message here . . . so I am including it so that you too can make it a focal point of your menus. All you need is a good-quality strip sirloin, aged rump or fillet steak – about 2 cm (¾ in) thick for each person at the table. The Roquefort Butter is simplicity itself.*

*Serves 4*

*4 sirloin strip (or rump) steaks, weighing 150 g/6 oz each,
2 cm/¾ in thick
Salt and freshly ground pepper
Olive oil
Roquefort Butter*

Preheat grill to maximum. Take steaks out of the refrigerator well in advance of cooking to bring to room temperature. Wipe them with a clean damp cloth. Trim off excess fat, then nick the remaining fat around edge of each steak to prevent meat curling up during cooking. Lay steaks on a wooden board and beat them on both sides with a wooden rolling pin, or meat bat, to tenderise the meat. Season steaks with salt and freshly ground pepper.

When ready to grill, oil grid of grill pan. Place steaks on grid and grill close to the heat for 1 minute on each side to seal the meat. Reduce heat to medium and grill for a further 2 minutes on each side for rare, 3 minutes for medium rare and 4 minutes each side for well done.

Meanwhile, slice Roquefort Butter into 4 neat pats. Transfer steaks to a heated serving platter and serve immediately garnished with pats of Roquefort Butter.

*The Robert Carrier Cookbook*

# Roquefort Butter

*50 g/2 oz Roquefort cheese
100 g/4 oz slightly softened butter
3–4 tablespoons finely chopped parsley,
chervil or chives
Juice of ½ lemon*

Pound Roquefort cheese with butter until smooth and well blended. Beat in finely chopped fresh herbs and lemon juice, to taste.
Shape into a roll and chill until firm.

*The Robert Carrier Cookbook*

# American Planked Steak

*The 'plank' is a thick wooden board approximately 30 x 45 cm (12 x 16 in) on which you present the steak together with its garnish. Before using a board for the first time, you will have to 'season' it – rather like an iron frying pan – by brushing it with olive oil, putting it into a cold oven and setting the thermostat to slow: 170°C (325 °F, Gas Mark 3). Leave the board in the oven for a total of 25 minutes; then remove it, brush with more oil and allow to cool. When a plank is not available, use a large, flat, heatproof serving platter that will allow you plenty of room for carving.*

*Serves 4 to 6*

*1 rump steak, 5 cm/2 in thick and
weighing 1 kg/2 lb
Freshly ground pepper
Melted butter
Olive oil
Salt
Finely chopped parsley
Grilled mushroom caps and halved
tomatoes, to serve*

If the steak is bought and cooked on the same day, it is better not to store it in the refrigerator so that it can lose the chill of the butcher's cold room. Slit fat around sides to prevent steak curling up as it cooks. Season both sides with freshly ground pepper (no salt at this stage) and put aside until required.

At least 20 minutes before you intend to start cooking steak, light the grill, set to maximum. Adjust rack of grill pan so that steak will be 13 cm (5 in) from sources of heat.

Test temperature of grill: it should be hot enough to toast a piece of fresh bread, set 8 cm (3 in) from heat, on one side within 35 to 40 seconds. Lay steak on rack of grill pan, 13 cm (5 in) from heat. Brush generously with a mixture of butter and oil. Grill for 7 to 8 minutes on each side if you like it 'blue', 10 minutes for rare, 12 minutes for medium and 15 to 16 minutes for well done. Brush steak with more butter and oil when you turn it, and at intervals if it appears to be drying out.

When steak is cooked to your liking, season it with salt and transfer to a hot serving dish (plank or platter). Spoon over pan juices. Coat top of steak with a blanket of finely chopped parsley. Garnish with grilled mushroom caps and tomatoes.

Cut steak diagonally into thin slices. If some of your guests prefer their steak more thoroughly cooked than others, carve their portions last of all. You will find that meat continues to 'cook' up to a stage further on the serving platter.

*Woman's Own*

# Porterhouse Steak with Pizzaiola Sauce

*Serves 2*

*1 porterhouse steak, 4 cm / 1½ in thick,*
*weighing 450 g / 1 lb*
*Freshly ground pepper*
*Salt*
*Melted butter*
*Olive oil*

## Pizzaiola Sauce

*1 tablespoon olive oil*
*1 garlic clove, sliced*
*225 g / 8 oz can Italian peeled tomatoes,*
*coarsely chopped*
*2 tablespoon finely chopped parsley*
*½ teaspoon dried oregano*
*Salt and freshly ground pepper*
*½ – 1 tablespoon Worcestershire sauce*

Wipe the steak with absorbent paper and beat it once or twice on each side with a meat bat. Season generously with freshly ground pepper and leave to come to room temperature.

## *To make the Pizzaiola Sauce*

Heat the olive oil in a small saucepan, add the sliced garlic and cook over low heat until the garlic is transparent. Add the coarsely chopped tomatoes and their juice, the finely chopped parsley and dried oregano. Season to taste with salt and freshly ground pepper. Simmer the sauce for 15 to 20 minutes, until slightly reduced and thickened. Stir in the Worcestershire sauce and correct the seasoning. Keep the sauce warm while you cook the steak.

## *To cook Steak*

Preheat the grill to high. Just before cooking, season the steak with salt and brush with melted butter and olive oil. Brush the grill grid with oil and place the steak on it. Grill 8 cm (3 in) from the heat until the steak is cooked to your taste (see page 97). Place the steak on a heated serving platter and serve the sauce in a heated sauce boat. Serve immediately.

*Great Dishes of the World*

## Steak au 'Tapis Vert'

*Serves 4*

*4 fillet steaks (225–450 g/½ –1 lb each)*
*4 tablespoons melted butter*
*50 g/2 oz butter*
*2 tablespoons cress*
*Coarsely chopped parsley, tarragon, chives*
*and green peppercorns*
*Crushed dried chillies*
*Salt and freshly ground pepper*

Trim excess fat from the steaks. Brush with butter and place on a very hot grill. Grill for 2 to 3 minutes on each side or until cooked to your liking. Add salt, freshly ground pepper and crushed dried chillies to taste.

While steaks are grilling, cream butter with finely chopped cress and green peppercorns and a little salt and pepper. Serve steaks immediately, topped with a green carpet of herbs and peppercorns.

*Carrier's*

## Tournedos with Corncakes

*This is another restaurant top favourite: tender tournedos grilled (or pan-fried) for minutes only and then served with golden corn pancakes right off the griddle. A great combination. Serve the corncakes, too, as a flavoursome base for baby lamb chops or homemade hamburgers.*

*Serves 6*

*6 tournedos steaks*
*Freshly ground pepper*
*Salt*
*Melted butter*
*Olive oil*
*75 g/3 oz Maître d'Hôtel Butter*

### Corncakes

*4 tablespoons butter*
*¼ Spanish onion, finely chopped*
*150 ml/5 fl oz cold Béchamel Sauce*
*200 g/8 oz can sweetcorn, drained*
*2 egg yolks, beaten*
*50 g/2 oz cornmeal*
*Salt and freshly ground pepper*

Wipe the steaks with absorbent paper and beat once or twice on each side with a meat bat. Season them generously with freshly

ground pepper and leave to come to room temperature.

Preheat grill to high. Season the steaks with salt and brush them generously with melted butter and olive oil. Brush the grill grid with olive oil and place the steaks on it. Grill 8 cm (3 in) from the heat until cooked to your taste (see page 97).

### *To make Corncakes*

Before grilling steaks, melt the butter in a small frying pan, add the finely chopped onion and sauté until the onion begins to take on colour. Add the cooked onion to the cooled Béchamel, together with the strained sweetcorn, egg yolks and cornmeal. Mix well and season to taste, with salt and freshly ground pepper.

When steaks are under the grill, heat 1 tablespoon oil and 1 tablespoon butter in a small frying pan. Spoon a little of the batter into the pan. Fry until just golden on the underside, turn with a fish slice and fry on the second side until golden. Add extra butter and oil as necessary and repeat with the remaining batter to make 12 Corncakes. Transfer the Corncakes to a heated serving platter as they are cooked and keep them hot.

When the steaks are cooked, arrange them on the serving platter with the Corncakes and top each one with a pat of *Maître d'Hôtel* Butter. Serve at once.

*Food, Wine & Friends*

# Maître d'Hôtel Butter

*100 g/4 oz slightly softened butter*
*2 tablespoons finely chopped parsley*
*Lemon juice*
*Salt and freshly ground pepper*
*Crushed dried chillies*

Pound slightly softened butter in a mortar with finely chopped parsley and lemon juice, salt, freshly ground pepper and crushed dried chillies, to taste.

Form loosely into a sausage shape on aluminium foil (or clingfilm); roll up and chill until firm.

*The Robert Carrier Cookbook*

# Chateaubriand

*This method of preparing beef fillet was invented by Montmirail, chef to Vicomte Chateaubriand. It is served with either Béarnaise Sauce (pages 42–3), or Chateaubriand sauce. It is traditionally garnished with château potatoes, which are 'turned' potatoes sautéed in butter and oil. A Chateaubriand steak can be cooked completely under the grill but, because of the thickness of the steak, it is usually better to start it under the grill to seal the juices and then cook it in a slow oven to retain a more even colour throughout.*

*Serves 2*

*Chateaubriand steak, 4 cm/1½ in thick, weighing 450 g/1 lb*
*Freshly ground pepper*
*Salt*
*Melted butter*
*Olive oil*
*450 g/1 lb Pommes au Beurre, to garnish*

## Sauce

*1 tablespoon Glace de Viande (page 102)*
*3 tablespoons beef stock*
*100 g/4 oz unsalted butter, diced*
*1–2 tablespoon lemon juice*
*Salt and freshly ground pepper*
*Cayenne pepper*

Wipe the steak with absorbent paper and beat it once or twice on each side with a meat bat. Season the steak with freshly ground pepper and leave to come to room temperature.

Heat the grill to high and the oven to 160°C (300°F, Gas Mark 2). Season the steak with salt and brush it with melted butter and olive oil. Brush the grill grid with oil and place the steak on it. Grill 8 cm (3 in) from the heat for 3 minutes on each side, to sear the surfaces. If your grid pan has heatproof handles, transfer the whole pan to the oven. If it does not, put the grid into a roasting tin and place in the oven. Cook for 10 minutes for blue steak, 15 minutes for rare, 20 minutes for medium or 25 minutes for well done.

Meanwhile, in a small saucepan, stir together the *Glace de Viande* (see page 102) and white stock, until well blended. Boil fast until reduced to 1 tablespoon. Reduce the heat to minimum and whisk in the diced butter a piece at a time, until the sauce thickens and emulsifies. The sauce should start to emulsify before the butter melts; if the sauce is too hot and melts the butter too quickly, remove from the heat while you whisk. When all the butter is incorporated add parsley and season with lemon juice, salt, freshly ground pepper and cayenne pepper.

Put the steak on to a carving board and carve it downwards at a slight angle, into 6 even slices. Transfer the slices to a heated dish, garnish with *Pommes au Beurre* (potatoes sautéed in butter) and serve the sauce separately.

## Glace de Viande

Meat glaze (*Glace de viande* in French kitchen terminology) is a very useful cook's aid. Just a tablespoon or two of this reduced glaze makes a simple sauce richer and more flavourful and just a little will enhance a grilled or sautéed dish of meat, poultry or seafood. Even pasta tastes better if a teaspoon of glaze is added to the sauce while it is cooking.

You will find that a rich, homemade glaze is very easily made in kitchens, where there are extra quantities of stock and bones at your disposal. Any good brown stock can be used, and the second boiling from meat and bones is almost preferable to freshly made stock, as it is more gelatinous. Free the stock from fat and put at least 1.2 l (1 quart) into a saucepan. Allow this to boil quickly, uncovered, skimming when necessary, until it is reduced to about 300 ml (10 fl oz). Strain through a very fine sieve (or through a piece of muslin placed over a colander). Then put stock into a smaller saucepan and reduce again until the glaze becomes syrupy, when it will be ready to use.

If not required at once, the glaze should be poured into a glass jar, and if a little melted butter (or lard) is poured over the surface, it will keep for weeks in the refrigerator. Use a glaze to enrich soups and sauces as well as to coat grilled meats, poultry or game.

*The Robert Carrier Cookbook*

## The No-Roast Roast Beef

*Lovers of perfectly rare beef, pink and juicy from end to end, with just the outer surface richly crusted, should try the following method when next cooking a larger joint. I have attempted to adapt it to smaller pieces of beef, too, but have had to admit defeat, which is sad, as the method is otherwise foolproof.*

*1 roast of beef (2.5 kg/5 lb or more)*
*Salt and freshly ground pepper*
*Butter*

At least 2 hours before you intend to roast beef, remove joint from the refrigerator. Turn the thermostat up to 250°C (500°F, Gas Mark 10) and give the oven at least 20 minutes to heat up before proceeding.

Rub joint all over with salt and freshly ground pepper, and spread it with 4 tablespoons dripping or butter. Lay it on a rack over a roasting tin. Place meat in the oven. Roast for 5 minutes per 450 g (1 lb); then, without opening the oven door, switch off the heat and leave for a further 2 hours. *Do not, under any circumstances, open the oven door during this time.*

When the 2 hours are up, open the door and, without removing the tin from the oven, touch the beef with your finger. If it feels hot, go ahead and serve it. However, as some ovens do not retain their heat as well as others (electricity is often rather better than gas in this instance), you may find the beef on the lukewarm side. If so, close the door, relight the oven, still set at 250°C (500°F, Gas Mark 10), and give it a further 10 minutes or so. This will raise the temperature of the beef without affecting its rareness.

Serve as usual, on a hot platter, accompanied by gravy made with the pan juices.

*Homes and Gardens*

# Old English Roast Beef with Yorkshire Pudding

*Serves 6*

*1 sirloin or rib roast of beef, (about 2.5 kg/5 lb)*
*4 tablespoons dripping or butter*
*1 tablespoon dry mustard*
*Coarsely ground pepper*
*2 tablespoons lightly browned flour*
*4 tablespoons warm water or red wine*
*1 recipe Yorkshire Pudding*
*(see page 104)*
*Salt*

At least 2 hours before you intend to roast beef, remove joint from the refrigerator. Preheat oven to fairly hot (220°C, 425°F, Gas Mark 7). Spread beef generously with dripping or butter, and sprinkle with a mixture of dry mustard, coarsely ground pepper and flour (which you have lightly browned in a frying pan or in the oven).

Prepare Yorkshire Pudding batter and put aside to set.

Place beef on a rack over a roasting pan and brown in the oven for 20 minutes. Lower heat to 170°C (325°F, Gas Mark 3); add warm water or red wine and continue to roast, basting occasionally, until beef is done to your liking: a further 16 minutes per 450 g (1 lb) for rare; 20 minutes per 450 g (1 lb) for medium and 30 minutes per 450 g (1 lb) for well done.

If you are going to make one large Yorkshire Pudding in roasting pan: 20 to 30 minutes before the end of cooking time, increase oven heat again, to 220°C (425°F, Gas Mark 7); lift the rack the joint and pour Yorkshire Pudding batter into the pan underneath. In this way, both will be ready at the same time. Or make Individual Yorkshire Puddings (see recipe opposite).

Remove Yorkshire Pudding from roasting tin and keep warm with beef while making gravy. Don't forget to salt beef just before serving.

*The Robert Carrier Cookery Course*

# Individual Yorkshire Puddings

*Yorkshire puddings look most attractive – and taste better too – if they are baked in individual round moulds instead of the usual large baking tin. If possible, use fluted tins measuring 7 to 8 cm (3 to 3½ in) across the top. The puddings should be timed to go into the oven when you remove the roast beef – allowing the latter 15 to 20 minutes to 'settle' before carving.*

*Makes 9 puddings*

*100 g/4 oz plain flour*
*Pinch of salt*
*2 eggs*
*150 ml/5 fl oz milk*
*3 tablespoons beef dripping or butter*

One hour before roast is done, sift flour and salt into a bowl and make a well in the centre. Break in eggs; add 2 tablespoons milk and work to a smooth paste with a wooden spoon. Then slowly add remaining milk, beating vigorously. Allow batter to rest.

Increase oven heat to 220°C (425°F, Gas Mark 7), remove roast beef from oven to 'rest' for 15 to 20 minutes while you bake Individual Yorkshire Puddings.

Put 1 teaspoon dripping or butter in the bottom of each fluted tin; lay tins on a baking

sheet and put them in the oven for 2 to 3 minutes to heat through. When fat has melted, remove tins from oven. Quickly pour 2 tablespoons batter into each tin; return tray to top shelf of oven and bake for 15 minutes, or until puddings are puffed and crisp, and golden brown on top. Serve immediately.

*The Robert Carrier Cookery Course*

(230°C, 450°F, Gas Mark 8); then drain off fat; turn tournedos over; add pinch of rosemary and salt and freshly ground pepper, to taste.

Pour 1 tablespoon cognac over each tournedo and continue cooking for a few minutes longer. Serve in casseroles.

*Daily Telegraph Magazine*

# Potted Tournedos

*Serves 4*

*4 thickly cut tournedos*
*2 tablespoons butter*
*6 shallots, finely chopped*
*French mustard*
*Worcestershire sauce*
*Rosemary*
*Salt and freshly ground pepper*
*4 tablespoons cognac*

Melt 1 tablespoon butter in a frying pan and sauté tournedos (thick slices of fillet of beef, trimmed and tied with a thin strip of fat) for 30 to 60 seconds on each side. Remove string and place in 4 individual heatproof casseroles and keep warm. Add remaining butter to pan and sauté finely chopped shallots until transparent. Add mustard and Worcestershire sauce, to taste, to the shallots; mix well and pour over tournedos. Cover casseroles and cook for about 10 minutes in a hot oven

# Bœuf à la Ficelle

*This is an up-market version of a famous nineteenth-century French bistro recipe – 'beef on a string' – the beef, in this case, 4 tournedos steaks, wrapped in 4 strips of pork fat, each tied with a piece of string long enough to hang over the sides of the pan so that the tournedos can be pulled out of the bouillon after 5 to 10 minutes, leaving the meat cooked on the outside and deliciously moist and pink on the inside.*

*Serves 4*

*450 g/1 lb carrots*
*450 g/1 lb small, sweet turnips*
*1.2 1/2 pints beef stock*
*225 g/8 oz small white button mushrooms*
*4 tournedos steaks, about 150 g/6 oz each*
*4 thin strips pork fat*
*Freshly ground pepper*
*4 teaspoons brandy*
*Finely chopped parsley*

Peel the carrots and cut them into 6 mm (¼ in) thick slices, then into batons 6 mm (¼ in) wide and 4 cm (1½ in) long. Peel the turnips and cut them into strips of the same size.

Select a wide pan which will take all the tournedos steaks comfortably side by side.

Pour in the beef stock and add the carrot strips. Bring to the boil and simmer for 4 minutes. Then add the turnips and simmer for 4 minutes longer.

Meanwhile, wipe or wash the mushrooms clean; trim the stems. Add them to the simmering pan and continue to cook gently for another 4 to 5 minutes, or until the vegetables are tender. Drain the vegetables and put them aside with a little stock. Return the remaining stock to the pan. Wrap a thin strip of pork fat round the middle of each tournedos. Cut 4 pieces of string long enough to go round each tournedos and hang over the side of the pan when submerged in stock. Tie one end of each string quite firmly round each tournedos to keep the pork fat in place.

Just before serving: bring the stock to the boil and lower in the tournedos side by side. Simmer for 5 minutes if you like them rare, 8 minutes for medium, and 12 minutes for well done.

When the tournedos are ready, fish them out by their strings. Drop the vegetables in the simmering stock to reheat them.

Remove the strings and strips of pork fat from the tournedos and arrange on a shallow, heated serving dish. Season each steak liberally with freshly ground pepper and sprinkle with a teaspoon of brandy. Garnish the dish with the reheated vegetables; moisten them with some of the cooking stock and sprinkle the vegetables with finely chopped parsley. Serve immediately.

*Carrier's*

# Glazed Fillet of Beef with Soy

*Serves 6*

*1 fillet of beef (1.25–1.4 kg/2½ –3 lb), stripped of fat*
*Freshly ground pepper*

## Soy Marinade

*100 ml/3 fl oz soy sauce*
*3 tablespoons olive oil*
*2 garlic cloves, finely chopped*
*3 tablespoons dry sherry*
*3 tablespoons water*

At least 2 hours before you intend to roast beef, remove joint from the refrigerator. Season fillet on all sides with generous amounts of freshly ground pepper. Combine Soy Marinade ingredients in an oval or rectangular baking dish large enough to hold fillet. Tie fillet neatly with string and place in marinade; spoon over marinade and marinate fillet for at least 4 hours, turning several times to ensure that it is impregnated with flavours.

Preheat oven to fairly 220°C (425°F, Gas Mark 7). Place fillet on a rack in a roasting pan; spoon over some of the marinade and roast in preheated oven, basting with marinade juices from time to time, for 10 to 12 minutes per 450 g (1 lb) for rare; 14 to 16 minutes per 450 g (1 lb) for medium rare; and 20 to 22 minutes per 450 g (1 lb) for well done.

### To serve

Remove string and place on warmed serving dish.

*Robert Carrier's Kitchen*

# Roast Fillet of Beef

*Serves 6 to 8*

*1 fillet of beef (1.25–1.4 kg/2½–3 lb),
stripped of fat
3 tablespoons melted butter, or dripping
Freshly ground pepper
24 fresh spikes of rosemary
1 bay leaf, crumbled
4 tablespoons warm water
Salt
350–450 g/¾–1 lb mushrooms, sliced
and sautéed in butter and lemon juice*

At least 2 hours before you intend to roast beef, remove from the refrigerator. Preheat oven to fairly hot (220°F, 425°C, Gas Mark 7).

Tuck the narrow end of fillet under to make roast evenly thick and tie roast neatly with string. Brush generously with melted butter, or dripping, and season with freshly ground pepper, to taste.

Sear meat on all sides in a hot shallow roasting pan until well browned (3 to 4 minutes in all). Place roast on rack in roasting pan and sprinkle with rosemary spikes and crumbled bay leaf; add warm water to pan and roast in preheated oven for 8 minutes to 10 minutes per 450 g (1 lb) for very rare to rare; 14 minutes per 450 g (1 lb) for medium rare to well done; and 20 to

22 minutes per 450 g (1 lb) if you like your meat very well done. Leave to rest for 15 minutes.

Just before serving: remove string and transfer roast to a heated serving dish; season with salt, to taste, and serve with sliced mushrooms which you have sautéed in butter and lemon juice.

*Robert Carrier's Kitchen*

# Fillet of Beef en Cochonailles

*There was a time – in the late Sixties – when every dinner party was centred around a fillet of beef in pastry. This is a recipe different enough (and good enough) to bring that old favourite back to our dinner tables with panache. Especially now that excellent flaky pastry can be bought so easily in all supermarkets. The cochonailles trick is to interleave the pre-cut fillet of beef with ham slices for extra colour and flavour.*

*Serves 6*

*1 kg/2 lb fillet of beef, cut from centre*
*1 teaspoon brandy*
*50–100 g/2–4 oz ham, cut into 11 pieces*
*2 Spanish onions*
*450 g/1 lb white button mushrooms*

*7 tablespoons butter*
*Salt and freshly ground pepper*
*100 g/4 oz puff pastry, homemade or frozen*
*1 egg, lightly beaten*

### To prepare Fillet

At least 2 hours before you intend to roast beef, remove joint from the refrigerator. Preheat oven to hot (230°C, 450°F, Gas Mark 8). Trim fillet of sinews and fat and brush with brandy. With a sharp knife cut fillet vertically into 12 even slices (i.e., 11 cuts) without taking knife right through so that slices remain attached along the bottom. Ease each cut open. Slice the pieces of ham to fit each gap in the fillet, and insert one piece in each gap. Pat fillet back into shape and pin slices together with 2 long skewers, one pushed in at either end. Trim ham edges level with edge of beef.

Finely chop onions and button mushrooms. In a large pan sauté finely chopped onions in 3 tablespoons butter over a moderate heat for 3 to 4 minutes until transparent. Add mushrooms and continue to sauté for 30 to 40 minutes until the mixture is dry, adding salt and freshly ground pepper, to taste. Leave to cool. Melt remaining butter in a roasting tin until butter is foaming, and brown fillet on all sides. Cool.

## Working the Pastry

Roll pastry out in rectangle roughly 40 x 25 cm (16 x 10 in). Trim edges and put trimmings aside to use as decoration. Spoon half the mushroom and onion mixture into the centre of the pastry. Remove metal skewers from meat. Transfer fillet to pastry and press remaining onion and mushroom mixture on to fillet. Seal fillet completely by folding one side of pastry over beef; spread a little beaten egg over upper surface and then fold over second side, overlapping the first. Roll pastry ends out flat, spread with beaten egg on upper side and fold ends over the roll.

Lay pastry-wrapped fillet on a heavy baking sheet, inverting it again so that main seam is underneath. Make 3 holes in top of pastry to allow steam to escape. Decorate around the holes with leaves, etc., made from discarded trimmings. Brush all over with beaten egg. Score surface of pastry attractively with a sharp knife.

Bake fillet for 20 minutes. Serve fillet in slices accompanied by Béarnaise Sauce (see pages 42–3) or Horseradish Chantilly (see page 33).

*Robert Carrier's Cookery Course*

# Corned Beef Hash with Poached Eggs

*Serves 6*

*2 tablespoons butter*
*1 tablespoon olive oil*
*1 Spanish onion, finely chopped*
*2 green peppers, cored, seeded and diced*
*700 g/1½ lb corned beef*
*300 g/12 oz potatoes, cooked and diced*
*6 tablespoons finely chopped parsley*
*2 tablespoons Worcestershire sauce*
*Salt and freshly ground pepper*
*6 poached eggs*

In a large frying pan heat the butter and olive oil. Add the onion and green pepper. Cook over a medium heat for 10 minutes or until soft, stirring occasionally.

Meanwhile, scrape any fat from the surface of the corned beef and mash to a paste. Add to the cooked vegetables, with the diced potato, chopped parsley, Worcestershire sauce and season with salt and freshly ground pepper to taste. Cook over a medium heat for 5 minutes or until the corned beef is heated through, stirring constantly.

Poach the eggs. Turn out the corned beef on to a serving platter and shape into a neat round. Arrange poached eggs at even intervals round the hash. Serve immediately.

*Robert Carrier's Kitchen*

# Beef Steak and Kidney Pudding

*This old-fashioned British steamed suet pudding, with its cargo of steak and kidneys enhanced, for modern times, with rich beef stock and a hint of dark caramel and Worcestershire sauce, is one of my favourite winter treats. One day I ran out of additional flour to dust the working surface when I was rolling out the pastry and used cornmeal (polenta) instead. The result was even more satisfying.*

*Serves 4 to 6*

*1 kg/2 lb good stewing steak*
*225 g/8 oz lamb's kidneys*
*2 tablespoons flour*
*Salt and freshly ground pepper*
*4 tablespoons finely chopped onion*
*225 g/8 oz self-raising flour*
*100 g/4 oz freshly grated or shredded suet*
*Butter for greasing*
*2 teaspoons sugar*
*150 ml/5 fl oz beef stock*
*1 teaspoon Worcestershire sauce*

Cut the stewing steak into 12 mm (½ in) cubes, removing all the fat and gristle. Slice the kidneys in half and remove the cores with a pair of scissors. Put the kidneys in a pan; cover with cold water; bring to the boil over

a moderate heat and drain thoroughly. Cut the kidneys horizontally into thin slices.

In a bowl, combine the meat and kidneys. Sprinkle with flour, tossing until the meat and kidneys are evenly coated, and season generously with salt and freshly ground pepper. Stir in the finely chopped onion.

Sift the self-raising flour into a large bowl. Stir in the suet; season with salt and freshly ground pepper, and add enough iced water, about 150 ml (5 fl oz), to make a soft but manageable mixture, rather like a scone dough. Knead lightly. Grease a 1.5 l (2½ pint) pudding basin with the butter.

Turn the suet dough on to a floured board. Roll out two-thirds of it fairly thickly, about 6 mm (¼ in) or more, and line the basin, taking the dough slightly over the rim. Fill the lined basin with the meat and kidney mixture.

## To make Pudding

Put the sugar in a small heavy-bottomed saucepan and shake over a low heat until it has melted and turned to a medium-dark caramel. (Remove from the heat for a few seconds before the caramel has cooked sufficiently, as it tends to continue cooking from the heat of the pan.) Cool slightly. Covering your hand with a cloth, carefully pour in the hot stock and stir until the caramel has melted, returning the pan to a

moderate heat if necessary. Cool slightly. Flavour the caramel to taste with the Worcestershire sauce and pour over the contents of the pudding basin.

Roll out the remaining dough and trim it into a circle to fit the top of the basin. Wet the rim with a little water and lay the dough in position; seal the edges thoroughly.

Cover the top of the pudding with greased greaseproof paper and a cloth – not too tightly, to leave room for expansion – and tie in position with string. Place the pudding in a steamer over a pan of boiling water, or in a saucepan with water to come halfway up the sides of the basin. Cover the steamer (or saucepan) tightly and cook for 3 hours, topping up with more boiling water as necessary. Remove the string and cloth, and gently run a knife round the rim of the suet pastry. Turn the pudding out on to a heated serving dish and serve immediately.

*The Sunday Times*

# Carbonnade of Beef

*Serves 4 to 6*

*700 g/2½ lb beef skirt*
*50 g/1 oz seasoned flour*
*50 g/1 oz butter*
*4 Spanish onions, thinly sliced*

*1 level tablespoon brown sugar*
*1 level tablespoon flour*
*2 cloves garlic, crushed*
*Salt and freshly ground pepper*
*Freshly grated nutmeg*
*300 ml/10 fl oz beer*
*150 ml/5 fl oz rich beef stock*
*1 tablespoon wine vinegar*

## Glazed Carrots (optional)

*450 g/1 lb carrots, thickly sliced*
*50 g/1 oz butter*
*4 tablespoons chicken stock*
*1 level tablespoon sugar*
*Salt*

Cut beef skirt into slices 2.5 cm (1 in) thick. Trim off any fat, and cut meat into 2.5 cm (1 in) wide strips across the grain. Roll strips in well-seasoned flour, shaking off excess.

Melt butter in a thick-bottomed, flameproof casserole; add thinly sliced onions and sprinkle with brown sugar. Sauté over a moderate heat until onions are golden brown and sugar is slightly caramelised. Remove onions from casserole. Brown meat well on all sides in fat remaining in casserole. Return onions to casserole; sprinkle with flour and add garlic. Season to taste with salt, freshly ground pepper and a generous pinch of freshly grated nutmeg. Add beer, stock and vinegar. Cover casserole tightly and simmer

in a very slow oven (135°C, 275°F, Gas Mark 1) for 2½ to 3 hours, or until meat is very tender.

### To prepare Glazed Carrots

As the casserole cooks, cover the carrots with cold water and blanch. Drain well. Simmer blanched carrots with butter, chicken stock, sugar and salt, to taste, until carrots have absorbed liquid without burning and have taken on a little colour.

### To serve

When meat is tender, skim sauce. If sauce is too thin, transfer meat to a heated dish with a slotted spoon and keep hot while you reduce sauce by letting it bubble briskly, uncovered, on top of the stove. Return meat to casserole together with carrots, heat through and serve.

*Daily Mirror*

# Mushrooms à la Bordelaise

*Serves 6*

*6–12 large, flat mushrooms, according to size*

*Olive oil*
*2–3 cloves garlic, finely chopped*
*2–3 level tablspoons finely chopped parsley*
*Salt and freshly ground pepper*

Wash mushrooms and trim stems. Drain. Sauté mushrooms in olive oil, cut side down, for 2 minutes; turn mushrooms over; sprinkle with finely chopped garlic and parsley; season with salt and freshly ground pepper, to taste, and continue to cook for a few minutes longer, until mushrooms are tender. Serve immediately.

*Homes and Gardens*

# Flemish Carbonnade of Beef

*Serves 4*

*1 kg/2 lb braising beef*
*Salt and freshly ground pepper*
*3 tablespoons butter*
*3 tablespoons olive oil*
*2 Spanish onions, thinly sliced*
*1 tablespoon wine vinegar*
*1 tablespoon light brown sugar*
*200 ml/7 fl oz beef stock*
*300 ml/10 fl oz pale ale*
*Bouquet garni*

## Beurre Manié

*1½ tablespoons butter*
*1½ tablespoons flour*

Cut the beef across the grain into fairly thin slices. Season generously with salt and freshly ground pepper. In a large flameproof casserole, heat the butter and olive oil. Brown the beef slices a few pieces at a time for 2 minutes on each side or until brown. Remove from the pan with a slotted spoon and keep warm. Repeat with the remaining meat.

Add the thinly sliced onions to the fat remaining in the pan and sauté over a moderate heat for 10 minutes or until a rich golden brown, stirring occasionally. Return the beef slices to the pan, add the wine vinegar and light brown sugar and cook for a further 1 to 2 minutes, stirring.

Add the beef stock, pale ale and *bouquet garni* and season with salt and freshly ground pepper to taste. Cover and simmer gently for 2 hours or until the beef is tender, stirring occasionally.

## To make a Beurre Manié

Mash the butter and flour together and add it to the beef carbonnade a little at a time, stirring it in well. Simmer gently for 1 to 2 minutes until the liquid has thickened, correct the seasoning and serve immediately.

*Daily Mirror*

# Tagine of Beef with Prunes and Almonds

*Moroccan cooking is full of recipes combining meat and fruits – a leftover from medieval times – as is the fine combination of sugar and spices. Try it and see.*

*Serves 4*

*1.25–1.4 kg/2½ –3 lb beef*
*2 large Spanish onions*
*2 tablespoons olive oil*
*1 teaspoon salt*
*½ teaspoon freshly ground pepper*
*1 teaspoon powdered cinnamon*
*¼ teaspoon powdered ginger*
*½ teaspoon saffron*
*100 g/4 oz butter*
*Water*
*450 g/1 lb dried prunes*
*4 tablespoons sugar*
*1 strip of lemon peel*
*2–3 short sticks cinnamon*
*350 g/12 oz blanched almonds, sautéed in butter*
*Sprigs of fresh mint or watercress*

Cut the meat into pieces about 4 cm (1½ in) square. Grate onions coarsely into a small bowl; add olive oil, salt, freshly ground pepper, powdered cinnamon and ginger and saffron and mix well. Spoon aromatics over meat and mix well, rubbing aromatics into each piece of meat with your fingers.

When ready to cook, transfer prepared meat to a thick-bottomed heatproof casserole and add butter and enough water just to cover meat and cook over a medium heat, covered, until meat is tender.

In the meantime, prepare the prunes. Cover the boiling water and allow prunes to infuse for 20 minutes. Drain. Remove 2 ladles of sauce from the casserole; skim off all fat; add 2 tablespoons sugar, lemon peel and cinnamon sticks and in a small saucepan cook prunes in this sauce for 20 minutes, or until prunes are soft and swollen.

Add 2 tablespoons sugar to casserole with meat. Stir well.

Transfer meat to a heated serving dish; garnish with prunes and their sauce. Reduce remaining sauce to half its original quantity over a high heat. Pour over meat and prunes; sprinkle with sautéed almonds and garnish dish with sprigs of fresh mint or watercress and serve immediately.

*Taste of Morocco*

# Japanese Beef with Fresh Ginger

*Rolf Widner, a young Swiss chef now cooking in Australia, once worked with me at Carrier's. This delightful cold appetiser was one of his creations. We served it often in the restaurant — to raves.*

*Serves 4*

*16 long thin slices rare sirloin
(21 x 5 cm/8 x 2 in)
3–4 tablespoons sesame seed oil
32 julienne strips of carrot, blanched
32 5 cm/2 in strips of chives, blanched*

## Marinade

*1 ginger root
Juice of 1 lime
4 tablespoons Mexican honey
4 teaspoons soy sauce*

Peel ginger root and cut into strips. In a small bowl combine lime juice, Mexican honey and soy sauce. Add julienne of ginger and leave for 2 hours.

Brush strips of beef with sesame seed oil. Lay 1 strip of beef with short edge towards you, fold short edges to middle and then fold over bottom edge to form a 5 cm (2 in) square. Repeat with remaining beef strips.

Place 4 pieces of beef on 4 individual serving plates with julienne of ginger and marinade in the centre. Garnish beef square with 2 pieces of carrot and chive, crossed diagonally.

*Quick Cook*

# Minute Sauté of Beef with Burgundy Garnish

*This was a recipe I first created for my old friend James Beard, America's best-loved cookery authority, when he visited me at Hintlesham Hall. The idea was to serve a main course right at the table in the kitchen after only 3 to 5 minutes of cooking in front of the guests. The chef's trick? Easy . . . with a little pre-prep of the traditional Burgundian sauce and garnish of sautéed bacon, button mushrooms and onions kept warm in pans on the stove, ready to be added at the last minute to the sautéed meats in the large frying pan and brought — triumphantly, of course — to the guests after only 3 to 4 minutes of 'cooking time'. Magic . . . or so it seemed.*

*Serves 4 to 6*

*1 kg/2 lb fillet of beef
Salt and freshly ground pepper
1 bay leaf*

115

6 tablespoons olive oil
2 tablespoons finely chopped parsley or
chives

## Bourguignonne Sauce
### *(Can be prepared 1 day ahead)*

2 tablespoons butter or lard
700 g/1½ lb shin of beef with bones,
coarsely chopped
2 large carrots, coarsely chopped
2 tablespoons flour
1 pint red wine
1 tablespoon tomato purée
2 bay leaves
2 garlic cloves, unpeeled and crushed
½ teaspoon dried thyme, crushed
Salt and freshly ground pepper
Cayenne pepper

## Bourguignonne Garnish
### *(Can be prepared 1 day ahead)*

18 button onions
2 tablespoons butter
Sugar
4 tablespoons red wine
12 button mushrooms
Lemon juice
1 bacon slice (12 mm/ ½ in thick),
cut into 12 strips
1 tablespoon olive oil

## To prepare Fillet of Beef

Cut fillet of beef into slices approximately 2.5 cm (1 in) thick. Trim each slice into 3 or 4 even-sized cubes. Reserve meat trimmings and scraps for sauce. Season beef cubes generously with salt and freshly ground pepper and place in an earthenware or porcelain (not metal) bowl. Add bay leaf and olive oil; toss well and leave beef cubes to marinate for at least 2 hours.

Meanwhile, make Bourguignonne Sauce. In a thick-bottomed saucepan, melt butter or lard over a medium heat and cook shin of beef and reserved trimmings and scraps from fillet until well browned on all sides. Pour off excess fats. Add coarsely chopped onions, carrot and celery stalks to pan and stir for 3 minutes; sprinkle with flour and stir for a further minute. Add 1.2 l (2 pints) water, 450 ml (15 fl oz) red wine, tomato purée, bay leaves, crushed unpeeled garlic and crushed dried thyme and simmer for 1 hour, skimming surface occasionally. Strain sauce into a measuring jug and measure, adding enough liquid to measure 600 ml (1 pint), or if there is too much liquid, strain sauce into a clean pan and reduce to 600 ml (1 pint).

Add remaining red wine to pan in which you cooked meat and vegetables and boil for 1 minute over a high heat, scraping in any crusty bits from bottom and sides of pan. Stir into sauce. Strain sauce again into a clean pan; season with salt and freshly ground pepper

and cayenne pepper, to taste, and reduce again to 600 ml (1 pint). Keep warm.

### To make Bourguignonne Garnish

Sauté button onions in 1 tablespoon butter with a little sugar until brown. Add red wine; cover and cook over a low heat until onions are just tender. Sauté button mushrooms in remaining butter with a little lemon juice until just tender. Sauté bacon strips in olive oil until crisp. Combine sautéed onions, mushrooms and bacon strips and keep warm.

### To sauté Beef at last minute

Using a slotted spoon, remove beef cubes from marinade. In a thick-bottomed frying pan, sear beef cubes in marinating oil on all sides until golden brown, but still quite rare. Pour off excess fats. Add warm Bourguignonne Sauce to pan and bring to the bubble. Add Bourguignonne Garnish; sprinkle with finely chopped parsley or chives and bring to the table.

*Note:* don't be afraid to experiment with wine in cooking. Think of it as just another of the necessary ingredients like butter, olive oil, onions and herbs. It will round out and add savour to your cooking.

*Hintlesham Hall*

# Bœuf Bourguignonne

*Serves 4*

*1 kg/2 lb beef*
*½ bottle red wine*
*225 g/12 oz carrots, sliced*
*25 g/1 oz shallots, finely chopped*
*50 g/2 oz onion, finely chopped*
*1–2 sprigs thyme*
*1–2 bay leaves*
*6 black peppercorns*
*Pinch quatre épices*
*225 g/8 oz green bacon, diced*
*12 button onions*
*12 baby carrots*
*1 tablespoon flour*
*1 glass water*
*2–4 cloves garlic*
*Bouquet garni*
*Salt and freshly ground pepper*
*12 button mushrooms*
*Butter*

Cut beef into bite-sized pieces and marinate overnight in red wine with carrots, shallots, onion, thyme, bay leaves, peppercorns and spices. Drain well. Dice green bacon and brown in a cocotte with small onions and carrots. When they are lightly coloured, remove them, and sauté drained beef in remaining fat until brown. Sprinkle with

flour, add red wine from marinade and a glass of water.

Return diced green bacon, onions and carrots and add garlic, a *bouquet garni* and salt and freshly ground pepper, to taste. Simmer gently until meat is tender and the sauce is reduced to half of its original quantity, about 2¾ to 3 hours. Ten minutes before the end of the cooking, add the mushrooms which you have previously browned in butter.

*Vogue*

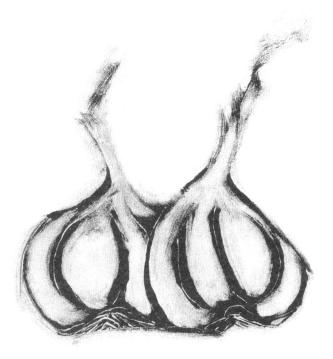

# Chile Con Carne

*In spite of repeated warnings this recipe seems to have caused more trouble than all the others put together, in a writing career spanning over 20 years! So please do not, repeat do not, confuse Mexican chile powder seasoning with powdered chillies. The former is a strong but pleasant Mexican blend of spices and peppers and the traditional seasoning for Chile Con Carne. The latter is so hot that more than a pinch or two renders a dish inedible.*

*Serves 4*

1 kg/2 lb lean beef
4 tablespoons bacon fat
1 Spanish onion, finely chopped
4 cloves garlic, finely chopped
450 ml/15 fl oz beef stock
150 ml/5 fl oz red wine
3 tablespoons Mexican chile powder
(see note above)
1 tablespoon flour
2 bay leaves
½ teaspoon powdered cumin
½ teaspoon dried oregano
Salt and freshly ground pepper
Mexican beans
Boiled saffron rice

Cut beef into bite-sized cubes, trimming fat as you go. Heat bacon fat in a large casserole and sauté meat for 3 to 4 minutes on each side. Remove with a slotted spoon and keep warm. In the remaining fat sauté finely chopped onion and garlic for 4 to 5 minutes until slightly golden. Return meat to casserole; cover with beef stock and red wine. Bring to the boil over a gentle heat; cover and simmer for about 1 hour.

With a wooden spoon blend chile powder and flour in a little of the hot pan juices and add to casserole together with bay leaves, powdered cumin, dried oregano, and salt and freshly ground pepper, to taste. Give a final stir to blend in seasonings. Simmer for 1 hour until meat is tender. Correct seasoning and serve with Mexican beans and rice.

*Great Dishes of the World*

# Yankee Pot Roast

*My Yankee grandmother, Udora Josephine Carrier, one of five sisters with equally extravagant names (my great aunts) used to make this American country dish to celebrate family visits when I was a boy living in Tarrytown, New York.*
*I still love it.*

*Serves 4 to 6*

*1 (1.4 kg/3 lb) piece of beef, boneless brisket or chuck*
*2 tablespoons lard*
*2 tablespoons olive oil*
*300 ml/10 fl oz well-flavoured beef stock*
*1 can (100 g/4 oz) Italian peeled tomatoes*

## Flavouring Vegetables

*4 large (or 8 small) carrots, quartered*
*2 Spanish onions, quartered*
*1 large (or 2 small) turnips, quartered*

## Aromatics

*4 whole cloves*
*2 whole allspice, or ¼ teaspoon ground allspice*
*1 tablespoon soy sauce*
*2 bay leaves*
*Salt and freshly ground pepper*
*Freshly grated nutmeg*

## Beurre Manié

*2 tablespoons butter*
*2 tablespoons flour*
*150 ml/5 fl oz red wine, reduced over a*
*high heat, to 4–6 tablespoons*

## Garnish

*4 carrots, peeled and cut in 5 cm/*
*2 in segments*
*12 button onions, peeled*
*3 turnips, quartered*
*A little stock (from pot roast)*
*4–6 small potatoes*

Brown roast well on all sides in lard and olive oil in a thick-bottomed casserole. Pour off excess fat; add beef stock and Italian peeled tomatoes (with juices) and bring to the boil. Skim; then reduce heat. Add quartered carrots, onions, turnips, cloves, allspice, soy sauce, bay leaves and salt, freshly ground pepper and freshly grated nutmeg, to taste; cover casserole tightly and cook over a very low heat for 2½ to 3 hours, or until meat is tender, checking often to see that the liquid in the casserole barely simmers (or the meat will be tough and dry) and only turning meat once during cooking time.

Thirty minutes before serving time, prepare Vegetable Garnish: poach prepared small carrots, onions and turnips in a little stock, or stock and water, until just tender.

Boil potatoes. Transfer meat with a slotted spoon to a heated serving dish and garnish meat with freshly boiled vegetables.

Skim fat from sauce in casserole, strain sauce into small saucepan; cook over a high heat until bubbling and then thicken sauce by adding *Beurre Manié* (made by mashing 2 tablespoons each butter and flour together to a smooth paste). Add reduced wine; correct seasoning by adding a little more salt and freshly ground pepper and freshly grated nutmeg, to taste. Spoon a little sauce over meat and vegetables. Serve remainder in a sauce boat.

*Daily Telegraph*

# Beef with Pappardelle and Orange Gremolata

*Serves 6*

## Beef

*1.4 kg/3 lb boned shoulder of beef top cut*
*(1.75 kg/4 lb before boning)*
*6 tablespoons flour*
*Salt and ground pepper*
*Paprika and cayenne*
*3 tablespoons butter*
*3 tablespoons olive oil*
*2 Spanish onions, quartered*
*2–3 tablespoons sugar*
*450 ml/15 fl oz beef stock*
*3 tablespoons tomato purée*
*3 small turnips, quartered*
*Bouquet garni*

## Garnish

*12 button onions*
*100 g/4 oz unsmoked bacon, diced*
*12 small potatoes, peeled*
*150 ml/5 fl oz red wine*
*150 g/6 oz frozen peas*
*225 g/8 oz pappardelle pasta, cooked*

Preheat the oven to 180°C (350°F, Gas Mark 4). Cut the beef into 4 cm (1 ½ in) cubes, discarding most of the fat and all of the gristle. Season flour generously with salt, ground pepper, paprika and cayenne to taste. Place half the seasoned flour in a large bowl and toss half the meat cubes in flour. Remove meat from bowl; add remaining seasoned flour to bowl and toss remaining meat until it is well coated. Heat 2 tablespoons butter and 2 tablespoons olive oil in a heatproof casserole. Brown the meat on all sides, in 4 batches; with a slotted spoon, transfer each batch as it is browned to a bowl and keep warm.

Add the quartered Spanish onion to the casserole with sugar. Brown sugared onion pieces on all sides in the casserole. Add the beef stock to the casserole and stir vigorously with a wooden spoon to incorporate all the crusty bits into the stock. Bring to the boil. Stir in the tomato purée and blend well. Add the quartered turnips and the *bouquet garni* and return the sautéed meat to the pan. Season with salt and ground pepper to taste. Cover and cook in the preheated over for 1 hour.

Meanwhile, in a small frying pan, melt the remaining teaspoon of butter and olive oil. Add the button onions and 1 teaspoon sugar and toss over a moderate heat for 5 to 7 minutes or until golden brown. Remove with a slotted spoon to a plate and keep warm.

Sauté the diced bacon in the remaining fat for 4 minutes or until golden. Add to the browned onions and keep warm.

Remove the beef cubes from the casserole

and keep warm. Strain the sauce and return it to the casserole. Skim off any fat and return it to the casserole. Return the beef to the pan with the sautéed onions and bacon and the peeled potatoes.

In a small saucepan, reduce red wine to about 4 tablespoons, add reduced wine to the casserole; cover and return to the oven for a further 30 minutes. Remove the lid; stir in the peas and cook for a further 5 to 10 minutes or until the meat and vegetables are tender. Correct the seasoning: stir in the cooked pappardelle, transfer to a heated serving dish; sprinkle with Orange Gremolata, and serve immediately.

*Cooking with Carrier*

# Orange Gremolata

*For a truly special flavour, generously sprinkle Gremolata mixture over beef just before serving. Lemon Gremolata also makes a lively seasoning for a tossed green salad.*

*Serves 6*

*4 tablespoons chopped parsley*
*2 teaspoons grated orange peel*
*1 clove garlic, finely chopped*
*Salt and freshly ground pepper*

### To make Gremolata

In a small bowl, combine parsley, orange peel, garlic and salt and freshly ground pepper, to taste. Toss until well blended.

*Note:* Gremolata is best prepared just before using, but it can be kept in a covered jar in the refrigerator for 1 or 2 more days.

*Cooking with Carrier*

# Saltimbocca all'Alfredo

*Serves 4*

*4 thin slices veal*
*Freshly ground pepper*
*12 small sage leaves*
*4 thin slices prosciutto (raw Parma ham)*
*3 tablespoons butter*
*3 tablespoons Marsala*

Between 2 sheets of clingfilm, flatten the slices of veal with a meat cleaver. Season both sides of the veal generously with freshly ground pepper. Cut each veal slices into 3 equal pieces, and place a sage leaf in the centre of each. Cut each slice of Parma ham into 3 and cover each piece of veal, trimming the ham to the same size. Roll up the veal with the Parma ham inside, and tie with fine string.

In a frying pan large enough to take the veal and ham rolls in one layer, heat the butter and sauté the meat for 2 minutes until golden brown all over, turning the veal once with a spatula. Add the Marsala, cover the pan and simmer gently for 3 minutes, or until the veal and ham rolls are tender, turning them occasionally.

Transfer to a heated serving dish and pour over the glaze.

*The Robert Carrier Cookbook*

# Pan-Fried Escalopes of Veal Savoyarde

*Serves 4*

*8 thin escalopes veal*
*1 tablespoon seasoned flour*
*25 g/1 oz fresh breadcrumbs*
*Salt and freshly ground pepper*
*1 egg, beaten*
*4 tablespoons butter*

## Savoyarde Mixture

*1 tablespoon butter*
*1 tablespoon flour*
*150 ml/5 fl oz milk*
*1 egg, beaten*
*100 g/4 oz Gruyère cheese, finely grated*
*Salt and freshly ground pepper*
*Freshly grated nutmeg*

### *To make Savoyarde Mixture*

Melt butter in a saucepan and add flour, stirring well. Cook for 1 minute, then gradually add milk; bring to the boil and allow to simmer for 5 minutes. Reduce heat; whisk in beaten egg and cook for 1 minute to allow sauce to thicken. Mix in finely grated Gruyère cheese to pan and season with salt and freshly ground pepper and freshly grated nutmeg, to taste.

## To prepare Veal

Put flour in a shallow dish and breadcrumbs in another shallow dish. Beat veal escalopes individually between 2 pieces of wet greaseproof paper (or clingfilm) with a rolling pin, or meat bat, to tenderise meat. Season both sides of escalopes with salt and freshly ground pepper. Spread 1 side of 4 escalopes generously with Savoyarde Mixture and cover with remaining escalopes. Toss escalopes in flour, shaking off excess. Dip in beaten egg and toss in breadcrumbs, patting coating on firmly.

Melt butter in a heavy frying pan and fry veal escalopes for 1½ minutes on each side. Transfer veal escalopes to a heated serving dish and serve immediately.

*Carrier's*

# Veal Parmesan 'Four Seasons'

*Serves 4 to 6*

*8 thin slices of veal (pounded as for Wiener Schnitzel or Scallopini)*
*Flour, seasoned with salt, freshly ground pepper and crushed dried chillies*
*3 eggs, well beaten*
*6 tablespoons fresh breadcrumbs*
*4 tablespoons freshly grated Parmesan*
*Grated rind of 1 lemon*
*Olive oil or butter, for frying*

Place 3 flat plates on working surface. Cover one with seasoned flour; cover the second with beaten eggs; and the third with a combination of fresh breadcrumbs, freshly grated Parmesan and grated lemon rind.

Dip thin slices of pounded veal in flour, then in beaten egg and finally in the mixture of breadcrumbs, cheese and lemon rind. Chill breaded veal slices in the refrigerator until ready to use.

When ready to cook: heat olive oil or butter (or a combination of the two) in a large heatproof frying pan. Or use two. Sauté veal slices on both sides in the fat until golden brown. Serve immediately.

*The Robert Carrier Cookbook*

# German Veal
# with Almonds

*Serves 4*

*4 veal escalopes, 100g/4–5 oz each*
*3 tablespoons butter*
*3 tablespoons olive oil*
*100 g/4 oz button mushrooms, thinly*
*sliced*
*Salt and freshly ground pepper*
*1½ tablespoons Madeira*
*100 g/4 oz cooked tongue*
*2 eggs, beaten*
*50 g/2 oz fresh white breadcrumbs*
*35 g/1½ oz flaked almonds,*
*roughly chopped*
*Flour*
*300 ml/8 fl oz  Hollandaise Sauce*
*(pages 23–4)*

In a medium-sized frying pan, heat 1 tablespoon each of the butter and olive oil and sauté the mushrooms for 5 minutes or until golden brown, turning them with a spatula. Season with salt and freshly ground pepper to taste. Sprinkle the Madeira over the mushrooms.

### To prepare Veal

Beat the veal escalopes between sheets of clingfilm with a meat bat until they are as thin as possible. Season the meat generously with salt and freshly ground pepper. Cut the tongue into thin strips. Divide it into 4 bundles and pile each bundle in the centre of an escalope. Spoon sautéed mushrooms over the top and fold each escalope into an envelope. Place the beaten eggs in a shallow dish, and the fresh white breadcrumbs and chopped flaked almonds, combined, in another shallow bowl.

Dust the veal envelopes with flour, dip into the beaten egg and coat with the almond and breadcrumb mixture, patting the mixture on firmly. Chill for about 15 minutes to set the coating.

### To cook Veal

Heat the remaining butter and olive oil in a frying pan large enough to take the envelopes of veal in one layer. Lay them in the hot fat side by side and cook over a low heat for 5 minutes each side, or until golden brown. Arrange them on a heated serving platter and serve immediately with the Hollandaise Sauce.

*Carrier's*

# Veal Escalopes Parmigiana

*Serves 4*

*4 veal escalopes, 100 g/4–5 oz each*
*Oil for deep-frying*
*2 tablespoons flour*
*Salt and freshly ground pepper*
*1 egg, beaten lightly*
*4 tablespoons single cream*
*25 g/1 oz fresh white breadcrumbs*
*8 tablespoons freshly*
*grated Parmesan*
*300 ml/10 fl oz Raw Tomato Sauce*
*(see page 127)*
*100 g/4 oz Mozzarella cheese, thinly*
*sliced*
*2 tablespoons finely chopped parsley*
*4 small bouquets of watercress*

Preheat the over to 230°C (450°F, Gas Mark 8), and heat the oil in a deep-fat fryer to 190°C (375°F).

### *To prepare Veal*

Place the veal escalopes between sheets of clingfilm and pound until thin with a meat bat.

Sprinkle the flour on to a plate and season with salt and freshly ground pepper. In a shallow bowl, combine the egg and single cream and mix to blend with a fork. Sprinkle the fresh white breadcrumbs into a separate shallow dish and mix with half of the freshly grated Parmesan cheese.

Toss each veal escalope in seasoned flour to coat and then in the egg and cream mixture, draining off the excess. Coat in the breadcrumb and Parmesan mixture, patting it on firmly with the palms of your hands. Lay them flat on a tray.

### *To cook Veal*

Deep-fry 2 veal escalopes at a time for 30 seconds on each side. Drain on absorbent paper and place in individual *gratin* dishes. Spread Raw Tomato Sauce evenly over each one and sprinkle with the remaining freshly grated Parmesan cheese. Top with thin slices of mozzarella and the finely chopped parsley.

Bake in the preheated oven for 10 minutes or until the cheese is melted and golden brown. Decorate each dish with a bouquet of watercress on one side. Serve immediately.

*Great Dishes of the World*

126

# Raw Tomato Sauce (Sauce vièrge)

*600 g/1½ lb ripe tomatoes, peeled,*
*seeded and chopped*
*8 tablespoons lemon juice*
*2 cloves of garlic, finely chopped*
*6 black olives, pitted and finely chopped*
*Salt and freshly ground pepper*
*1 tablespoon each finely chopped tarragon,*
*chives and flat-leafed parsley*

In a medium-sized bowl, combine the tomatoes, olive oil, lemon juice and garlic, and add salt and freshly ground pepper, to taste. Set aside for 2 hours to allow flavours to blend. Just before serving, stir in the chopped black olives and herbs.

*Feasts of Provence*

# Wiener Schnitzel

*The famous Viennese dish which gives breaded star quality. You might find it difficult to persuade your local butcher to cut slices of escalope for you across the grain from a leg of veal. If so, the ideal alternative is boned veal cutlets, or fillets, both of which can be pounded out to the required thinness without shredding. And while on the subject of thinness, a schnitzel should be thin, but not transparent; you do not want to end up with a fried breadcrumb sandwich.*

*Serves 4*

*2 veal cutlets, boned (about 275 g/10 oz each), or 4 thin slices veal fillet*
*25 g/1 oz plain flour*
*1 egg, beaten*
*75 g/3 oz fine dry breadcrumbs*
*4–6 oz butter*
*2 tablespoons olive oil*
*Salt and freshly ground pepper*
*4 anchovy fillets*
*4 stuffed olives*
*1 lemon, cut in wedges*

If boned cutlets are used, cut each one into 2 thin slices, slanting the knife so that you cut as much across the grain as possible. Lay pieces of veal between two sheets of

greaseproof paper and pound them until very thin.

Dust each *schnitzel* with flour. Dip in beaten egg, draining off excess, and coat with fine dry breadcrumbs, patting them in firmly with a palette knife or the palm of the hand. Chill in the refrigerator for at least 30 minutes to 'set' coating. Use one very large frying pan or two smaller ones which hold each schnitzel comfortably in one layer. Heat butter with olive oil until foaming; sprinkle lightly with salt and freshly ground pepper; add *schnitzels*. Fry over a steady, moderate heat for 3 to 5 minutes on each side, turning them once, until breadcrumb casing is crisp and golden and veal inside cooked but still very juicy.

Transfer *schnitzels* to a large heated serving dish. Place 1 anchovy-wrapped olive in centre of each *schnitzel* and garnish dish with lemon wedges.

*Robert Carrier's Kitchen*

# Pan-Fried Veal Chops 'Grandmère'

*Serves 4*

*4 thick veal chops (350 g / 12 oz each)*
*Salt and freshly ground pepper*
*16 button onions*
*100 g / 4 oz diced bacon*
*100 g / 4 oz button mushrooms, quartered*
*4 tablespoons butter*
*2 tablespoons olive oil*
*4 tablespoons well-flavoured beef stock*
*2 tablespoons finely chopped parsley*

Place button onions and diced bacon in a saucepan of cold water and bring to the boil. Drain. Heat 2 tablespoons butter and olive oil in a heavy frying pan over a high flame and brown veal chops for 2 minutes on each side. Reduce heat; cover pan and cook chops gently for 6 to 8 minutes. Meanwhile, melt remaining butter in a heavy frying pan and sauté onions and bacon for 5 minutes. Add mushrooms and cook for a further 2 to 3 minutes. When cooked, transfer veal chops to a heated serving dish. Deglaze pan with beef stock. Add onion/bacon/mushroom mixture and season with salt and freshly ground pepper, to taste. Pour over veal chops. Sprinkle with finely chopped parsley and serve immediately.

*The Robert Carrier Cookbook*

# Cotelettes 'Pojarsky'

*Serves 4*

*450 g/1 lb boned shoulder of veal*
*Salt and freshly ground pepper*
*300 ml/10 fl oz double cream*
*Flour*
*4–5 tablespoons butter*
*150 g/6 oz fresh morilles if possible, or*
*mushrooms, sliced*
*150 ml/5 fl oz dry white wine*
*Beurre manié (1 tablespoon each butter and*
*flour mashed to a smooth paste)*

Remove nerves and skin from meat and cut meat into small pieces. Mince in electric food processor until very fine. Add a generous seasoning of salt, freshly ground pepper and 150 ml (5 fl oz) double cream to meat and blend again for a few minutes only, until purée is very fine.

Sprinkle working surface with flour. Divide the minced veal into 8 portions and form each into a miniature cutlet about 6 mm (¼ in) thick. Chill in the refrigerator for 2 hours. Heat 2 tablespoons of butter and sauté sliced mushrooms until just soft.

Melt remaining butter in a large frying pan, add cutlets and sauté them for 4 to 5 minutes, or until they are golden brown on both sides. Lift out and drain and keep warm.

Add dry white wine to the frying pan and scrape up all the crunchy bits from bottom and sides of the pan. Add remaining double cream and the sautéed mushrooms. Stir and blend everything over a gentle heat. Add *beurre manié* a little at a time, stirring it in well. When all the *beurre manié* is added heat the sauce gently for 2 or 3 minutes. Pour the mushroom sauce over the cotelettes.

*Grand Hôtel du Commerce, Lamastre*

# Veal Avesnoise

*No one ever believes just how quick this recipe is to make. I find it a wonderful dinner party treat when I have a moist, pink roast of veal to serve as the base for the golden cheese and cream topping. Also good with pork.*

*Serves 4*

*4 large slices roast veal*
*100 g / 4 oz Gruyère cheese, finely grated*
*2 teaspoons tomato purée*
*½ teaspoon Worcestershire sauce*
*2 tablespoons double cream*
*Salt and freshly ground pepper*
*Tabasco sauce*
*Olive oil*

Preheat the grill to high. In a bowl, mix the finely grated Gruyère cheese with the tomato purée, Worcestershire sauce and enough cream to make a smooth mixture. Season generously with salt, freshly ground pepper and Tabasco.

Brush the grill grid with olive oil and place the veal slices on the grid. Spread each piece with a quarter of the cheese mixture and grill, 8 cm (3 in) from the heat for 1 to 2 minutes, until the sauce is golden and the meat heated through. Serve immediately.

*The Robert Carrier Cookbook*

# Vitello Tonnato

*One of my favourite summer dishes is Vitello Tonnato, a boned breast of veal larded with thin strips of anchovy and simmered in dry white wine and stock until tender. The veal is then sliced and covered with a delicious tuna-, anchovy- and caper-flavoured mayonnaise. A quicker version uses sliced roast veal (cooked until just pink and tender) served with the highly flavoured sauce.*

*Serves 6*

*Boned breast of veal 1.25–1.5 kg /*
*2½ –3 lb*
*10 anchovy fillets*
*Bay leaves*
*1 Spanish onion, sliced*
*2 carrots, sliced*
*2 stalks celery, sliced*
*2 sprigs parsley*
*2 cloves*
*Salt and freshly ground pepper*
*300 ml / 10 fl oz dry white wine (optional)*

# Tuna Fish Sauce

*125 g (7 oz) can tuna fish*
*6 anchovy fillets*
*1 teaspoon capers*
*2 tablespoons lemon juice*
*Freshly ground pepper*
*150 ml/5 fl oz mayonnaise*
*Olive oil (optional)*

# Garnish

*12 lemon slices*
*6–12 capers*

Start this dish the day before you intend to serve it. Have your butcher bone and tie a piece of breast of veal to make a joint weighing 1.25 to 1.5 kg (2½ to 3 lb) when boned and trimmed.

Cut anchovy fillets into small pieces; push these into holes pierced in surface of meat. Lay several bay leaves along top of joint.

Place meat in a heatproof casserole with sliced onion, carrots, celery, parsley sprigs and cloves. Season to taste with salt and freshly ground pepper. Pour in dry white wine and add just enough water to cover meat (or use water only). Bring to the boil. Skim; lower heat so that liquid barely simmers; cover casserole and simmer gently for 2½ to 3 hours. When veal is tender, remove string and return veal to stock. Leave to become quite cold.

## To make Tuna Fish Sauce

Drain tuna and pound with anchovy fillets and capers to a smooth paste, add lemon juice and freshly ground pepper to taste. Combine with mayonnaise in an electric blender and blend until sauce is smooth. Add a little strained veal stock if sauce seems too thick.

Drain cold veal thoroughly, reserving stock, and place veal in a bowl. Cover with prepared Tuna Fish Sauce; cover bowl with clingfilm and leave to marinate in refrigerator overnight.

One hour before serving, remove veal from sauce; scrape excess sauce into bowl. Cut veal into thin slices and arrange them in a row, slightly overlapping, on a shallow, oval serving dish. Mask slices with sauce, thinned down with a little more stock or olive oil if necessary, and refrigerate until ready to serve.

Serve garnished with lemon slices and capers.

*Robert Carrier's Kitchen*

# Calf's Liver with Sage and Avocado

*Albert Stockli was the head chef of New York's famous Four Seasons restaurant. There he created many famous recipes. My favourite is Calf's Liver with Avocado. I served this light main course often at Carrier's with the addition of sage leaves and a spoonful or two of Glace de Viande (see page 102) to give substance and flavour to the sauce.*

### Serves 4

*4 very thin slices calf's liver*
*1 avocado pear (not too ripe)*
*2 tablespoons lemon juice*
*4 tablespoons flour*
*Salt and freshly ground pepper*
*2 tablespoons butter*
*1 tablespoon olive oil*
*6 sage leaves*
*1–2 tablespoons Glace de Viande,*
*or 8 tablespoons beef stock reduced*
*to 2 tablespoons*

Peel and cut avocado in half; remove stone. Cut 3 thin slices from avocado half parallel to cut surface. Brush slices with 1 tablespoon lemon juice to preserve colour. Combine flour with salt and freshly ground pepper on a plate. Coat liver slices with seasoned flour.

Melt butter and olive oil in a frying pan; add sage leaves and sauté liver for 30 seconds on each side, turning with a fish slice. Remove liver slices from pan and place on a heated platter; keep warm.

Add *Glace de Viande* or reduced beef stock, to juices left in pan and simmer for 1 minute. Stir in lemon juice to taste, and pour over liver slices. Top liver slices with sliced avocado and serve immediately.

*Carrier's*

# Alain Senderens' Rognons de Veau aux Echalotes Rôties

*Alain Senderens is the undisputed king of Parisian cuisine. He used to serve this delicious dish in his elegant restaurant, L'Archestrate, on the rue de Varenne. It was one of his favourite dishes.*

### Serves 4

*36–44 large pink shallots*
*3 tablespoons melted butter*
*Salt and freshly ground pepper*
*½ teaspoon caster sugar*
*450 g/1 lb chicken bones, wing tops and giblets (neck, liver, heart, gizzard)*

*Butter*
*2 tablespoons olive oil*
*100–150 g /4–6 oz carrots, cut into 6*
*mm/¼ in dice*
*100–150 g/4–6 oz onions, cut into*
*6 mm/¼in dice*
*2–3 celery stalks, cut into 6 mm/¼ in dice*
*1 bouquet garni (1 thyme sprig, 1 bay leaf,*
*2 parsley roots)*
*700 g/1½ lb tomatoes, skinned and diced*
*100 g/4 oz button mushrooms, cut into*
*6 mm/¼ in dice*
*1 beef stock cube, crumbled*
*2 veal kidneys, trimmed of fat*
*2 sheep's caul strips,*
*or 4 streaky bacon rashers*
*6–8 tablespoons double cream*
*Cooked spinach*

Preheat oven to fairly hot (220°C, 425°F, Gas Mark 7). To prepare shallots, line a baking tray with foil. Arrange shallots on foil, brush with melted butter and sprinkle with 1 teaspoon salt, caster sugar and 10 grinds of pepper. Cover with another sheet of foil and cook in preheated oven for 1 hour, or until tender, turning 2 to 3 times. After half cooking time, reduce heat to moderately hot (200°C, 400°F, Gas Mark 6).

## To make the Sauce

Begin by making a stock; cut chicken bones, wing tips and giblets into small pieces. In a shallow thick-bottomed casserole, melt 2 tablespoons butter with olive oil and sauté chopped chicken bones, wing tips and giblets until golden brown. Add diced carrots, onions and celery and *bouquet garni* to casserole and continue to cook for 4 minutes, stirring constantly, or until vegetables begin to take on colour.

Add diced tomatoes and mushrooms to casserole and season generously with salt and freshly ground pepper. Lower heat to medium and cook for 6 minutes. Lower heat to a simmer and cook until liquids have reduced. Pour 450 ml (12 fl oz) water over chicken bones, wing tips, giblets and vegetables; add crumbled beef stock cube and bring to the boil. Lower heat and simmer for 15 minutes, skimming surface 2 to 3 times. Turn heat to lowest possible and cook for 15 minutes.

Meanwhile, when shallots are tender, remove from oven and reserve 24 of the best shallots for garnish. Keep warm. To peel remaining shallots, use a sharp knife, cut off base of each shallot and holding a shallot in a tea towel to protect your fingers, mash flesh into a bowl. Repeat with remaining shallots. Coarsely chop shallot flesh.

To cook kidneys, season them generously with salt and freshly ground pepper. Wrap each kidney in a sheep's caul strip or 2 streaky bacon rashers, and place in a heatproof *gratin* dish with a little butter and cook in preheated oven for 10 minutes. Turn and cook for a further 8 minutes.

Skim any remaining froth or fat from stock. Pass through a fine sieve into a clean casserole, pressing down on chicken bones, wing tips, giblets and vegetables with a wooden spoon to extract all the juices. Bring to the boil. Stir in coarsely chopped shallot flesh and double cream; lower heat and simmer for 10 to 15 minutes, or until sauce has thickened slightly. Pass sauce through a fine sieve, pressing down on shallot flesh to extract all the juices. Correct seasoning.

### To serve

Have ready 4 heated serving plates. Spoon a little sauce on to each plate. Remove and discard caul strip or bacon rashers from kidneys. Thinly slice kidneys and season with a little salt and freshly ground pepper. Arrange thinly sliced kidneys in an overlapping circle around each plate; place a little cooked spinach in centre and garnish with 6 reserved cooked shallots.

*Sunday Express Magazine*

# Blanquette de Veau

*French bourgeois cooking – with its long simmered casseroles of meat, poultry and game – was my first great culture shock when I came to live in Paris so many years ago. I was astounded at the ease of making these wonderful dishes so full of flavour and so easy to serve . . . and perfect with a little boiled rice or a selection of green vegetables. Blanquette de Veau with its acidulated creamy sauce is one of my favourites.*

*Serves 4 to 6*

*1.25 kg/2½ lb boned shoulder
or breast of veal
1 lemon
2 pints veal or chicken stock
2 carrots, coarsely chopped
2 leeks, white part only, coarsely chopped
Bouquet garni (2 sprigs parsley, 1 sprig thyme, 1 small bay leaf)
1 Spanish onion, stuck with 2 cloves
24 small button mushrooms
Butter
Lemon juice
24 button onions
Salt and freshly ground pepper
25 g/1 oz flour
2 egg yolks
4 level tablespoons double cream
2 level tablespoons finely chopped parsley*

## To prepare Veal

Cut shoulder or breast of veal, or a combination of the two, into 4 cm (1½ in) cubes, discarding fat and gristle. Place in a large bowl with the juice and rind of 1 lemon; cover with cold water and allow veal to 'blanch' for 12 hours, changing water two or three times.

Drain veal and place in a casserole. Add stock and bring to simmering point. Add coarsely chopped vegetables, the *bouquet garni* and the onion stuck with cloves. Cover and simmer over a low heat for 1½ hours, or until veal is tender. Wash button mushrooms, trim stalks and simmer mushrooms in a frying pan in 25 g (1 oz) melted butter, sprinkling them with a few drops of lemon juice to preserve their colour. Cover and simmer gently until softened. Melt another 25 g (1 oz) of butter in another pan and sauté button onions until golden, adding 2 tablespoons stock from the pan of veal. Season to taste with salt and freshly ground pepper.

When veal is tender, remove pieces from pan with a slotted spoon and keep hot. Strain pan juices through a fine sieve into a bowl. Rinse the pan and dry it thoroughly.

## To make Sauce

Melt 25 g (1 oz) butter in the pan; add flour and stir over a low heat for 2 or 3 minutes to make a pale roux. Gradually add strained pan juices and bring to the boil, stirring constantly until sauce is smooth, then simmer for 2 or 3 minutes longer. Add mushrooms and onions to the sauce; mix well and simmer for 10 minutes.

Beat egg yolks with cream and 1 tablespoon lemon juice. Beat in a few tablespoons of the hot sauce; then pour back into the pan and stir over a low heat until sauce thickens, taking care not to let it come to the boil, or it may curdle. Season with salt and freshly ground pepper, to taste. Add veal to the sauce and heat through for a few minutes longer, taking the same care not to let the pan come to boiling point. Serve *Blanquette* immediately, garnished with finely chopped parsley, and accompanied by plain boiled or steamed rice.

*The Robert Carrier Cookery Course*

# Osso Buco à l'Orange

*Italian country cooking at its best. Rounds of shin of veal simmered with an onion-and-garlic-flavoured tomato sauce until meltingly tender. The secret ingredient that gives this dish its unique flavour: a gremolata of finely chopped anchovy, garlic and parsley and finely grated orange and lemon peel. Delicious!*

*Serves 4 to 6*

*4–6 thick slices shin of veal, with bone*
*Salt and freshly ground pepper*
*25–50 g/½ oz flour*
*4–6 tablespoons olive oil*
*3 cloves garlic, finely chopped*
*1 Spanish onion, finely chopped*
*150 ml/5 fl oz hot chicken stock*
*150 ml/5 fl oz dry white wine*
*6 tablespoons tomato purée*
*4–6 anchovy fillets, finely chopped*
*2–3 tablespoons finely chopped parsley*
*Grated rind of ½ orange*
*Grated rind of ¼ lemon*

Choose shin of veal with plenty of meat and ask for it to be sawed across the bone into pieces 5 cm (2 in) thick. Season generously on both sides with salt and freshly ground pepper; dredge with flour and simmer in olive oil in a large heatproof casserole until meat is lightly browned on all sides (5 minutes). All slices must touch the base. If they do not, use two pans.

Add 2 cloves finely chopped garlic and the finely chopped onion to veal; pour over hot stock, dry white wine and tomato purée; cover casserole and simmer very gently for 1½ hours, or until veal is tender. Add finely chopped anchovy fillets and remaining finely chopped garlic clove to veal. Correct seasoning and blend thoroughly. Heat through and serve sprinkled with finely chopped parsley and grated orange and lemon rind. Serve with Saffron Rice (see page 59).

*Carrier's*

# Hungarian Veal Gulyas

*Serves 4 to 6*

*1.25 kg/2½ lb boned leg of veal*
*2 Spanish onions, finely chopped*
*2 cloves garlic, finely chopped*
*4 level tablespoons lard*
*2 tablespoons paprika*
*¼ teaspoon caraway seeds*
*½ teaspoon cayenne pepper*
*Generous pinch each of marjoram and thyme*
*Salt and freshly ground pepper*
*2 bay leaves, crumbled*
*4 sweet red peppers*

450 g / 1 lb button mushrooms
1 can peeled tomatoes
(about 400 g / 14 oz)
*Paprika*
*Finely chopped parsley*
300 ml / 10 fl oz sour cream

Preheat oven to 110°C (250°F, Gas Mark ½ ). Cut veal into neat 4 cm (1½ in) cubes, discarding any fat or gristle. In a heavy, flameproof casserole, sauté finely chopped onions and garlic in lard for 3 to 4 minutes, or until soft and transparent. Add veal and continue to sauté until meat is golden on all sides.

Sprinkle with paprika, caraway seeds, cayenne pepper, marjoram and thyme, and salt and freshly ground pepper, to taste. Add crumbled bay leaves; mix well and cook gently for 10 minutes, stirring occasionally. Core and seed peppers and slice thinly. Wash mushrooms, trim stems and slice thinly.

Add peppers, mushrooms and canned tomatoes. Stir lightly and bring to simmering point over a very low heat.

Cover casserole tightly; transfer to the preheated oven and cook for about 2 hours, or until veal is tender, stirring casserole occasionally. Dust gulyas with paprika and finely chopped parsley, and serve with sour cream.

*Great Dishes of the World*

# Stuffed Breast of Veal Provençale

*A rustic green stuffing (chopped spinach and minced pork, seasoned with dried herbs and grated Parmesan) makes this colourful roast a winner. Serve it hot as a main course or cold as a first course or lunch or supper dish.*

*Serves 6 to 8*

1.25–1.75 kg/2½ –3 lb boned breast
of veal, bones reserved
Salt and freshly ground pepper
1 onion, coarsely chopped
3 whole garlic cloves
1 carrot
1 bay leaf
Parsley sprigs
10 black peppercorns
Stock (optional)

## Stuffing

1½ slices white bread, crusts removed
150 ml/5 fl oz milk
1 tablespoon butter
½ Spanish onion, finely chopped
100 g/4 oz lean pork, minced
100 g/4 oz fresh pork fat, minced
2 tablespoons freshly grated Parmesan
cheese
100 g/4 oz frozen leaf spinach, thawed

¼ *teaspoon dried marjoram*
¼ *teaspoon dried thyme*
½ *tablespoon salt*
*1 egg, lightly beaten*
*Freshly ground pepper*
*50 g/2 oz shelled pistachio nuts, skinned*

## To prepare Stuffing

Put the white bread in a bowl, cover with the milk and leave to soak for about 10 minutes. Melt the butter in a frying pan and sauté the finely chopped onion for 2 to 3 minutes or until it is transparent. In a bowl, combine the cooked onion, minced pork and pork fat, the grated Parmesan cheese, spinach, dried marjoram, dried thyme, salt, and the beaten egg, and season with freshly ground pepper. Mix well.

Squeeze the excess milk from the bread and mix the bread into the spinach mixture. Fold in the pistachio nuts.

## To stuff breast and cook

Season the inside of the veal with salt and freshly ground pepper. Spread the stuffing over the veal and sew up the meat to form a neat roll. Place the veal bones (if available), coarsely chopped onions, garlic, carrot, bay leaf, parsley and black peppercorns in a large saucepan and lay the stuffed veal on top of

them. Add enough stock or water to cover the meat completely. Bring to the boil, reduce the heat and simmer as gently as possible for 40 minutes, or until the veal is tender when pierced with a fork.

Allow the meat to cool in the liquid and then transfer to the refrigerator in its liquid until it is completely cold (preferably overnight). Drain well and carve into 6 mm (¼ in) slices.

*Carrier's*

# Lamb

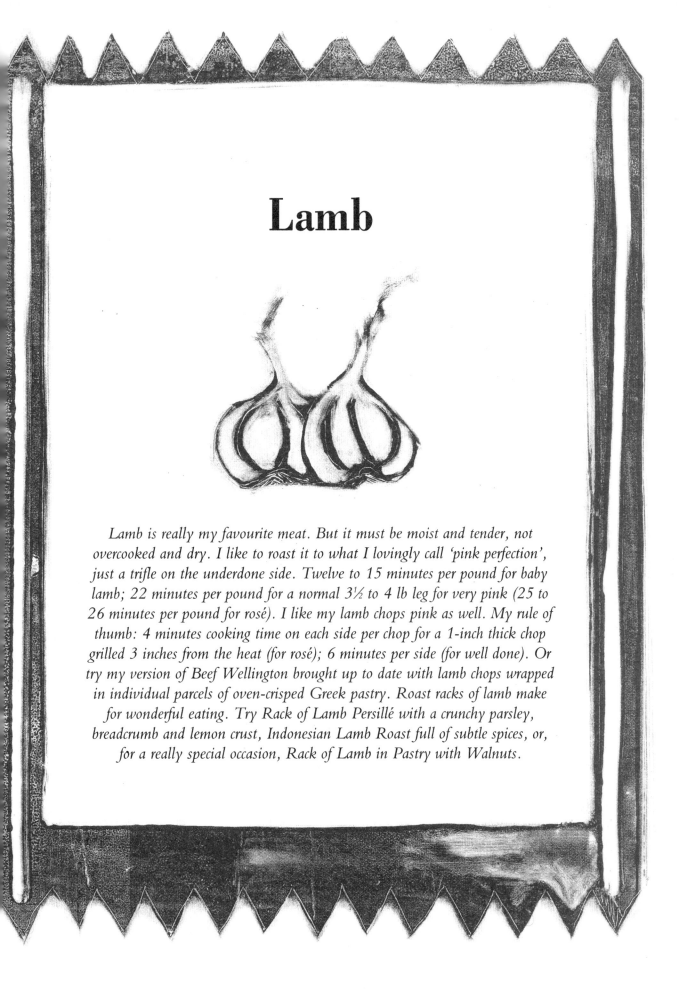

Lamb is really my favourite meat. But it must be moist and tender, not overcooked and dry. I like to roast it to what I lovingly call 'pink perfection', just a trifle on the underdone side. Twelve to 15 minutes per pound for baby lamb; 22 minutes per pound for a normal 3½ to 4 lb leg for very pink (25 to 26 minutes per pound for rosé). I like my lamb chops pink as well. My rule of thumb: 4 minutes cooking time on each side per chop for a 1-inch thick chop grilled 3 inches from the heat (for rosé); 6 minutes per side (for well done). Or try my version of Beef Wellington brought up to date with lamb chops wrapped in individual parcels of oven-crisped Greek pastry. Roast racks of lamb make for wonderful eating. Try Rack of Lamb Persillé with a crunchy parsley, breadcrumb and lemon crust, Indonesian Lamb Roast full of subtle spices, or, for a really special occasion, Rack of Lamb in Pastry with Walnuts.

# Moroccan Skewered Lamb

*Finely chopped onion and coriander with Moroccan spices (cumin, ginger, cayenne, paprika and pepper) make these brochettes special. Try this 'dry' marinade recipe, too, for brochettes of chicken or monkfish.*

*Serves 4*

*350 g/12 oz lamb*
*350 g/12 oz lamb fat*
*1 leek*
*½ Spanish onion*
*1 tablespoon chopped chervil*
*1 level teaspoon salt*
*1 level teaspoon each of powdered cumin and ginger, and crushed pepper*
*Cayenne pepper and paprika*
*2 tablespoons olive oil*

Cut lamb and fat into equal-sized cubes about 2 cm (¾ in) square and place in a large bowl. Pound white part of leek, onion, chervil and salt in a mortar; add to meat and sprinkle with powdered cumin, ginger, crushed pepper, cayenne and paprika, and oil. Mix well and let meat marinate in this mixture for 2 hours.

Place meat and fat alternately on metal skewers and grill over charcoal or under a gas or electric grill until lamb is cooked through.

*Vogue*

# Grilled Marinated Lamb Chops with Green Butter

*If you were a regular at Carrier's or Hintlesham Hall, you know how good baby lamb chops marinated in an olive oil and dry white wine marinade can be. Especially when served with a chilled garlic, parsley and lemon flavoured Green Butter.*

*Serves 4 to 6*

*8–12 small loin lamb chops*
*Salt and freshly ground pepper*
*2–3 bay leaves, crumbled*
*2–3 tablespoons finely chopped onion*
*6 tablespoons olive oil*
*6 tablespoons dry white wine*

## Green Butter

*100 g/4 oz butter*
*1–2 cloves garlic, crushed*
*Finely chopped parsley*
*1–2 tablespoons lemon juice*
*Salt and freshly ground pepper*

Have your butcher cut and trim 8 to 12 baby loin lamb chops.

Arrange chops in a large flat dish and season to taste with salt and freshly ground pepper. Add crumbled bay leaves, finely chopped onion, olive oil and dry white wine

and marinate chops in this mixture, turning them once or twice, for at least 2 hours.

### *To make Green Butter*

Cream butter with crushed garlic and 1 to 2 tablespoons finely chopped parsley. Season to taste with lemon juice, and salt and freshly ground pepper. Roll into balls about the size of a marble. Chill in the refrigerator until firm; roll again into more perfect shapes and then roll in finely chopped parsley. Each ball should be completely covered with parsley. Chill until ready to serve.

### *To cook Lamb*

Preheat grill for 15 to 20 minutes; rub grid with pieces of lamb fat; place chops on grid and grill for 2 to 3 minutes on each side (longer, if chops are larger). Serve immediately with Green Butter.

*Carrier's*

# Quick Sauté of Lamb

*Cubed lamb (cut from 2 racks of lamb) marinated in herb-flavoured olive oil, quickly sautéed and then finished in a sauce made of lamb trimmings and bones, tomato purée, onions, crumbled bay leaves and white wine.*

*Serves 4*

*2 racks of lamb, trimmed*
*Salt and freshly ground pepper*
*2 bay leaves*
*4 tablespoons olive oil*
*2 tablespoons finely chopped parsley*
*1 tablespoon finely chopped chives*

## Sauce

*Bones and meat trimmings from racks of lamb*
*1 chicken stock cube*
*2 tablespoons tomato purée*
*½ large onion, finely chopped*
*2 bay leaves*
*4 tablespoons dry white wine*
*2 teaspoons flour*
*2 teaspoons butter*
*Salt and freshly ground pepper*
*Crushed dried chillies*

Cut meat from bones of lamb, making 2 'fillets' of lamb. Cut each 'fillet' into 2.5 cm (1 in)-thick slices. Trim a little fat from each slice and cut into 2 or 3 even-sized cubes, according to size of lamb. Reserve bones and meat trimmings for sauce. Place lamb slices in a bowl and season generously with salt and freshly ground pepper. Add bay leaves and olive oil; toss well and leave lamb to marinate for at least 2 hours in a cool place.

### To make Sauce

Chop lamb bones coarsely and place in a thick-bottomed saucepan, or small casserole, with trimmings, chicken stock cube, tomato purée, finely chopped onion, bay leaves and dry white wine. Add 900 ml (1½ pints) water and simmer gently for 30 minutes. Strain stock into a clean saucepan and cook over a high heat for 15 minutes until it is reduced to half of its original quantity. Whisk in *beurre manié* (made by creaming flour and butter together to form a smooth paste) and simmer for 2 to 3 minutes until thickened. Season with salt, freshly ground pepper and crushed dried chillies to taste. Keep warm.

### To cook Lamb

Drain lamb marinade into a large frying pan. Heat and sauté lamb in 2 batches, cooking for 8 to 10 minutes, or until golden brown,

turning with a spatula. Remove lamb with a slotted spoon and place into sauce. Keep warm. Repeat with remaining lamb. Sprinkle sauté of lamb with finely chopped parsley and chives; correct seasoning. Spoon into a warmed serving dish and serve immediately.

*Hintlesham Hall*

# Lamb in Greek Pastry

*It has been said that if Greece ever gave a knighthood for creating a Greek-inspired recipe, I would now be a Greek Sir Robert. This recipe – which combines a duxelles stuffing and crisp Greek phyllo pastry with lightly browned lamb chops – was a menu favourite at both my restaurants for many years. Try it next time you give a dinner party. It is surprisingly easy. Greek pastry known as 'phyllo' or 'filo' is an almost transparent paper-like pastry, very similar to strudel dough in appearance. Always brush Greek pastry with a little melted butter before using it*
*(to make pastry more pliable).*

*Serves 6*

*6 lamb cutlets*
*Salt and freshly ground pepper*
*1 tablespoon butter*
*1 tablespoon olive oil*
*6 sheets (about 125 g/5 oz) Greek pastry,*

*or if unavailable, 150 g/6 oz shortcrust or puff pastry*
*Melted butter or beaten egg yolk*
*75 g/3 oz pâté de foie gras, cut into 6 small rounds*

## Mushroom Duxelles

*1 tablespoon butter*
*½ Spanish onion, very finely chopped*
*50 g/2 oz mushrooms, very finely chopped*
*50 g/2 oz cooked ham, very finely chopped*
*Salt and freshly ground pepper*

Season lamb cutlets with salt and freshly ground pepper, and brown them in a mixture of butter and olive oil for 2 to 3 minutes on each side. Remove from pan and leave to cool.

### *To prepare Mushroom Duxelles*

Melt butter in a pan and sauté finely chopped onion until transparent. Add finely chopped mushrooms and continue to sauté gently until soft. Stir in finely chopped ham; season with salt and freshly ground pepper, to taste, and remove from heat. Cool.

### *To prepare Lamb in Pastry*

Preheat oven to hot 220°C (425°F, Gas Mark 7). If using Greek pastry, take one sheet at a time and fold it in half to make a rectangle. Brush lightly all over with melted butter. Place a round of pâté de foie gras in the centre, cover with 1 tablespoon Mushroom Duxelles and lay a sautéed lamb cutlet on top so that the nut of the cutlet covers duxelles. Fold nearside edge of pastry up over the cutlet and the two sides in towards the centre. Brush again with melted butter and twist pastry round cutlet neatly to seal it completely. Lay on a baking sheet, seam side down, and brush all over with melted butter.

If using shortcrust or puff pastry, divide into 6 equal pieces. Roll each piece out very thinly into a rectangle about 20 x 13 cm (8 x 5 in), depending on size of cutlet. Proceed as above, using beaten egg to seal joins and trimming off excess pastry as you go.

Lay parcels on baking sheet seam side down and brush tops with beaten egg to glaze them. Bake parcels for 25 to 30 minutes, or until well puffed and golden brown. Serve immediately.

*Carrier's*

# Rack of Lamb Persillé

*Serves 6*

*2 racks of lamb, each with 6 cutlets,*
*trimmed*
*Salt and freshly ground pepper*
*2–3 teaspoons English mustard*
*1 tablespoon dry white wine*
*6 tablespoons fresh breadcrumbs*
*3 tablespoons finely chopped parsley*
*½ teaspoon finely chopped garlic*
*1 tablespoon butter, diced*

Preheat oven to 200°C (400°C, Gas Mark 6).
Season trimmed racks of lamb generously
with salt and freshly ground pepper, and roast
in preheated oven for 20 minutes.
Meanwhile, in a small bowl, combine English
mustard and dry white wine, to form a paste.
In another bowl combine breadcrumbs,
chopped parsley and garlic.

Remove racks from oven and brush with
mustard and dry white wine paste, then pat
on breadcrumb mixture. Dot racks with
butter, return meat to oven and roast for 8 to
10 minutes.

Serve immediately.

*Robert Carrier's Kitchen*

# Rack of Lamb in Pastry with Walnuts

*Serves 4*

*1 rack of lamb*
*(8 chops about 1 kg, 2 lb in weight)*
*Salt and freshly ground pepper*
*2 tablespoons softened butter*
*½ Spanish onion, finely chopped*
*½ tablespoon butter*
*½ tablespoon olive oil*
*100 g/4 oz mushrooms, finely chopped*
*1 slice cooked ham, finely chopped*
*50 g/2 oz coarsely chopped walnuts*
*225 g/8 oz puff pastry,*
*homemade or frozen*
*1 egg, beaten*

Ask your butcher to trim off fat from rack of
lamb, and to chine bone (cut meat away from
the backbone) and trim away top half of
bone. Preheat oven to moderate 190°C,
(375°F, Gas Mark 5). Season lamb generously
with salt and freshly ground pepper. Brush
with 1 tablespoon softened butter. Place in a
roasting pan, so that rack is supported by its
bones, and roast in preheated oven for 20
minutes, or a little longer if you prefer lamb
well cooked. Allow meat to cool completely.

Sauté finely chopped onion in butter and
olive oil until onion is transparent; add finely

chopped mushrooms and continue to cook, allowing juices to run from mushrooms; cook for about 30 minutes, stirring frequently, until mixture is almost dry. Add finely chopped ham and chopped walnuts; season with salt and freshly ground pepper to taste and cook for 1 minute more. Allow mixture to cool.

Press chopped onion, mushroom, ham and walnut mixture firmly on to base and back of cold meat; brush with about 1 tablespoon softened butter. Roll out puff pastry into a thin sheet and wrap lamb neatly in it, allowing bones to protrude from pastry. Make 2 or 3 attractive holes in pastry, about 2 cm (¾ in) across, to allow steam to escape. Use some beaten egg to seal pastry securely. Decorate with 'leaves' and 'tassels' cut from any spare pastry trimmings, fixing them on with a little beaten egg. Brush pastry with water and cover exposed bones loosely with a little aluminium foil. Place a slightly crumbled piece of foil over 'leaves' and 'tassels' to prevent over-browning.

Raise to oven temperature 230°C (450°F, Gas Mark 8). Place lamb on a baking sheet and bake in a preheated oven for 20 minutes, or until crust is browned. Serve immediately.

*Food, Wine & Friends*

# Indonesian Lamb Roast

*Trader Vic's was a well-known restaurant chain in America with a branch at the London Hilton. This recipe was one of its most famous creations. I still make it when I want to serve lamb with a Javanese honey and spice sauce. Try it.*

*Serves 4*

*Best end of lamb*
*(about 8 ribs weighing*
*about 800 g/1lb 12oz)*

## Javanese Satay Sauce

*1 Spanish onion, finely chopped*
*2 teaspoons salt*
*1 clove garlic, finely chopped*
*1 tablespoon curry powder*
*½ teaspoon each powdered turmeric,*
*coriander and Mexican Chile powder*
*(not cayenne pepper, or powdered chilli)*
*6 tablespoons lemon juice*
*1–2 tablespoons clear honey*
*Freshly ground pepper*

Ask the butcher to chine and trim away top half of rib bones. Preheat oven to moderate 190°C (375°F, Gas Mark 5). Cut lamb into four portions. Wrap rib bones in aluminium foil to prevent burning.

### To prepare Sauce

Combine ingredients for Javanese Satay Sauce in a large bowl and marinate lamb in this mixture for at least 12 hours.

### To cook Lamb

When ready to cook lamb, place on a rack over a roasting tin and spoon all over the marinade mixture. Cook in preheated oven for 30 to 35 minutes (for pink meat), or until tender, turning the lamb over after about 15 minutes, and basting it now and then with the marinade from the bottom of the tin.

Serve with the cooked onion marinade.

*The Sunday Times*

---

# Roast Leg of Lamb Boulangère

*Serves 6*

*1 leg of lamb, about 2 kg/4 lb*
*Butter*
*6 cloves garlic*
*700 g–1 kg/ 1½–2 lb potatoes, peeled*
*Salt and freshly ground pepper*
*4–6 tablespoons finely chopped parsley*
*300 ml/10 fl oz rich chicken stock*

Preheat oven to slow 170°C (325°F, Gas Mark 3). Butter a shallow fireproof casserole or *gratin* dish just large enough to hold leg of lamb comfortably and rub lightly with a cut clove of garlic. Discard garlic. Bring peeled potatoes to the boil and cook until almost tender. Drain and slice potatoes thickly and cover bottom of casserole, or *gratin* dish, with overlapping slices. Sprinkle generously with salt and freshly ground pepper.

Chop remaining garlic cloves finely and combine with finely chopped parsley; sprinkle over potato slices.

Lay leg of lamb on potatoes and moisten with chicken stock. Roast in preheated oven for 1¼ to 1½ hours, or until lamb is pink and tender and potatoes are cooked through, but not disintegrating. Turn lamb occasionally while roasting and increase cooking time if you prefer it less pink. Serve very hot.

*The Robert Carrier Cookbook*

---

# Roast Saddle of Lamb à l'Arlésienne

*Serves 6 to 8*

*1 saddle of lamb*
*Softened butter*
*Salt and freshly ground pepper*
*Crushed rosemary*
*450 ml/15 fl oz water*

450 ml/15 fl oz hot beef stock
1 level tablespoon butter
1 level tablespoon flour

## L'Arlésienne Garnish

*6–8 medium-sized courgettes*
*6–8 medium tomatoes, sliced*
*1 Spanish onion, finely chopped*
*Sprigs of thyme*
*Cloves of garlic, unpeeled*
*Olive oil*

## To serve

*24 new potatoes, boiled*
*and sautéed in butter*
*6 tablespoons finely chopped mushrooms*
*2 tablespoons each finely chopped parsley*
*and truffles, sautéed in butter*
*Watercress*

Spread saddle of lamb with softened butter and sprinkle with salt, freshly ground pepper and crushed rosemary, to taste. Place in moderately hot oven 200°C (400°F, Gas Mark 6); pour water into roasting pan and roast for 1 hour, basting frequently.

Remove roast from oven; discard fat from pan; add beef stock and a *beurre manié* (1 level tablespoon butter mashed to a smooth paste with 1 level tablespoon flour) and cook over a high flame, stirring all crusty bits from sides of pan into sauce, until sauce is smooth and thick. Strain and keep warm.

## L'Arlésienne Garnish

Slice each baby marrow lengthways into 4 or 5 slices, without cutting all the way through, to make a fan shape. Place a thin slice of tomato in each opening. Place partially roasted saddle of lamb in baking tin, oiled and scattered with finely chopped onion; add sprigs of thyme, garlic and salt and freshly ground pepper, to taste. Surround with prepared marrows; sprinkle with a little olive oil and continue to roast meat for about 45 minutes, or until meat is tender.

## To serve

Place lamb on a large heated serving dish with baby marrows at one end, sautéed potatoes at the other. Sprinkle vegetables with finely chopped mushrooms, parsley and truffles sautéed in butter. Garnish with watercress. Serve sauce separately.

*The Sunday Times*

## Irish Stew

*There is only one Irish stew, according to the Irish, and the recipe is simplicity itself: shoulder or neck of mutton, potatoes and onions, parsley and thyme, and sometimes a bit of barley. I add carrots and celery to lend a touch of colour and sweetness to this savoury broth.*

*Serves 4 to 6*

*1.4 kg/3 lb shoulder of mutton*
*450 g/1 lb onions*
*1 kg/2 lb potatoes*
*2 stalks celery*
*225 g/8 oz carrots*
*Salt and freshly ground pepper*
*Water or light stock, to cover*
*2–3 tablespoons chopped parsley*

Cut mutton in 6 cm (2½ in) cubes; peel and slice onions and potatoes thickly. Trim and slice celery; peel and slice carrots. Place a layer of sliced onions, celery and carrots on the bottom of a heatproof casserole; cover with a layer of meat, and then a layer of potatoes, and continue filling casserole in alternate layers, finishing with potatoes. Season each layer to taste with salt and freshly ground pepper. Add water or light stock to cover; bring to the boil; skim; lower heat and simmer, covered, until tender (almost

3 hours). Just before serving, sprinkle with chopped parsley.

*The Sunday Times*

## Lancashire Hot Pot

*Serves 4*

*700 g/1½ lb best end neck of lamb*
*6 lamb's kidneys*
*700 g/1½ lb potatoes, thinly sliced*
*Salt and freshly ground pepper*
*1 Spanish onion, thinly sliced*
*300 ml/10 fl oz pint chicken stock*
*2 tablespoons butter*

Preheat the oven to 180°C (350°F, Mark 4). Cut the best end neck of lamb into chops and cut away most of the fat, scraping the bones clean with a sharp knife. Cut the lamb's kidneys in half; remove the membrane and snip away the core with a pair of scissors.

In a medium-sized casserole, overlap one-third of the potato slices to cover the bottom of the casserole and season with salt and freshly ground pepper. Lay half the best end neck of lamb chops and the halved kidneys on top. Season generously with salt and freshly ground pepper. Sprinkle over half the onion slices. Repeat the procedure, seasoning each layer with salt and freshly ground pepper. Finish with an overlapping layer of potatoes.

Pour in the chicken stock, put buttered paper on top of the potatoes and cover with a lid. Bake in the preheated oven for 1½ hours.

Uncover the casserole and remove the buttered paper. Dot the potatoes with butter and cook for a further 30 minutes or so until the potatoes are browned and the meat is tender. Serve immediately.

*Robert Carrier's Kitchen*

# Scots Hotch Potch

*This traditional Highland hot pot from Scotland used to be made from mutton and took up to 2 hours to cook. Today we use lamb for this dish — from the neck or the middle neck for tenderness — and the hotch potch is cooked in under an hour*

*Serves 4 to 6*

*1.25 kg/2½ lb neck of lamb (or middle neck)*
*1.1 l/2 pints water or light stock*
*2 Spanish onions, coarsely chopped*
*Salt and freshly ground pepper*
*450 g/1 lb fresh peas*
*225 g/8 oz young broad beans*
*4–6 young turnips, diced*
*4–6 young carrots, diced*
*1 small cauliflower (or 2 baby cauliflowers)*
*2–4 tablespoons chopped parsley*

Place neck of lamb in a saucepan with water (or stock), coarsely chopped onions and salt and freshly ground pepper, to taste. Bring slowly to the boil and skim carefully. Add half the quantity of peas and the broad beans and diced carrots and turnips. Bring to the boil again; skim carefully; lower heat and simmer gently, covered, for 45 to 60 minutes.

In the meantime, wash cauliflower well and separate into 'florets'. Twenty minutes before serving, add prepared cauliflower and remaining peas, and continue cooking until vegetables are tender. Just before serving, remove lamb; cut into serving pieces and return to pan with chopped parsley. Correct seasoning and serve immediately.

*Vogue*

# Ragoût of Lamb

*Serves 4 to 6*

*1 kg/2 lb shoulder of lamb, boned*
*3 tablespoons rendered fresh pork fat,*
*or cooking oil*
*2 tablespoons flour*
*1 teaspoon salt*
*½ teaspoon freshly ground pepper*
*750 ml/1¼ pints water*
*1 small clove garlic, crushed*
*¼ –½ teaspoon crushed dried rosemary*
*1 bouquet garni (consisting of 2 parsley*
*sprigs, 1 bay leaf and ⅛ teaspoon dried*
*thyme, tied in a piece of cheesecloth)*
*8 small potatoes, peeled and sliced*
*12 button onions, blanched*
*12 small whole carrots*

Cut lamb into 5 cm (2 in) cubes. Heat the fat or cooking oil, in a large, heavy saucepan. Add the lamb cubes, a few pieces at a time, and brown on all sides. As the cubes are done lift them out of the pan with a slotted spoon, place in a dish and keep warm. When all the pieces of lamb have been browned, return them to the pan and sprinkle with the flour, salt and freshly ground pepper. Toss the pieces of meat with a spoon to coat them with the other ingredients. Cook over a moderate heat, mixing occasionally, until the flour is lightly browned.

Add the water, the garlic, crushed rosemary and the *bouquet garni*. Cover the saucepan and bring to the boil. Lower the heat and simmer for 40 minutes. Add the sliced potatoes, onions and carrots. Replace the lid and simmer for another 45 minutes to 1 hour or until the meat is tender when pierced with a fork and the vegetables are cooked. Turn vegetables frequently to ensure the potatoes are covered with liquid, otherwise they will not cook. Taste the stock and add more seasoning if necessary.

To serve, remove the *bouquet garni*, skim off the fat, put the meat and vegetables into a warmed serving dish and pour the stock over.

*Robert Carrier's Kitchen*

# Daube de Mouton

*A daube is made in a daubière. Makes sense, doesn't it? It does if you were a country cook in the heart of France sometime during the past century. But today, daubes (French cooking terminology for country casseroles of lamb or beef) can be cooked in any pot or casserole as long as they are lovingly simmered with aromatics (usually including a strip of dried orange peel for extra savour) and red or white wine. The trick with a daube is to cook it as gently as you can (at the very lowest of temperatures) and for a very long time, so that the meat is meltingly tender and the sauce of meat juices and wine and aromatics has reduced to a glaze of pure flavour.*

### Serves 6 to 8

*1 leg of lamb*
*225 g/8 oz bacon, thinly sliced*
*225 g/8 oz bacon, in one piece*
*Olive oil*
*Salt and freshly ground pepper*
*Dried thyme, marjoram, crumbled bay leaf*
*Red wine*
*4 tablespoons olive oil*
*2 finely chopped carrots*
*1 finely chopped Spanish onion*
*4 cloves garlic, mashed*
*1 bay leaf*

*2 sprigs thyme*
*1 sprig rosemary*
*4 sprigs parsley*
*4 tablespoons finely chopped onion*
*Dried thyme and crumbled bay leaf*
*1 bouquet garni*
*(parsley, thyme, celery, etc.)*
*1 strip dried orange peel*
*Well-flavoured stock*
*Flour and water*

Bone leg of lamb and cut it into large pieces weighing about 75 g (3 oz) each. Cut half of bacon slices into 6 mm (¼ in) strips. Lard each of the lamb pieces with 2 strips of bacon which you have rubbed with a little olive oil, salt, freshly ground pepper and dried thyme, marjoram and crumbled bay leaf. If you do not have a larding needle, cut 2 holes in meat cubes with a thin bladed knife and insert strips of well-seasoned bacon into holes with the point of a skewer.

### To marinate Meat

Place prepared lamb cubes in a large earthenware bowl and add enough red wine just to cover meat. Add 4 tablespoons olive oil, 2 finely chopped carrots and 1 finely chopped Spanish onion, 4 mashed garlic cloves, 1 bay leaf, thyme, rosemary, parsley, and salt and freshly ground pepper, to taste. Marinate for at least 4 hours.

### *To cook Daube*

Dice uncut bacon and blanch it with remaining bacon rashers. Cover the bottom of a large earthenware ovenproof casserole with a layer of lamb cubes; sprinkle with 4 tablespoons finely chopped onion, diced blanched bacon and season with a pinch each of dried thyme and crumbled bay leaf. Cover with a layer of lamb; sprinkle with onion, bacon and dried herbs as above; drop in a *bouquet garni* and a strip of dried orange peel. Then cover with a final layer of lamb cubes right to the very top of the casserole. Pour in strained marinade juices and a little stock. Top with remaining thin bacon slices; cover casserole and wrap a band of dough (made with flour and water) around join to seal it completely. Cook for 4 hours in a very slow oven (130°C, 300°F, Gas Mark 1).

### *To serve*

Remove pastry 'join' and cover; remove bacon strips and *bouquet garni*, skim fat and serve from casserole.

*Vogue*

# Pork

*Pork – except for bacon and gammon – isn't really appreciated in this country.
In America and on the continent (Spain and Germany particularly)
it is of prime importance. And in China, it is a favourite meat.
I think the reason why Britain, as a country, is not more pork-minded
is because all our pigs are raised with bacon in mind: to be lean. To be tender
and tasty, pork must be fat. But we can still make delicious dishes from the
pork we have available if we remember to moisturise it before and/or during
cooking: Italian Roast Pork, Pot Roast of Pork and Pork Cooked like Game
are three cases in point. I like, too, to cook a loin of pork on a gratin of
potatoes: French Pork Boulangère prepared like a French Gigot, but pre-roasted
before being placed sumptuously on its bed of sliced potatoes. For a quicker and
lighter pork dish, try thin strips of pork, rubbed with oil and spices and then
grilled in the Thai manner, or Italian Grilled Pork Chops with Mozzarella.*

# Thai Pork Satays with Peanut Sauce and Cucumber Relish

*On my first visit to Singapore I fell in love with the satay stalls in the centre of the city. Particularly the spicy satays of pork and chicken served with Thai Peanut Sauce and Cucumber Relish. Since then, I have used this same recipe theme and accompaniments for satays of Monkfish and even Aubergine, when I'm feeling in a 'vegetarian' mood.*

*Serves 4*

## Pork Satays

*550 g/1¼ lb fillet of pork*
*1 tablespoon curry powder*
*¼ teaspoon coriander powder*
*¼ teaspoon turmeric powder*
*Cayenne pepper*
*Salt*
*Peanut oil*

## Thai Peanut Sauce

*100 g/4 oz fine-cut desiccated coconut*
*100 g/4 oz salted peanuts*
*½ teaspoon turmeric powder*
*½ teaspoon curry powder*
*⅛ –¼ teaspoon cayenne pepper*
*2 tablespoons sugar*
*1 teaspoon lemon juice*
*Salt*

## Thai Cucumber Relish

*½ cucumber, peeled*
*2 tablespoons thinly sliced shallots*
*½ hot green chilli, very thinly sliced*
*2–3 tablespoons lemon juice*
*4–6 teaspoons sugar*

### *To prepare Pork Satays*

Cut pork into thin slices, approximately 6 mm (¼ in) thick, and then cut each slice into rectangles approximately 2.5 x 5 cm (1 x 2 in). Place meat in a bowl and add curry, coriander, turmeric and cayenne pepper and salt, to taste.

Wet your hands and gently knead the spices into the meat, adding 1 teaspoon each peanut oil and water to help work spice mixture into meat. Knead again. Cover bowl and leave for 2 hours.

## To make Thai Peanut Sauce

Place fine-cut desiccated coconut in a bowl; add 450 ml (¾ pint) water and knead with hands for 3 minutes. Strain coconut through a fine sieve, pressing coconut milk into a bowl with a wooden spoon. You'll end up with a little over 300 ml (10 fl oz).

Grind peanuts coarsely (I use an electric coffee grinder). Add turmeric, curry, cayenne pepper and sugar to coconut milk and cook over a medium heat, stirring, until sauce comes to the boil. Reduce heat to low and add ground peanuts. Continue to cook, stirring constantly, for about 2 minutes. Add the lemon juice and salt, to taste; remove sauce from heat and allow to cool.

## To make Thai Cucumber Relish

Cut cucumber in half lengthways and then cut each half into very thin slices. Put sliced cucumber in a bowl, add thinly sliced shallots and green chilli, lemon juice and sugar. Chill until ready to serve.

## To grill Pork Satays

Thread 4 pieces of pork along each thin metal or bamboo skewer (2 skewers for each person). The skewer should enter the meat 2 or 3 times. Preheat grill to high. Brush pork satays with peanut oil and grill 10 cm (4 in) from heat, turning frequently, until satays are cooked through: 4 to 6 minutes on each side.

## To serve Satays

Serve 2 skewers on an individual plate for each person as a first course; 3 as a main course. Garnish each plate with Thai Peanut Sauce and Cucumber Relish.

*Robert Carrier's Kitchen*

# Italian Roast Pork

*Serves 6*

*1 piece loin of pork (1.5–2 kg/3–4 lb)*
*2 fat cloves garlic*
*½ Spanish onion, finely chopped and*
*mixed with 2 tablespoons olive oil*
*12 tiny rosemary sprigs (just the tips)*
*Salt and freshly ground pepper*
*2 bay leaves, crumbled*
*Water*

Ask your butcher to remove the rind and about half the fat from loin of pork. Cut each garlic clove into 6 slivers. Pierce pork loin in 12 places with a thick skewer and insert a garlic sliver, a little chopped onion mixture and 1 tiny rosemary sprig in each hole.

Rub the meat with salt, freshly ground pepper and crumbled bay leaves, and place it in a roasting pan with about 4 cm (1½ in) water. Roast meat in a preheated moderate oven (170°C, 325°F, Gas Mark 3), topping up with water if necessary, for about 35 minutes to the pound, or until the meat is tender and moist.

Skim fat from pan juices and serve with pork roast.

*Robert Carrier's Kitchen*

# Pot Roast of Pork with Grapes

*A pork pot roast with gin and grapes*
*sounds way out – and perhaps it is – but if*
*you try it, you'll love its unique*
*combination of flavours. It makes a great*
*Sunday dinner dish.*

*Serves 4 to 6*

*Lean loin of pork (1.8 kg/4 lb)*
*Salt and freshly ground pepper*
*3 tablespoons gin*
*150 ml/5 fl oz unsweetened grape juice*
*150 ml/5 fl oz dry white wine*
*2 tablespoons butter*
*2 tablespoons flour*

## Marinade

*8 juniper berries, crushed*
*2 cloves, crushed*
*1 clove garlic, crushed*
*3 tablespoons olive oil*
*6 tablespoons dry white wine*

## Garnish

*2 tablespoons butter*
*450 g/1 lb seedless white grapes*

Ask your butcher to skin, bone and roll a lean loin of pork. The rolled joint should weigh just under 1.4 kg (3 lb) after being prepared. Combine marinade ingredients. Pour over joint in a deep dish, cover and leave to marinate, at the bottom of the refrigerator, for 24 hours. Turn pork several times to keep it thoroughly coated with marinade.

## To cook Pork

When ready to cook pork, preheat oven to moderate (190°C, 375°F, Gas Mark 5). Drain pork, reserving marinade, and put in a roasting tin. Sprinkle pork with salt and freshly ground pepper. Pour about 150 ml (5 fl oz) cold water around it and roast, basting occasionally until cooked through but still moist. It will take about 1¾ hours, or 35 minutes per 450 g/1 lb.

## To prepare Garnish

Ten minutes before taking pork out of the oven, prepare garnish by melting butter in a large deep frying pan and sautéing grapes for 4 to 5 minutes, until golden brown. Reserve.

## To flambé Pork

When pork is cooked, transfer to a deep hot heatproof serving dish. Pour 3 tablespoons gin over it, stand well back and set alight with a match. (Or pour gin into a heated metal ladle, set it alight and quickly pour all over the meat.) Return pork to the turned-off oven to keep hot while you prepare sauce.

## To prepare sauce

Skim fat from juices left in roasting tin. Pour back into the tin any juices that have collected around the pork on the serving dish.

Add grape juice, white wine and reserved marinade to the roasting tin and bring to the boil on top of the stove, scraping bottom and sides of tin with a wooden spoon to dislodge any crusty bits stuck there. Allow to simmer for 2 to 3 minutes longer.

Meanwhile, work butter and flour to a smooth paste in a small cup to make a *beurre manié*. Strain sauce into the frying pan over sautéed grapes and, over low heat, stir in *beurre manié* in small pieces. Continue to stir until sauce comes to the boil and simmer for 3 to 4 minutes longer to cook the flour. Season with salt and freshly ground pepper.

## To serve

Spoon sauce and grapes over and around pork. Any excess sauce and grapes should be served with the meat in a heated sauce boat or bowl. Serve pork very hot, cut into thick slices.

*Entertaining*

# Pork Cooked Like Game

*Serves 6*

*1 loin of pork*
*Olive oil*
*Aromatic spices*
*1 teaspoon salt*
*½ teaspoon powdered nutmeg*
*¼ teaspoon powdered cloves*
*2 bay leaves, crumbled*
*½ teaspoon thyme*
*12 peppercorns, crushed*
*2 large onions, thinly sliced*
*4 fat cloves garlic, thinkly sliced*
*1 bottle red Burgundy*
*Peel of 1 orange*
*300 ml / 10 fl oz chicken stock*

Ask your butcher to trim a loin of pork (6–8 chops) and to score the fat.

Rub the pork with olive oil and then with aromatic spice mixture. Place pork on a serving dish large enough to hold it; and keep in refrigerator for 24 hours to allow flavours to permeate meat.

Remove pork from refrigerator; place it in a large, deep container (not metal) with sliced onions and garlic, red wine, 300 ml (10 fl oz) olive oil, orange peel and chicken stock.

Marinate pork in this mixture for 2 to 3 days, turning the meat in the marinade twice each day.

Preheat oven to slow (170°C, 325°F, Gas 3).

When ready to cook roast remove from marinade (reserve marinade for later use) and pat meat dry with kitchen towels. Sprinkle with olive oil and place meat on rack in roasting pan. Roast for 25 minutes per pound, or until cooked through.

## To make Sauce

Cook reserved marinade juices over a high heat until reduced by a half; strain into a bowl and serve with meat.

Remove meat from oven; transfer to a heated platter and keep warm. Strain pan juices into sauce.

*Homes and Gardens*

## Bauernschmaus

*Serves 6*

*1 loin of pork (cut into 6 chops)*
*Lard*
*Salt and freshly ground pepper*
*Crushed dried chillies*
*1 kg/2 lb sauerkraut, with juices*
*Beer to cover*
*1 teaspoon cumin or caraway seeds*
*1–2 cloves garlic*
*2 large raw potatoes, grated*
*2 Spanish onions, sliced*
*1 piece back bacon, cut in thick slices*
*12 frankfurter sausages*

In a large heatproof casserole, sauté pork chops in 2 tablespoons lard until they are golden on all sides. Season with salt, freshly ground pepper and crushed dried chillies, to taste. Add sauerkraut with juices and stir well. Then add beer, cumin seeds (or caraway), garlic and salt and freshly ground pepper, to taste. Simmer casserole for 1½ hours. Then, stir in grated raw potatoes, moistened with a little cold water. Cook for 2 to 3 minutes more. Sauté sliced onions in 2 tablespoons lard until transparent and add to casserole with back bacon and frankfurters and simmer for 1 hour longer, adding water, or more beer, if necessary.

### To serve

Drain the sauerkraut, reserving juices, and pile on a large wooden platter. Surround with 3 kinds of meat. Garnish platter with 6 large Dumplings and serve the gravy separately, seasoned to taste.

*The Sunday Times*

## Dumplings

*Serves 6*

*6 rolls*
*150 ml/5 fl oz milk*
*2 eggs, beaten*
*2 tablespoons finely chopped parsley*
*Salt, pepper and nutmeg, to taste*
*30 g/1½ oz sifted flour*

Break up rolls into small pieces and soak in milk. Squeeze bread almost dry. Add eggs, chopped parsley and salt, pepper and nutmeg, to taste. Then add flour and work mixture into a dough with your hands, adding more flour if the dough is too moist to handle.

Shape dough into 6 balls and drop them into a large saucepan of boiling salted water. Boil for 12 to 15 minutes, uncovered, until dumplings rise to the surface. Skim dumplings from water and drain well.

*The Sunday Times*

# Loin of Pork Boulangère

*Serves 6 to 8*

*1 loin of pork (6–8 cutlets)*
*Salt and freshly ground pepper*
*Rubbed rosemary and thyme*
*6–8 large potatoes*
*300 ml / 10 fl oz milk*
*1 Spanish onion, finely chopped*
*2 tablespoons finely chopped parsley*
*1–2 teaspoons dried herbs of Provence*
*Softened butter*
*200 ml / 8 fl oz hot beef stock*

Season pork generously with salt, freshly ground pepper and rubbed rosemary and thyme, to taste. Place pork on the rack of roasting pan and roast in a fairly hot oven (220°C, 425°F, Gas Mark 7) for 1 hour, or until pork is half cooked, basting it from time to time.

While pork is cooking, peel and slice potatoes thinly and simmer them in 300 ml (10 fl oz) each milk and water for 10 minutes, or until potatoes are partially cooked. Drain potatoes and place them in a large oval or rectangular *gratin* dish (large enough to hold loin of pork). Sprinkle with finely chopped onion, parsley and herbs of Provence. Season generously with salt and freshly ground pepper. Remove pork from oven.

Spread potatoes with 4 tablespoons softened butter, and place pork roast on top. Add beef stock and bring the liquid to a boil (over an asbestos mat). Return *gratin* dish to a moderate oven (200°C, 400°F, Gas Mark 6) and cook for 30 minutes longer, or until meat is done, the liquid has almost cooked away, and the potatoes are tender. Serve immediately.

*Robert Carrier's Kitchen*

# Pork Chops 'Ardennaise'

*Take 4 thick pork chops: cut off excess fat and sauté them in butter and lard (for extra savour). Make a Beef Velouté Sauce with Juniper Berries from the Ardennes. And for a final country touch, serve the pork chops with sautéed new potatoes, mixed with bacon bits and finely chopped onion for extra flavour.*

*Serves 4*

*4 thick pork chops*
*Salt and freshly ground pepper*
*2 tablespoons butter*
*1 tablespoon lard*
*6 tablespoons dry white wine*

2–3 crushed juniper berries
6 tablespoons beef stock
1 tablespoon butter
1 tablespoon flour
Sautéed potatoes, mixed with bacon bits
and finely chopped onion sautéed in butter

### To cook Pork

Trim excess fat from 4 good-sized pork chops; season and sauté in butter and lard until they are tender. Remove chops and keep warm.

### To make Sauce

Skim excess fat from the pan and add wine, stirring crusty bits from sides of pan into sauce. Add crushed juniper berries, beef stock and a *beurre manié* (made by mashing the butter and flour to a smooth paste). Bring to the boil; boil for a few minutes; correct seasoning and pour over chops.

Serve with sautéed potatoes mixed with bacon bits and finely chopped onion sautéed in butter.

*The Sunday Times*

# Grilled Pork Chops with Mozzarella

*The Italians look at pork chops in a different manner. Double cream, diced Fontina or Mozzarella cheese, and ham give a northern Italian touch to this easy-to-make recipe.*

*Serves 4*

4 loin pork chops,
weighing 150 g/6 oz each
100 ml/3 fl oz double cream
100 g/4 oz Fontina
or Mozzarella cheese, diced
50 g/2 oz ham, cut in fine julienne strips
Freshly ground pepper
Pinch of nutmeg
1 egg, beaten
Salt
Olive oil

### To prepare Sauce

Heat grill to high. In a double saucepan heat double cream with diced Fontina or Mozzarella cheese. When the cheese is melted, add ham, freshly ground pepper and nutmeg. Stir in beaten egg.

### *To cook Pork*

Season pork cutlets with salt and freshly ground pepper and brush with olive oil. Place on preheated grill pan 8 cm (3 in) from heat and cook for 5 to 6 minutes on each side. When cooked, place cutlets on a heatproof serving dish, spoon sauce over cutlets and glaze under grill.

*Robert Carrier's Kitchen*

# Pork Tournedos with Grilled Mushrooms

*Serves 4*

*450 g / 1 lb pork fillet*
*4 slices streaky bacon*
*Freshly ground pepper*
*Salt*
*Oil*
*100 g / 4 oz button mushrooms,*
*stalks removed*

Cut the pork fillet into four 6 cm (2 ½ in) pieces. Flatten the pork pieces with your hand until 5 cm (2 in) in diameter and 2.5 cm (1 in) deep. Wrap a piece of bacon round each steak and tie in place with string. Season generously with freshly ground pepper and allow to come to room temperature.

When ready to serve, heat the grill to high. Brush the grill grid with oil and place the pork tournedos on the grid. Season with salt and drizzle with oil. Grill 8 cm (3 in) from the heat, for 15 minutes, turning once during cooking, and brushing again with oil. Five minutes before the end of the cooking time, place the mushrooms on the grid, brush with oil and cook for 5 minutes, brushing with oil occasionally. Remove the string from the steaks, arrange on a heated serving platter with the mushrooms and serve immediately.

*Robert Carrier's Kitchen*

# Homemade Sausage Patties

*The perfect idea for a special Sunday breakfast or brunch. These Southern-style homemade sausage patties are the ideal fare. Serve them with soft scrambled eggs, breakfast pancakes or waffles, or cooked oatmeal porridge, served with freshly grated cheese and melted butter (like polenta). I can hear them asking for more.*

*Serves 6*

1 kg/2 lb lean pork
½ teaspoon powdered sage
½ teaspoon powdered cumin
¼ teaspoon powdered ginger
2 bay leaves, crumbled
Salt and freshly ground pepper
Crushed diced chillies
2 tablespoons butter
2 tablespoons olive oil

Ask your butcher to mince the pork. Mix ground meat with sage and spices, crumbled bay leaves, salt, freshly ground pepper and crushed dried chillies, to taste. Form mixture into 12 to 18 small patties and sauté in butter and olive oil until well browned on both sides.

*Vogue*

# Grilled Gammon Steaks with Grapefruit

*Serves 4*

4 gammon steaks, 12 mm/½ in thick,
about 150 g/6 oz each
Milk, optional
Freshly ground pepper
1–2 grapefruit
4 tablespoons clear honey
Oil

If the gammon steaks are salty, soak them in milk for 1 to 2 hours before cooking. Dry the steaks with absorbent paper and trim off any excess fat. Leave a narrow border of fat round the steaks and slash it at intervals with a sharp knife. Season with freshly ground pepper and allow to come to room temperature.

Heat the grill to high. Peel the grapefruit, removing all white pith, and cut into segments. You need 16 segments in all.

Brush the grill grid with oil and place the gammon steaks on the grid. Pour ½ table-spoon honey over one side of each steak and grill 8 cm (3 in) from the heat for 5 minutes.

Turn the steaks and pour over the remaining honey. Grill for a further 3 minutes. Place 4 grapefruit segments on each steak, brush with oil and grill for a further 2 minutes. Season with freshly ground pepper .

*The Robert Carrier Cookery Course*

# Creole Jambalaya

*Serves 6*

*350 g/12 oz cooked ham*
*350 g/12 oz large frozen prawns*
*225 g/8 oz Chorizo sausage*
*(or pork or garlic sausage)*
*4 tablespoons olive oil*
*2 tablespoons butter*
*2 tablespoons lard*
*1 Spanish onion, finely chopped*
*2 cloves garlic*
*350 g/12 oz risotto rice*
*2 stalks celery, thinly sliced*
*1 green pepper, diced*
*1 (225 g/8 oz) can Italian peeled*
*tomatoes, diced*
*6 tablespoons tomato concentrate*
*1 bay leaf, crumbled*
*½ teaspoon thyme, or oregano*
*⅛ teaspoon ground cloves*
*Salt and freshly ground pepper*
*Cayenne pepper*
*1–1.5 l/2–2½ pints chicken stock*
*4–6 tablespoons dry white wine*
*4 tablespoons finely chopped parsley*
*12 pitted black olives*

Cut ham into 2.5 cm (1 in) squares; defrost prawns and slice Chorizo sausage into 12 mm (½ in) pieces. Heat olive oil in a thick-bottomed frying pan and sauté ham chunks, prawns and sausage in separate batches until they are golden brown. Remove with a slotted spoon and reserve.

Melt butter and lard in the bottom of large heatproof casserole and sauté finely chopped Spanish onion and whole garlic cloves until onion and garlic are transparent. Stir in risotto rice and cook over a low heat, stirring gently until the rice is transparent. Stir sautéed ham, prawn and sausage mixture into rice; stir in sliced celery stalks, diced green pepper, tomatoes and their juice, and tomato concentrate. Add crumbled bay leaf, thyme (or oregano and ground cloves) and season with salt, freshly ground pepper and cayenne to taste.

Bring well-flavoured chicken stock to boil and pour over Jambalaya mixture. Cover casserole and simmer over a low heat for 15 to 20 minutes, or until the rice is tender, but still separate, adding a little more liquid from time to time if necessary.

Just before serving, stir in dry white wine, correct seasoning and keep warm in the lowest of ovens, or on a candle warmer, until ready to serve. Add finely chopped parsley, pitted black olives and serve immediately.

*Harper's Bazaar*

# Poultry and Game

*I love farmyard fare: farm-raised (and fed) chickens, ducks, guinea fowl, pigeons and rabbits. Roast Chicken with a Richly Aromatic Stuffing or with a more unusual Watercress Stuffing, or chicken-in-the pot. Perhaps the simplest, and most satisfying of them all is not-so-plain Boiled Chicken with Rice, thanks to its creamy Velouté Sauce and its accompaniment of colourful boiled vegetables. I like, too, the curried chicken theme for a dinner party – so flavourful, and so easy to cook and serve. Magrets de Canard, that famous French restaurant speciality, are now available in this country. I give you two versions – Grilled Magret with Soy and Honey and a Pan-Fried Magret with Cassis (a special favourite of Delia Smith and her husband, Michael Wynne Jones). Try, too, my mother's Roast Duck with Sauerkraut and Apple Stuffing, a dish from my childhood which I still make when feeling a trifle nostalgic for home delights.*

# Old English Devilled Chicken

*Serves 4*

*1 (1.25kg/2½ lb) chicken*
*50 g/2 oz fresh white breadcrumbs*

## For the Devil Mixture

*5 tablespoons butter*
*1 tablespoon curry powder*
*1 teaspoon caster sugar*
*1 teaspoon dry mustard*
*½ teaspoon salt*
*½ teaspoon paprika*
*1 pinch crushed dried chillies*
*1 teaspoon Worcestershire sauce*

Joint the chicken into 4 serving portions. Preheat the grill to high and the oven to 180°C (350°F, Gas Mark 4).

In a small saucepan, melt the butter over a low heat. Stir in the remaining Deveil Mixture ingredients.

Lay the chicken portions on the grid of the grill pan and brush both sides with a little of the Devil Mixture. Grill for 5 minutes on each side, 8 cm (3 in) away from the heat. Transfer the chicken portions to a heatproof *gratin* dish large enough to take them in one layer. Pour the juices from the grilling pan into the remaining Devil Mixture. Add the

fresh white breadcrumbs and stir to blend. Spoon the devilled crumbs evenly over the chicken portions and bake in the preheated oven for 30 minutes, or until the chicken portions are cooked and the breadcrumbs crisp. Serve immediately.

*The Sunday Times*

# Country Fried Chicken

*Some fried chicken and rabbit recipes just seem to cry out to be fried in lard for extra richness of flavour. Country Fried Chicken is a case in point. However, if you are one of the more 'health-minded' cooks who insist on Mediterranean oils for cooking, go for it.*

*Serves 2 to 4*

*1 tender young chicken (1.4 kg/3 lb)*
*Juice of ½ lemon*
*Salt and freshly ground pepper*
*½ level teaspoon paprika*
*2 eggs*
*2 tablespoons water*
*Flour*
*Fine breadcrumbs*
*Lard for deep-frying*
*1 lemon, cut into wedges*

Cut young chicken into 4 pieces. Rub chicken pieces with lemon juice, salt, freshly ground pepper and paprika. Beat eggs with

water until well beaten. Dust chicken pieces with flour; dip in beaten eggs and water mixture and then in fine breadcrumbs.

Melt lard in a large frying pan to a depth of at least 2.5 cm (1 in). Carefully place chicken pieces into the boiling fat and fry them to a golden brown on all sides.

Lower heat and continue to cook chicken until tender, without taking on any more colour, about 10 to 15 minutes.

Remove chicken pieces from fat with a slotted spoon and allow them to drain on a pan lined with kitchen paper to absorb excess fat. Serve fried chicken on a heated serving dish with lemon wedges.

*The Robert Carrier Cookery Course*

# Chicken à la Kiev

*Kiev was the military academy of Tsarist Russia. It was there that this intriguing recipe for deep-fried stuffed chicken breasts was created – named, it is said, after the famous academy because the chicken breasts were arranged like little 'firing cannons' placed on deep-fried 'carriages' of bread with cannon 'wheels' made of deep-fried rounds of bread.*

*Serves 4*

*4 raw-winged chicken breasts,
weighing not less than 200 g/7 oz each*

*2 tablespoons flour
Salt and freshly ground pepper
2 medium-sized eggs, beaten
Fine dry breadcrumbs
Oil, for frying
Mustard mayonnaise*

## Seasoned Butter

*100 g/4 oz butter
Grated zest of ½ lemon
Juice of ½ lemon
1 garlic clove, crushed
1 tablespoon finely chopped parsley
1 tablespoon finely chopped chives
or tarragon
Salt and freshly ground pepper
Cayenne pepper*

### To make Seasoned Butter

Combine butter with grated lemon zest, lemon juice, crushed garlic and finely chopped parsley and chives or tarragon and mash with a fork to a smooth paste. Season with salt, freshly ground pepper and cayenne pepper, to taste. Form mixture into a sausage about 6 cm (2 ½ in) long, wrap in foil and chill until firm.

## To prepare Chicken

Cut wings off chicken breasts below the first joint. Remove skin and all other bones. Lay chicken breasts flat, cut side uppermost, with the thickest side towards you. With a sharp knife, cut a horizontal pocket along the centre of each breast to within 2.5 cm (1 in) of either end, taking care not to cut right through flesh.

Cut Seasoned Butter into 4 fingers and insert 1 piece lengthways into each pocket. Press open edges of pocket together to enclose butter completely.

Season flour generously with salt and freshly ground pepper. Toss chicken breasts in seasoned flour, shaking off excess, then in beaten eggs, draining carefully, and then in breadcrumbs, patting coating on firmly. Repeat this process again, then chill for at least 1 hour to 'set' coating. All this may be done on the day before serving.

When ready to cook: heat oil in a deep-fat fryer to 180°C (350°F). Lower chicken breasts two at a time into fat and fry for 12 to 15 minutes, or until chicken breasts are golden brown and tender. Drain on absorbent paper. Transfer chicken breasts to a heated serving dish; slip a cutlet frill on each wing joint and serve immediately with mustard mayonnaise.

*Woman's Own*

# Old-Fashioned Roast Chicken with Aromatic Stuffing

*This is one of the best poultry stuffings I know – rich in flavours and textures – the onion, sausage and breadcrumb mixture flavoured with chopped anchovies, apple, herbs and lemon juice and enriched with sautéed chopped poultry livers. Use it (as here) for roast chicken, or roast duck, guinea fowl and turkey.*

*Serves 4 to 6*

*1 (2 kg/4 lb) roasting chicken with giblets*
*Salt and freshly ground pepper*
*40 g/1½ oz softened butter*
*½–1 tablespoon flour*
*Sprigs of watercress*
*300 ml/10 fl oz chicken stock*
*(made from ½ chicken stock cube and reserved giblets)*

## Aromatic Stuffing

*2 tablespoons lard*
*1 Spanish onion, finely chopped*
*225 g/8 oz sausage meat*
*2 tablespoons finely chopped parsley*
*4 anchovy fillets, finely chopped*
*2 eggs, beaten*

*Juice of ½ lemon*
*Generous pinch each of dried thyme and*
*dried marjoram*
*1 medium-sized cooking apple, finely*
*chopped*
*Salt and freshly ground pepper*
*225 g/8 oz poultry livers, chopped*
*75 g/3 oz dry breadcrumbs*

Preheat oven to fairly hot (220°C, 425°C, Gas Mark 7).

## To make Aromatic Stuffing

Melt lard in a frying pan and sauté finely chopped onion for 5 to 10 minutes or until transparent. Add sausage meat and sauté with onion for about 10 minutes more. Remove with a slotted spoon.

Combine onion and sausage meat mixture in a bowl with finely chopped parsley, finely chopped anchovy fillets, beaten eggs, lemon juice, dried thyme and marjoram, finely chopped apple, salt and freshly ground pepper, to taste. Sauté chopped poultry livers in fat remaining in pan for about 5 minutes. Add breadcrumbs and sauté for a further 5 minutes. Combine with other ingredients, and reserve.

## To prepare Chicken

Wipe bird clean both inside and out with a damp cloth, or absorbent paper. Season cavity with salt and freshly ground pepper. Loosen the skin at the neck end of chicken as much as possible from the breast; insert some of the stuffing evenly over the flesh of the breast and fill the loose skin of the neck with as much as it will hold. Fold the skin over and fasten with a few stitches. Stuff body cavity as well and sew up. Pass a skewer through the 2 wings to hold them neatly together.

Season the chicken all over with salt and freshly ground pepper. Spread breast and thighs of chicken with softened butter.

Lay chicken on its side in a roasting tin and roast in preheated oven for 20 minutes until slightly browned. Turn bird on to its other side and roast for a further 15 to 20 minutes. Remove bird from oven.

Reduce oven to moderate (180°C, 350°F, Gas Mark 4). Turn bird on its back and sieve over a dusting of flour. Baste with 3 or 4 tablespoons boiling water and continue to roast for about 1 hour, or until chicken is tender, basting frequently. If you push a skewer through the thickest part of the inside leg, the juices should run quite clear and golden, with no hint of pink.

When chicken is tender, remove trussing skewer, string, etc. Drain bird and transfer to a heated serving dish. Garnish with sprigs of watercress.

Pour away the fat from the roasting pan in which bird was roasted; add chicken stock (made from stock and giblets) and stir over a high heat until boiling, scraping in any brown bits from sides of pan. Season to taste with salt and freshly ground pepper, and serve in a sauceboat with chicken.

*Robert Carrier's Kitchen*

# Roast Chicken with Watercress Stuffing

*Serves 4*

*1 roasting chicken (1.5–2 kg/3½ to 4 lb)*

## Stuffing

*6 tablespoons finely chopped onion*
*6 tablespoons finely chopped celery*
*6 tablespoons butter*
*1 bunch watercress, finely chopped*
*Salt and freshly ground pepper*
*Crushed dried chillies*
*100 g/4 oz dry breadcrumbs*

## To prepare Stuffing

Simmer onion and celery in half the butter until soft. Add finely chopped watercress and season with salt, freshly ground pepper and crushed dried chillies, to taste. Cook until all liquids evaporate. Melt remaining butter, stir in breadcrumbs and add to watercress mixture.

Stuff chicken with this mixture and roast in preheated oven as for Old-Fashioned Roast Chicken (pages 168–70).

*The Robert Carrier Cookbook*

# Grilled Spring Chicken

*Serves 4*

*2 tender young chickens (1 kg/2–2½ lb each)*
*Salt, freshly ground pepper and paprika*
*Lemon juice*
*Melted butter*
*6 tablespoons breadcrumbs, browned in 2 tablespoons butter*
*Sprigs of watercress and lemon wedges*

Split cleaned chickens open through the back, flatten out and trim birds, cutting off feet and wingtips; wipe with a damp cloth, and season generously with salt, freshly ground pepper, paprika and a little lemon juice. Skewer birds open; brush both sides with melted butter and sprinkle with fine browned breadcrumbs.

Grill over charcoal (or under grill) for 25 to 30 minutes, turning the birds occasionally and basting frequently with melted butter. Serve very hot, garnished with watercress and lemon wedges

*The Robert Carrier Cookbook*

# Lemon Barbecued Chicken

*Serves 6*

*2 young fryer chickens (1 kg/2–2½ lb each)*
*Salt and freshly ground pepper*

## Lemon Barbecue Sauce

*150 ml (5 fl oz) olive oil*
*8 tablespoons lemon juice*
*2 tablespoons finely chopped onion*
*1–2 teaspoons dried tarragon or rosemary*
*1–2 teaspoons finely chopped parsley*
*Salt, freshly ground pepper and Tabasco*

Quarter chickens. Sprinkle quarters with salt, freshly ground pepper, and marinate in Lemon Barbecue Sauce for at least 4 hours, turning chicken quarters at least once.

When ready to grill: drain chicken pieces, reserving marinade juices, and place on barbecue grill about 15 cm (6 inches) from coals. Or, if you are using an electric or gas grill, place drained chicken pieces on grill. Brush with marinade juices and cook slowly until tender (25 to 35 minutes) turning chicken pieces and basting with the marinade juices from time to time.

*The Robert Carrier Cookbook*

# Barry Wine's Marinated Chicken

*Each year Barry Wine and his wife Karen visit the best restaurants in France and bring back ideas for their New York restaurant. In the Quilted Giraffe, Wine presents such delights as ravioli stuffed with wild mushrooms, a rose-pink rack of lamb with Chinese mustard – and marinated chicken breast, grilled, sliced and served on a bed of deep-fried sweet potato chips and accompanied by a lightened Aïoli. The combination of new flavours and textures makes a memorable festive dish.*

*Serves 4*

*1 young chicken (1–1.5 kg/2½ to 3 lb)*
*4 tablespoons olive oil*
*4 tablespoons sesame seed oil*
*100 g/4 oz garlic cloves, finely chopped*
*100 g/4 oz root ginger, peeled*
*and finely chopped*
*Salt and freshly ground pepper*

## Aïoli

*1 teaspoon lemon juice*
*1 egg yolk*
*2 tablespoons olive oil*
*2 tablespoons sesame seed oil*
*2 tablespoons peanut oil*
*2 tablespoons double cream*
*2 garlic cloves, finely chopped*
*Salt and freshly ground pepper*

## Sweet Potato Chips

*1 kg/2 lb sweet potatoes*
*Salt*
*Oil, for deep-frying*

### To marinate Chicken

In a thick-bottomed frying pan, combine olive oil, sesame seed oil and finely chopped garlic cloves and root ginger and cook over a low heat for 10 minutes, stirring occasionally. Pour garlic and ginger marinade into a porcelain or earthenware (not metal) dish. Using a sharp knife, cut chicken into 6 serving pieces: 2 drumsticks, 2 thighs and 2 breasts. (Save carcass and wings for another use.) Season chicken pieces generously with salt and freshly ground pepper; place in marinade, spooning it over, and leave in a refrigerator for at least 3 hours, turning several times.

## To make Aïoli

Beat together lemon juice and egg yolk. Gradually beat in olive oil, sesame seed oil and peanut oil. Add double cream and garlic; season with salt and pepper and beat until smooth.

## To prepare Sweet Potato Chips

Scrub sweet potatoes and cook in boiling salted water for 10 minutes. Drain. Cut into strips, 5 cm (2 in) long and 6 mm (¼ in) wide. Dry with absorbent paper.

## To cook Chicken

Preheat grill to high. Drain chicken pieces. Brush grid of a grill pan with olive oil and lay chicken drumsticks and thighs, fleshy side up, on grid. Grill 13 cm (5 in) from heat for 5 minutes. Place chicken breasts fleshy side up on grid with drumsticks and thighs; brush all pieces with marinade and continue to grill for a further 15 minutes, or until chicken pieces are cooked through, turning and brushing with marinade once more.

## To cook Sweet Potato Chips

Meanwhile, heat oil in a deep-fryer to 180°C (350°F). Using a small quantity of chips at a time, deep-fry for 3 minutes, or until crisp and golden brown with a soft centre. Drain on absorbent paper.

## To serve

Slice each chicken breast crosswise into 4 to 6 thick slices. Sprinkle chips with salt. Have ready 4 heated serving plates. Scatter one-quarter of the chips on each plate; arrange 1 drumstick or thigh on each plate and half a chicken breast each. Dribble a little Aïoli over chicken and garnish plates with colourful vegetables. Serve with remaining Aïoli separately.

*Sunday Express Magazine*

# Chicken with 40 Cloves of Garlic (Poulet à l'Ail)

*In this dish, garlic plays the role of a vegetable garnish as well as an aromatic. There is no need to feel apprehensive about 40 cloves of garlic – cooked in this way they are, if anything, less indigestible than a couple of finely chopped raw cloves would be. After all, we happily eat cooked stuffed onions as a dish in themselves, so why not garlic? It makes an unforgettable dish – rich and nutty and, strangely enough, not particularly strong in garlic flavour.*

*Serves 4*

*1 (1.4 kg/3 lb) chicken*
*Salt and freshly ground pepper*
*40 plump whole cloves garlic*
*3 tablespoons olive oil*
*3 tablespoons butter*
*Whites of 4 fat leeks, thinly sliced*
*1 bay leaf*
*6–8 tablespoons dry white wine*
*6–8 tablespoons chicken stock*

Preheat the oven to 110°C (225°F, Gas Mark ¼). Wipe the chicken clean with a damp cloth and season both inside and out with salt and freshly ground pepper. Truss the chicken.

Remove the papery skins from the garlic cloves, but leave them whole. Put the garlic cloves in a small pan, cover with cold water, bring to boiling point and drain thoroughly. Choose a heavy, flameproof casserole just large enough to hold the chicken comfortably, and equipped with a tight-fitting lid. In it heat 2 tablespoons each olive oil and butter, add the blanched garlic cloves and sauté for 3 to 4 minutes, stirring frequently. Take the greatest care not to let the garlic cloves brown, or they will impart an unpleasantly bitter flavour to the whole dish. Remove the garlic cloves from the casserole with a slotted spoon and reserve.

Add the thinly sliced leeks to the casserole and sauté gently until the slices are soft and a rich golden colour. Remove with a slotted spoon and put aside with the garlic cloves. Add the remaining oil and butter to the casserole. Raise the heat and brown the chicken steadily and thoroughly on all sides (approximately 10 minutes).

Return the sautéed garlic cloves and leeks to the casserole, season to taste with salt and freshly ground pepper; add the bay leaf. Put the dry white wine and chicken stock in a saucepan and bring to the boil. Pour the liquid over the chicken; cover the casserole tightly and transfer to the oven. Bake for 1½ hours, or until the chicken juices run clear when the leg is pierced through the thickest part close to the body, and the leeks have disintegrated to make a sauce.

### To serve

Remove the chicken from the casserole and place on a heated serving dish. Remove the trussing string. Garnish with the garlic cloves. Skim the fat from the pan juices; spoon some over the chicken and serve the remainder in a heated sauceboat.

*Robert Carrier's Kitchen*

# Poulet aux Poivrons

*Serves 4*

*1 (1.6 kg/3½ lb) roasting chicken*
*2 tablespoons butter*
*2 tablespoons olive oil*

*½ level teaspoon paprika*
*Salt and freshly ground pepper*
*Cayenne pepper*
*2 Spanish onions, finely chopped*
*4 cloves garlic, finely chopped*
*1 kg/2 lb ripe tomatoes, peeled,*
*seeded and chopped*
*1 kg/2 lb red and green pepper,*
*seeded and thinly sliced*
*2 bay leaves*
*2 sprigs thyme*
*2 sage leaves*
*4 sprigs parsley*

Clean chicken and cut into 8 serving pieces. Melt butter and olive oil in a large heatproof casserole and sauté chicken pieces in fats until golden. Season with paprika and salt, freshly ground pepper and cayenne pepper, to taste.

Add onions and garlic, tomatoes, peppers, bay leaves, thyme, sage and parsley. Cook, covered, over a gentle heat, or in a slow oven (130°C, 300°F, Gas Mark 1) for 1¼ hours, or until chicken is tender.

### To serve

Remove herbs and correct seasoning (the dish should be very highly spiced). Serve in casserole accompanied by boiled or steamed rice.

*Feasts of Provence*

# Poulet au Blanc

*Serves 4*

*1 plump chicken (1.4–1.3 kg/3–3½ lb*
*600 ml/1 pint good white stock*
*Salt and freshly ground pepper*
*4 tablespoons butter*
*12 mushroom caps*
*Juice of 1 lemon*
*2 tablespoons flour*
*2 egg yolks*

Preheat oven to 110°C (225°F, Mark ¼). Place chicken in an earthenware casserole. Add enough stock to half-cover chicken. Season with salt and freshly ground pepper, to taste. Cover exposed part of chicken with a piece of buttered paper; place lid on casserole and simmer in preheated oven for about an hour, or until chicken is tender.

Simmer mushroom caps in 2 tablespoons butter and lemon juice in a small saucepan; keep warm. Remove chicken from casserole; keep warm. Make a white roux with remaining butter and flour. Strain 600 ml (1 pint) of liquid in which chicken has been cooked into roux to make a Velouté Sauce (see page 182). Remove sauce from heat and stir in the egg yolks. Carve chicken into serving pieces and place in a clean casserole; add Sauce and mushroom caps; correct seasoning; warm and serve in casserole.

*The Sunday Times*

# Boiled Chicken and Rice

*Boiled chicken and rice? You can bet your boots on it. This simple recipe of a whole tender boiled chicken, served in a rich cream sauce and surrounded by colourful clusters of boiled rice and steamed or boiled vegetables is one of my favourite ways of dealing with Sunday lunch. I sometimes add a little saffron to the cream sauce for a more special occasion.*

*Serves 6*

*1 (1.4 kg/3 lb) chicken, cleaned*
*1 Spanish onion, stuck with 2 cloves*
*2 large carrots, quartered*
*Bouquet garni*
*2 celery stalks, coarsely chopped*
*180 ml/6 fl oz dry white wine*
*1.2 l/2 pints chicken stock*
*Salt*
*Black peppercorns*
*1 tablespoon butter*
*1 Spanish onion, finely chopped*
*225 g/8 oz rice*
*600 ml/1 pint hot water*
*Freshly ground pepper*
*Steamed carrots*
*Steamed green beans*

# Cream Sauce

*2 tablespoons butter*
*2 tablespoons flour*
*450 ml / 12 fl oz double cream*
*Salt and freshly ground pepper*
*Freshly grated nutmeg*

Place chicken in a casserole with onion stuck with cloves; add quartered carrots, *bouquet garni* and coarsely chopped celery. Pour over dry white wine and chicken stock. Season with salt, to taste; add a few black peppercorns and simmer gently for about 1 to 1½ hours until chicken is tender. Remove chicken from casserole and keep warm. Strain stock and use for cooking rice and Cream Sauce.

## *To cook Rice*

Melt butter in a saucepan; add finely chopped onion and stir over gentle heat for 4 to 5 minutes until translucent. Stir in rice, 300 ml (10 fl oz) strained chicken stock and hot water. Season to taste with salt and freshly ground pepper, bring the boil, and stir to dislodge any grains of rice stuck to the pan. Simmer gently, covered, for about 25 minutes until tender but not mushy.

## *To make Cream Sauce*

Melt butter in a heavy pan; blend in flour smoothly with a wooden spoon and stir over a low heat for 2 to 3 minutes to make a pale roux. Gradually add 150 ml (5 fl oz) strained chicken stock and double cream, stirring vigorously with a wire whisk to prevent lumps forming. Bring to the boil, stirring, and simmer for 5 to 10 minutes until sauce is thick and smooth. Season to taste with salt and freshly ground pepper, and freshly grated nutmeg.

## *To serve*

Place boiled chicken in the centre of a large heated serving platter. Surround with clusters of steamed whole carrots, green beans and rice. Pour a little Cream Sauce over chicken and serve the remainder separately.

*Robert Carrier's Kitchen*

# Jamaican Chicken Curry

*My valet René was from Jamaica. This is his recipe for one of the best chicken curry recipes I know – full-blooded, highly spiced and wonderful to look at – prepared as only Jamaican cooks know how.*

*Serves 4 to 6*

*1–1½ tender chickens (about 1.4 kg/ 3 lb each), jointed into 4 to 6 pieces*
*6 black peppercorns*
*1 small piece fresh root ginger, peeled and chopped (or ¼ teaspoon ground ginger)*
*½ teaspoon coriander seeds*
*4 cardamom seeds and 2 bay leaves*
*2 dried red chillies*
*2–3 tablespoons curry powder*
*½ teaspoon ground nutmeg*
*Salt*
*2–3 tablespoons olive oil*
*2–3 tablespoons butter*
*1–1½ Spanish onions, finely chopped*
*1 large clove garlic, finely chopped*
*1 small green pepper, diced*
*2–3 tomatoes, peeled and chopped*
*1 stick cinnamon*
*Grated rind of 1 lemon*
*Juice of ½ lemon*
*1 sprig thyme*
*450 ml/12 fl oz chicken stock*
*1 tablespoon cornflour*

Grind peppercorns, chopped root ginger, coriander and cardamom seeds in a mortar. Break the bay leaves and dried red chillies with your fingers, add to pestle and mortar and break up further; add powdered ginger, if you're using it, 1 tablespoon curry powder, nutmeg and salt to taste. Rub spice mixture into chicken pieces. Leave for 2 hours.

In a large heatproof casserole sauté chicken pieces in olive oil and butter until golden. Remove chicken and sauté finely chopped onion and garlic in remaining fat until transparent; add diced green pepper and chopped tomatoes, cover and continue cooking until green pepper is just soft; add cinnamon, broken into 3 or 4 pieces, lemon rind and lemon juice and thyme; add chicken stock. Stir well, cover and simmer for 20 to 30 minutes until chicken is almost done.

Skim off excess fat, add remaining curry powder and continue to cook, uncovered, for 10 to 15 minutes, or until chicken is tender. Remove chicken pieces and keep hot.

### *To prepare Sauce*

Remove pieces of cinnamon stick and sprig of thyme. Blend cornflour with some of the chicken liquor. Return to hot liquor and whisk constantly over a high heat until boiling, then allow to simmer for 5 minutes.

Serve the chicken pieces with the hot sauce ladled over.

*Food, Wine & Friends*

# Ceylonese Chicken Curry

*On the chicken curry theme again – this time the recipe is from Ceylon where half the hot curry spices are rubbed into the chicken pieces before they are gently simmered in a rich coconut cream. As a flavour surprise, the remaining aromatic spices are sprinkled over the curry just before serving.*

*Serves 8*

*2 (1.4 kg/3 lb) roasting chickens*
*2 teaspoons curry powder*
*2 teaspoons ground coriander*
*½ teaspoon ground ginger*
*½ teaspoon saffron*
*Crushed dried chillies*
*2 Spanish onions, finely chopped*
*3–4 cloves garlic, finely chopped*
*2 bay leaves*
*1 cinnamon stick, broken in four pieces*
*2 teaspoons salt*
*6 tablespoons peanut oil*
*300 ml/10 fl oz Coconut Milk*
*(made with 125 g/5 oz fine-cut*
*desiccated coconut)*
*½ teaspoon sugar*
*1–2 teaspoons fresh lime juice, or lemon juice*

## Aromatic spice blend

*½ teaspoon each freshly ground cardamom and cinnamon*
*½ teaspoon each freshly ground cloves and coriander*

### To prepare Chicken

Cut each chicken into 8 to 10 serving pieces. Mix next 10 ingredients; add peanut oil and rub well into chicken pieces. Allow chicken to marinate in this aromatic flavouring mixture overnight.

### To make Coconut Milk

Place 125 g (5 oz) fine-cut desiccated coconut in a bowl; add 450 ml (15 fl oz) water and knead with hands for 3 minutes. Strain coconut through a fine sieve, pressing coconut milk into a bowl with a wooden spoon. You'll end up with a little over 300 ml (10 fl oz).

### To cook Chicken

When ready to cook, put chicken pieces and aromatics in a large heatproof casserole and cook, stirring constantly, until chicken pieces and onion are golden brown, adding a little more oil, if necessary. Add coconut milk,

stirring in all the crusty bits from the bottom and sides of the casserole; cover and simmer gently for 35 to 45 minutes, or until chicken is tender, stirring contents of casserole from time to time to prevent sticking.

Transfer chicken pieces to a heated serving dish with a slotted spoon. Add 1 teaspoon sugar to pan juices; turn up heat under casserole to high and cook sauce until it is reduced to half its original quantity.

Remove casserole from heat; add lime, or lemon juice; stir well; strain sauce over chicken pieces; sprinkle chicken with an aromatic blend of freshly ground spices. Serve with rice and other accompaniments.

*Robert Carrier's Kitchen*

# Curry Side Dishes

- Diced fresh tomatoes (peeled and seeded), flavoured with finely chopped onion and green pepper, and lemon juice, salt and freshly ground black pepper, to taste.
- Diced cucumber (peeled and seeded), flavoured with chopped spring onion (green and white parts) and salt and freshly ground pepper, to taste.
- Yoghurt, flavoured with finely chopped mint and garlic, and lemon juice and salt and freshly ground pepper, to taste.
- Browned desiccated coconut, flavoured with salt, to taste.
- Currants and sultanas, soaked in a little sherry and mixed with finely chopped onions and almonds fried in butter.
- Diced crisp-fried bacon.
- Chopped hard-boiled eggs flavoured with finely chopped spring onion and green pepper, and lemon juice and salt and cayenne pepper, to taste.
- Various chutneys.
- Quarters of fresh limes.

# Old English Chicken Pie

*Lemon and herb white 'forc'dmeat' balls, liver and sausage 'forc'dmeat' balls and quartered hard-boiled eggs lend an authentic nineteenth-century touch to this deep-dish chicken pie. A Sunday lunch favourite.*

*Serves 4 to 6*

*1 (about 1.4 kg/3 lb) tender roasting chicken*
*1/2 Spanish onion, sliced*
*1 bay leaf*
*6 tablespoons flour*
*2 tablespoons butter*
*Salt and freshly ground pepper*
*2 hard-boiled eggs, quartered*
*Flaky pastry for 1-crust pie*
*Chicken Velouté Sauce (see recipe page 182)*

## White Forc'dmeat

*100 g/4 oz stale bread*
*1 teaspoon finely chopped parsley*
*¼ teaspoon finely chopped thyme*
*Grated rind of ½ lemon*
*Pinch of freshly grated nutmeg*
*½ teaspoon salt and freshly ground pepper*
*50 g/2 oz butter, diced*
*1 egg yolk*

## Sausage Forc'dmeat

*Liver and heart of the chicken*
*100 g/4 oz sausage meat*
*1 teaspoon each finely chopped parsley and chives or onion greens*

### To cook Chicken

Bone chicken. Make a light stock by simmering wings, neck and bones in a little water with sliced onion and bay leaf for 2 minutes. Re-form boned pieces of chicken; roll in flour and sauté in 2 tablespoons butter until golden. Add salt and freshly ground pepper; cover and cook over a low heat for 20 minutes, turning occasionally.

### To prepare White Forc'dmeat

Grate bread and mix it with finely chopped parsley and thyme, grated lemon rind, and grated nutmeg, salt and freshly ground pepper, to taste. Add diced butter and egg yolk, and work to a smooth paste with fingers.

### To prepare Sausage Forc'dmeat

Mince liver and heart of chicken with sausage meat. Combine with chopped parsley and chives. Form small balls out of two mixtures and brown lightly in butter in another pan.

Garnish a deep pie dish with chicken pieces, forc'dmeat balls and quartered hard-boiled eggs.

Stir 6 tablespoons stock into a pan in which chicken was cooked, blending it well with butter and remaining juices. Pour this over the contents of pie dish and cover with layer of pastry.

Moisten edges of pie dish with water; press pastry to edge; crimping edge of crust with a fork. Cut one or two slits in the centre of crust to allow steam to escape. Decorate pastry crust as desired.

Bake in a moderate oven (190°C, 375°F, Gas Mark 5) for 30 minutes, or until done. Serve with Chicken Velouté Sauce.

*Daily Telegraph Magazine*

# Basic Velouté Sauce

*This sauce forms the basis for a number of the best white sauces, which take their distinctive names from the different ingredients added. It can be used by itself, but in that case, it is much improved by the addition of a few tablespoons of double cream and/or an egg yolk.*

*Serves 4 to 6*

*2 tablespoons butter*
*2 tablespoons flour*

*2 tablespoons finely chopped onion*
*600 ml/1 pint of water*
*Salt*
*White peppercorns*
*Mushroom peelings or stems*
*Lemon juice*

Melt butter in the top of a double saucepan; add onion and simmer until onion is transparent. Add flour and cook for a few minutes to form a pale roux. Add boiling water, salt, peppercorns and mushroom peelings or stems; reduce heat and simmer gently, stirring occasionally, and skimming from time to time, until the sauce is reduced to two-thirds of the original quantity and is thick but light and creamy. Flavour with lemon juice and strain through a fine sieve.

*The Robert Carrier Cookbook*

# Basic Chicken or Fish Velouté Sauce

Proceed as for Basic Velouté Sauce above, substituting 600 ml (1 pint) chicken or fish stock for the water.

# Chicken Pot Pie

*Serves 4*

*1.4 kg/3 lb chicken*
*2 tablespoons flour*
*Salt and freshly ground pepper*
*2 tablespoons olive oil*
*3 tablespoons butter*
*12 small onions*
*600 ml/1 pint chicken stock*
*Bouquet garni*
*Juice of 1 lemon*
*24 button mushrooms*
*225 g/8 oz packet frozen peas*
*1 tablespoon flour*
*300 ml/10 fl oz double cream*
*225 g/8 oz shortcrust pastry*
*1 egg yolk*

Cut chicken into 8 portions. Put flour into a shallow dish and season with salt and freshly ground pepper. Toss each chicken portion in flour, shaking off excess. Heat olive oil and 1 tablespoon butter in a large frying pan. Sauté chicken portions in 2 batches for 2 to 3 minutes on each side, or until lightly golden. Transfer to a casserole and keep warm. Repeat with second batch.

In the same pan sauté onions for 3 to 4 minutes, or until lightly browned, shaking pan to ensure even cooking. Remove with a slotted spoon and add to casserole. Pour chicken stock over chicken portions and onions; add *bouquet garni* and season with salt and freshly ground pepper, to taste. Cover casserole and simmer gently for 1 to 1¼ hours, or until chicken portions are tender. Remove chicken portions from casserole; strain and reserve 300 ml (10 fl oz) of stock.

Meanwhile, heat 1 tablespoon butter in a clean large frying pan; add lemon juice and button mushrooms and cook for 4 to 5 minutes, or until tender, turning mushrooms with a fish slice. Remove with a slotted spoon. Simmer frozen peas in a saucepan of salted water for 2 minutes; drain.

## *To make Sauce*

Melt remaining butter in the top of a double saucepan. Blend in flour with a wooden spoon. Pour reserved stock from the casserole into pan, whisking continuously. Add double cream; season with salt and freshly ground pepper, to taste, and cook for a further 10 minutes, or until sauce thickens slightly.

## *To assemble and cook Pie*

Preheat oven to moderate, 190°C (375°F, Gas Mark 5). Place a pie funnel in the centre of a 1.5 l (2 ½ pint) pie dish and arrange chicken portions around it. Add onions, mushrooms and peas; correct seasoning and pour over sauce. Leave to cool slightly.

Roll pastry out a little larger than pie dish. Moisten rim of dish with a little beaten egg yolk. Place pastry over dish and cut off any excess with a sharp knife. Flute edges and make decorations from any scraps. Cut vents in pastry to allow steam to escape; brush with beaten egg yolk and bake in preheated oven for 20 minutes, or until pastry is golden brown. Serve immediately.

*Daily Telegraph Magazine*

# Magret de Canard au Cassis

*A thick 'skin' of glazed apple slices and a delicate blackcurrant-flavoured sauce make this a special recipe for a company dinner party. It takes time to apply the paper-thin apple slices to the sautéed duck breasts. But it's fun . . . and well worth the effort.*

*Serves 4*

*4 boneless breasts of duck*
*(125–150 g/5–6 oz each)*
*Salt and freshly ground pepper*
*1 tablespoon olive oil*
*2 tablespoons butter*
*2 tart dessert apples*
*4 tablespoons blackcurrants*
*Sprigs of watercress*

## Glaze

*Carcass and trimmings of duck*
*6 tablespoons butter*
*2 chicken stock cubes*
*1 tablespoon tomato purée*
*1 carrot, finely chopped*
*½ Spanish onion, finely chopped*
*150 ml/5 fl oz dry white wine*
*Freshly ground pepper*
*2 tablespoons Crème de Cassis*

### To prepare Glaze

Chop the duck carcass and trimmings coarsely with a chopper. Melt the butter in a saucepan, add the chopped carcass, the ½ chicken stock cube and tomato purée with the finely chopped carrot and onion and sauté until the ingredients are well browned. Stir in 600 ml (1 pint) water and the dry white wine and cook, skimming the surface from time to time, until the liquid is reduced to half its original quantity. Strain the sauce into a small saucepan, pressing the vegetables and bones to extract all the juice. Continue to cook the sauce over a low heat until it is reduced to about 150 ml (5 fl oz). Season with freshly ground pepper, add the Crème de Cassis and keep warm.

## To prepare Duck

With a sharp knife, slash the fat on each duck breast diagonally at 6 mm (¼ in) intervals in both directions to form a lattice pattern. Season the duck breasts with salt and freshly ground pepper. Heat 1 tablespoon butter and oil in a large, heavy, thick-bottomed frying pan over a high heat. Sear the fat side of each breast for about 30 seconds to brown, then remove from the pan and pour off the fat.

Return them to the pan, cover and cook over a low heat for 10 to 12 minutes, turning once during cooking. The duck should still be slightly pink in the middle. Remove the duck from the pan and, using a kitchen towel to protect your hands from the heat of the cooked duck, remove the skin, or remove it with a very sharp knife. Place the duck breasts in a flameproof serving dish or shallow casserole (an oval enamelled iron *gratin* dish is very good for this as it can go directly on to the heat). Keep warm in the oven (not for too long or it will go on cooking).

## To decorate Duck

Peel and core the apples and slice them thinly. Melt 2 tablespoons butter in a small frying pan, add the apple slices and sauté gently until golden brown, adding a little more butter if necessary. Make a new 'skin' for each breast of duck by covering it with overlapping slices of sautéed apple. Place the serving dish over a medium heat to reheat the duck breasts; brush the apple slices with a little of the glaze.

## To serve

Add the blackcurrants to the remaining sauce and pour it around the duck breasts in the serving dish. Garnish with watercress and serve at once.

*The Robert Carrier Seminar of Cooking*

## Grilled Magrets de Canards with Soy and Honey

*Serves 4*

*4 boneless duck breasts, wings removed*
*(225 g/8 oz each)*
*Freshly ground pepper*
*Olive oil*

### Soy-Honey Marinade

*2 tablespoons soy sauce*
*8 tablespoons dry sherry*
*3 tablespoons clear honey*
*3 tablespoons peanut oil*
*A little finely chopped fresh ginger*
*Pinch or two or crushed dried chillies*
*Finely grated peel of 1 orange*
*½ Spanish onion, finely chopped*

With a sharp knife, cut diagonally through the skin and dot on each duck breast, in both directions, to make a diamond pattern.

In a shallow dish, combine the ingredients for the Soy-Honey Marinade. Add the duck breasts and turn them to coat well. Cover and leave to marinate for 4 hours, turning them from time to time to ensure they remain coated. Preheat the grill to high.

Brush the grill grid with olive oil and place the duck breasts on the grid, fat side up. Grill 8 cm (3 in) from the heat for 15 to 20 minutes, turning them once and brushing frequently with the marinade. The breasts should be crisp on the outside but still pink in the centre. Cook them a little longer if you prefer, but avoid prolonged cooking or the meat will toughen.

*Vogue*

## Duck with Sauerkraut and Apple Stuffing

*Serves 4*

*1 (2–2.5 kg/4–5 lb) duck*
*150 g/6 oz fat salt pork*
*1 large onion, coarsely chopped*
*550 g/1¼ lb cooking apples*
*25g/1 oz dark brown sugar*
*1 teaspoon caraway seed*
*Salt and freshly ground pepper*
*¼ –½ teaspoon dried thyme*
*700 g/1½ lb sauerkraut*

Preheat oven to moderate (180°C, 350°F, Gas Mark 4). Dice salt pork and heat in a frying pan until transparent. Add coarsely chopped onion and fry until transparent. Add apples which have been peeled, cored and diced, and toss with onion and salt pork. When apples and onions are golden, add brown sugar, caraway seed, and salt, freshly ground pepper and thyme, to taste. Remove from heat.

Wash sauerkraut in water and squeeze out liquid with your hands, and toss with apple and onion mixture. Wash duck inside. Rub cavity with a little salt and freshly ground pepper. Stuff with apple-sauerkraut and truss. Prick well with a fork and place duck on rack over a roasting pan. Roast in preheated oven for about 2 to 2 ½ hours, pricking duck from time to time to allow fat to escape. When the leg joint moves freely, the bird is done.

*Great Dishes of the World*

# Denys Gentes' Duck with Fresh Figs and Wild Strawberries

*Denys Gentes' little restaurant on a tree-shaded street in Montmartre is not very busy at lunchtime – it is too far away from commercial Paris – but it is packed to bursting every evening. The last time I was there they were squeezing a tiny round table for two in a place not really big enough for one. 'I couldn't refuse them,' whispered Denys, 'they came from so far away.' The dish they enjoyed that night – as did I – was Duck with Fresh Figs and Wild Strawberries. The bird is roasted at a medium temperature until just tender; the lacquered duck is then served with a colourful garland of fresh figs and wild strawberries and a tangy wine-flavoured sauce.*

*Serve 4*

*1 duck (2.5–3 kg / 5–6 lb)*
*Salt and freshly ground pepper*
*Lemon juice*
*1 garlic clove, cut in half*
*4 tablespoons sugar*
*1 glass red wine vinegar*

4–6 crushed peppercorns
450 ml (12 fl oz) chicken stock
*Fresh figs cut into 'flower' shapes and a few
wild strawberries*

## Aromatics

*½ onion, sliced
½ apple, peeled and sliced
3–4 celery leaves*

Preheat the oven to moderate (190°C, 375°F, Gas Mark 5).

### *To prepare Duck*

Trim wing tips and cut off neck of duck. Wipe with a damp cloth inside and out and sprinkle salt and freshly ground pepper into cavity. Rub cavity of duck with lemon juice and stuff with aromatics: sliced onion, sliced apple, celery leaves. Truss duck. Prick skin of duck with a fork; rub with cut garlic clove and sprinkle with salt and freshly ground pepper. Place duck, breast side up, on rack in a roasting tin and cook in preheated oven for 35 minutes. Transfer duck to a heated dish. Keep warm.

### *To make Sauce*

Skim off all but 2 tablespoons fat from roasting tin. Cook sugar, red wine vinegar and crushed peppercorns together until a light caramel is formed, then stir into tin juices, scraping in all the crusty bits from bottom and sides of tin. Pour in chicken stock and continue to cook, stirring constantly, until mixture is reduced to a light sauce. Correct seasoning.

### *To serve*

Remove trussing string from duck; return duck to roasting tin and baste with sauce. Return tin to oven and continue to cook until duck is tender, basting occasionally. Discard aromatics and transfer duck to a heated serving dish. Surround with a garnish of fresh fig 'flowers' and wild strawberries (raspberries can be used as an alternative). Strain sauce over duck.

*Homes and Gardens*

# Cold Duck
# with Orange Jelly

*Serves 8*

*2 (2 kg/4 lb each) tender ducklings*
*6 tablespoons butter*
*2 tablespoons olive oil*
*300 ml/10 fl oz dry white wine*
*900 ml/1½ pints chicken stock*
*Salt and freshly ground pepper*
*Bouquet garni (2 sprigs thyme,*
*1 stalk celery, 2 bay leaves)*

## Garnish

*8–10 cubes bacon, cut*
*from bacon 12 mm (½ in) thick*
*8–10 button onions*
*150 g/6 oz button mushrooms (about 36)*

## Aspic

*2 egg whites*
*100 g/4 oz raw minced beef*
*2 small carrots, chopped*
*2 sticks celery, chopped*
*2 tomatoes, seeds removed and chopped*
*½–1 oz gelatine (optional)*
*2 fl oz Madeira or port*
*Grated rind and strained juice of 1 orange*
*and ½ lemon*

*Cayenne pepper*
*Thin strips green leek, tarragon*
*or fennel leaves*

### *To cook Duck*

Clean ducklings and cut into serving pieces, removing the backbone. Sauté duck pieces, a few at a time, in 4 tablespoons butter and olive oil in a large heatproof casserole, until golden on all sides. Return all the duck pieces to the casserole and moisten with dry white wine; add chicken stock and bring to the boil. Add salt, freshly ground pepper and *bouquet garni*; reduce heat and simmer gently.

Sauté bacon cubes in remaining butter until golden; remove and sauté button onions in resulting fat until golden.

Combine sautéed bacon and button onions with button mushrooms and add to casserole with duck pieces. Simmer, covered for about 30 minutes, or until duck is tender, basting pieces from time to time. While duck pieces are still moist and hot remove all the bones, leaving the skin on.

Transfer duck pieces to a rack placed over a baking sheet and allow to cool. Reserve bacon cubes, mushrooms and onions.

## To make Aspic

Strain hot stock through a sieve into a bowl; allow to become cold and remove fat from surface. To clarify stock, beat egg whites until frothy. Heat stock in a saucepan and remove any remaining fat with kitchen paper, taste and season stock. Add minced beef, chopped carrots, chopped celery and tomatoes and frothy egg whites. Set pan over a moderate to low heat, bring slowly to boil, whisking continuously with a balloon whisk – this takes about 10 minutes. When boiling, stop whisking, let egg white rise to top of pan, turn heat very low and simmer for 10 to 15 minutes. (If stock was not jellied when cold sprinkle gelatine on to 2 to 4 tablespoons water. When water has been absorbed, place bowl in a pan of boiling water until gelatine dissolves.)

Carefully ladle flavoured stock from beneath egg white, taking care not to disturb or break egg white, into a bowl through a conical sieve lined with a layer of fine muslin, add gelatine, if used, and Madeira or port and orange and lemon rind and juice. Place in the refrigerator until Aspic is just on the point of setting.

## To prepare Duck

Sprinkle the pieces of duck with cayenne pepper to taste and garnish the skin attractively with thin strips of green leek, tarragon or fennel leaves that have been dipped in boiling water. Coat each piece of duck with Aspic, allowing two or three coats in all returning pieces to the refrigerator each time to allow the coat to set. If during this work the unused aspic sets, gently reheat it and allow it to cool to the point of setting once more before continuing the coating.

## To serve

Serve the cold duck with orange jelly garnished with bacon cubes and button onions and mushrooms. A tossed green salad with crisp mushroom slices and apple and potato salad accompany this dish.

*Sunday Times*

# Duck and Orange Salad

*Serves 4*

*1 roasted duck (about 2 kg/4 lbs)*
*4 shallots, finely chopped*
*2 stalks celery, sliced*
*6–8 tablespoons olive oil*
*2–3 tablespoons red wine vinegar*
*Salt and freshly ground pepper*
*¼ –½ teaspoon chopped*
*fresh rosemary leaves*
*4 small oranges, peeled*
*and separated into sections*
*Lettuce*
*8–10 black olives*

### To prepare Duck

Dice flesh of duck into cubes about 12 mm (½ in) square. Combine diced duck, finely chopped shallots and sliced celery with a dressing made from 6 tablespoons olive oil to 2 tablespoons red wine vinegar. Season to taste with salt and freshly ground pepper and chopped fresh rosemary. Toss well. Allow duck to marinate in this mixture for at least 2 hours.

### To serve

Just before serving, add orange sections; toss again, adding a little more dressing, made from the remaining olive oil and red wine vinegar, if required. Line a glass salad bowl with lettuce leaves; fill with salad and garnish with black olives.

*Robert Carrier's Kitchen*

# Roast Turkey with Orange Gravy

*Serves 8*

*1 medium-sized turkey*
*(about 5 kg/10 lb dressed weight), giblets*
*reserved*
*2 tablespoons olive oil*
*¼ teaspoon dried oregano*
*¼ teaspoon dried rosemary*
*Salt and freshly ground pepper*

## Basting Sauce

*225 g/8 oz butter*
*150 ml/5 fl oz dry white wine*
*Juice of 2 small oranges*
*1 clove garlic, finely chopped*
*1 chicken stock cube*

## Giblet Stock

*1 Spanish onion, coarsely chopped*
*1 bay leaf*
*4 sprigs each celery tops and parsley*
*Salt and freshly ground pepper*
*150 ml/5 fl oz dry white wine*

## Orange Gravy

*2 tablespoons butter*
*2 tablespoons flour*
*Salt and freshly ground pepper*

Preheat oven to fairly hot (220°C, 425°F, Gas Mark 7). Wipe turkey both inside and out with a damp cloth or absorbent paper. Pick off any stray feathers or quills.

Sew or skewer vent tightly to prevent juices escaping. Draw neck skin over back, not too tightly, and fasten in place with metal skewers or wooden toothpicks. Cut off ends of wings to use for the Giblet Stock. Tie legs together with string.

Rub turkey all over with olive oil and season with dried oregano and rosemary, and salt and freshly ground pepper. Lay bird in a roomy roasting tin breast side up. Melt butter for Basting Sauce in a heavy pan. Remove from heat before it starts to sizzle.

Cut a piece of double-thick muslin large enough to drape over and cover turkey, legs and all. Rinse muslin under the cold tap and wring out as dry as possible. Soak muslin in melted butter and gently squeeze out excess. Drape muslin over turkey. Roast turkey on lowest shelf of preheated oven for 15 minutes.

While turkey is roasting make Basting Sauce: add dry white wine, orange juice and finely chopped garlic to remainder of melted butter. Crumble in chicken stock cube for seasoning and stir until dissolved.

Reduce temperature of oven to moderate (180°C, 350°F, Gas Mark 4) for the rest of the cooking time, turn bird on its breast for 15 minutes to allow back to take on some colour; then reverse bird to original position.

Baste turkey with some of the Basting Sauce at the end of the first 30 minutes, and every 15 minutes thereafter, making sure that the muslin is completely remoistened with this buttery liquid (or the pan juices) each time. Forty-five minutes before the end of cooking time remove muslin to allow turkey to brown.

### *To make Giblet Stock*

While turkey is roasting, prepare a stock with the giblets: wash neck, heart, gizzard and wing tips and place them in a pan with coarsely chopped onion, bay leaf, celery tops and parsley, and a little salt and freshly ground pepper. Add dry white wine and enough water to cover. Bring to the boil; skim; lower heat and simmer gently for 1½ hours, topping up with more water as necessary. Wash and add turkey liver and simmer for 30 minutes

longer. Strain Giblet Stock and reserve. Chop giblet meats finely and reserve.

## To make Orange Gravy

When turkey is tender remove strings, skewers, etc. used to truss the bird. Transfer bird to a hot serving dish and keep hot in a turned-off oven while you prepare Orange Gravy. Like roast beef, turkey is easier to carve if it is left for 15 minutes to allow juices to 'settle'.

Pour juices and crusty bits from roasting tin into a bowl. Leave for a minute to allow all the fat to come to the surface so that you can skim it off.

Melt butter in a heavy pan; blend in flour and stir over a low heat for 2 minutes to make a pale roux. Gradually add 300 ml (10 fl oz) strained Giblet Stock and skimmed pan juices, whisking vigorously with a balloon whisk to prevent lumps forming. Bring to the boil and simmer, stirring, until gravy has thickened and flour is cooked, 6 to 8 minutes. Add chopped giblets; heat through and correct seasoning. Pour Orange Gravy into a hot sauce boat and serve with turkey.

*The Robert Carrier Cookbook*

# Pigeon Prince Rainier III

*A dark-coloured pigeon is thought to have the highest flavour, and a light-coloured one the most delicate. The legs should be of a pinkish colour; when they are large and deeply coloured the bird is old. The breast should be fat and plump. The tame pigeon is smaller than the wild species and is better for cooking. Tame pigeons should be cooked at once, as they soon lose their flavour, but wood pigeons may be hung for a few days.*

*A squab is a young pigeon.*

*Serves 4*

*4 small pigeons*
*4 cubes truffle*
*4 cubes mousse de foie gras*
*225 g/8 oz minced raw pork*
*100 g/4 oz minced raw veal*
*Salt and freshly ground pepper*
*Dash of Cayenne pepper*
*Cognac*
*2 tablespoons butter*
*150 ml/5 fl oz dry white wine*
*4 tablespoons demi-glace sauce*
*(or 1 level tablespoon cornflour or arrowroot)*
*Small croûtons of fried bread*
*Pommes Cocotte*
*(small new potatoes tossed in butter)*
*Finely chopped parsley*

Completely bone pigeons before cooking (or, as our pigeons are often not as tender as French ones, substitute *petits poussins* or very young chickens), then stuff each with a cube of truffle, a cube of foie gras (I often use pâté de grives or one of the less expensive pâtés) and the heart and liver of the bird. Finish with a stuffing made of minced raw pork and veal which you have flavoured to taste with salt, freshly ground pepper, cayenne and a little cognac. Stuff the pigeons with this mixture, forming birds into their original shape. Sew stuffing in.

Roast pigeons in a pan with a little butter. When half cooked, remove threads and continue cooking until birds are tender. Remove birds. Pour in dry white wine and cook over a high flame, stirring in all crusty bits from side of pan until sauce is reduced to three-quarters of original quantity. Add 1 to 2 tablespoons cognac; stir in demi-glace sauce (or 1 level tablespoon cornflour or arrowroot which you have mixed with a little water). Cook until sauce is thickened.

### To serve

Serve the pigeons on small croûtons of fried bread. Surround with a few *Pommes Cocotte* (see page 000), strain sauce over birds and sprinkle with finely chopped parsley.

*The Sunday Times*

# Glazed Pigeons with Grapes

*Serves 4*

*4 pigeons*
*Salt and freshly ground pepper*
*4–6 tablespoons cognac*
*175 ml/6 fl oz melted chicken fat or lard*
*Few drops water*
*4 rectangular canapés (each large enough to hold a pigeon)*
*1 small tin mousse de foie gras*
*Peeled and seeded white grapes*
*Aspic jelly*

Season pigeons with salt and freshly ground pepper and flame with cognac.

Melt chicken fat with a few drops of water over a low heat. As soon as the fat is nearly melted, add pigeons; bring to a moderate boil and simmer for 45 minutes to 1 hour.

Remove pigeons from fat; place them in an earthenware crock, cover with strained fat, and cool.

Spread 4 rectangular canapés with *mousse de foie gras* and place 1 pigeon (from which you have removed the fat) in the centre of each. Surround each pigeon with 6 large peeled and seeded white grapes and glaze with aspic jelly.

*The Robert Carrier Cookery Course*

# Guinea Fowl with Exotic Fruits

*Serves 4*

*1 (1 kg/2 lb) guinea fowl*
*4 passion fruit*
*Salt and freshly ground pepper*
*1 tablespoon butter*
*4 tablespoons Glace de Viande*
*(see page 101)*
*4 tablespoons dry white wine*
*4 tablespoons Madeira*
*50 g/2 oz cold butter, diced*

## Stuffing

*Pulp from 4 passion fruit (see below)*
*4 tablespoons fresh breadcrumbs*
*1 medium onion, chopped*
*1 tablespoon softened butter*
*1 tablespoon chopped parsley*
*Salt and freshly ground pepper*

## Garnish

*1 kiwi fruit, sliced*
*4 strawberries, sliced*
*1 pawpaw, sliced*

Preheat oven to moderate (180°C, 350°F, Gas Mark 4). Trim guinea fowl. Cut passion fruit in half; scoop out pulp and pass through a sieve. Reserve juice for sauce and use pulp for stuffing.

Mix stuffing ingredients together in a bowl. Stuff guinea fowl and tie up. Season with salt and freshly ground pepper, to taste, and spread with butter. Roast bird in preheated oven for 45 minutes, or until tender.

Meanwhile, reduce *Glace de Viande* with dry white wine and Madeira to half its original quantity. Add passion fruit juice and season sauce with salt and freshly ground pepper, to taste.

Take guinea fowl from oven and remove string; discard stuffing. Cut guinea fowl into 4 or 8 pieces. Keep warm.

Bring sauce to the boil; remove from heat and whisk in cold diced butter, a little at a time. Pour sauce over guinea fowl portions; garnish with sliced kiwi fruit, strawberries and pawpaw and serve immediately.

*The Robert Carrier Seminar of Cooking*

# Guinea Fowl with Pears

*Serves 4*

*2 firm pears, peeled, cored and halved*
*1 (1 kg/2 lb) guinea fowl, dressed*
*75 g/3 oz butter*
*1 onion, thinly sliced*
*Salt and white pepper*
*150 ml/5 fl oz white wine*
*120 ml/4 fl oz port*
*1–2 teaspoons lemon juice*
*1 tablespoon cornflour*
*Watercress*

## Syrup

*225 g/8 oz sugar*
*Juice and pared rind of ½ lemon*

To make the syrup, put the sugar, lemon rind and juice and 450 ml (15 fl oz) water in a saucepan and stir over gentle heat until the sugar is dissolved. Then boil for 10 minutes. Remove the lemon rind. Poach the pears in the syrup for 10 minutes, or until slightly softened, then remove with a slotted spoon and drain.

Heat the butter in a flameproof casserole and sauté the guinea fowl until golden on all sides. Remove from the pan.

Sauté the thinly sliced onion in the casserole until transparent. Return the guinea fowl to the casserole; season generously with salt and white pepper, cover and cook at medium heat, turning the guinea fowl frequently, for 10 to 15 minutes. Add the white wine, port and poached pears. Simmer for a further 10 to 15 minutes at the same heat, until the guinea fowl is tender. Add salt, white pepper and a little lemon juice to taste. Remove the guinea fowl and keep warm.

In a small bowl, blend the cornflour with 2 tablespoons cold water, then stir in 2 tablespoons hot syrup. Return the cornflour mixture to the sauce and simmer for 1 to 2 minutes, or until the sauce thickens, stirring constantly.

Cut the guinea fowl into quarters. Present the guinea fowl on a round heated serving dish, decorated with the pear halves. Spoon the syrup over the guinea fowl pieces and pears and decorate with a bunch of watercress in the centre.

*Robert Carrier's Kitchen*

# Roast Grouse

*Serves 1*

*1 young grouse (450 g / 1 lb) dressed*
*weight, trussed, with liver*
*Butter*
*1 teaspoon lemon juice*
*Salt and freshly ground pepper*
*2 thin slices fat salt pork*
*or unsmoked bacon*
*1 slice bread, 6–12 mm / ¼ –½ in thick,*
*trimmed, to serve as base for grouse*
*1 tablespoon clarified butter*
*1 tablespoon olive oil*
*Cayenne pepper (optional)*
*Sprigs of watercress, to garnish*

## To prepare Grouse

Preheat oven to fairly hot (220°C, 425°F, Gas Mark 7). Wipe bird carefully both inside and out with a damp cloth or absorbent paper. Reserve liver. In a small bowl or cup, blend 1 level tablespoon softened butter with lemon juice and a generous seasoning of salt and freshly ground pepper. Stuff seasoned butter into body cavity of grouse.

Bard breast of grouse with thin slices of fat salt pork or bacon and tie in place with fine string. Rub bird all over with salt and freshly ground pepper. Butter a small roasting tin or baking dish. Lay grouse in it.

## To cook Grouse

Roast grouse for 35 to 45 minutes, depending on its size and whether you prefer it slightly pink or well done. Test by piercing flesh between leg and breast with a fine skewer or toothpick. You will be able to judge the state of the bird from the colour of the juices. For well-done meat they should run quite clear.

Ten to fifteen minutes before grouse is ready, fry bread in a mixture of clarified butter and olive oil until crisp and golden brown on both sides. Drain well on absorbent paper. Place on a heated serving dish and keep hot. In a small pan, sauté grouse liver for 2 to 3 minutes in 1 level teaspoon hot butter, mashing with a fork. Scrape contents of pan into a small bowl. Add 1 level tablespoon butter and mash to a smooth paste. Season to taste with salt and freshly ground pepper or a pinch of cayenne.

## To serve

Spread fried bread *croûte* with liver mixture. Remove grouse from the oven; discard trussing thread and barding strips, and place bird on *croûte*. Skim pan juices of fat if necessary and spoon over bird. Garnish with sprigs of watercress and serve immediately. Bread sauce or browned breadcrumbs, game chips and redcurrant jelly are the usual accompaniments.

*The Robert Carrier Cookery Course*

# Gilbert Harding's Roast Grouse

*Gilbert Harding was one of our first panel-game TV stars with an irascible temper. But he also had a heart of gold. One night at dinner at his home in Brighton, he served roast grouse stuffed with sliced raw apple, raw onion and raw beef steak. The aromatic 'stuffing' was not for eating . . . but gave incredible moisture and flavour to the birds.*

*Serves 2 to 4*

*2 young grouse (each 450 g/1 lb dressed), trussed, with livers*
*Butter*
*2 teaspoons lemon juice*
*Salt and freshly ground pepper*
*1 apple, sliced*
*½ Spanish onion, sliced*
*2 small pieces of raw beef steak*
*2 thin slices fat salt pork*
*or unsmoked bacon*
*2 slices bread, 6–12 mm/¼ –½ in thick, trimmed, to serve as base for grouse*
*1 tablespoon clarified butter*
*1 tablespoon olive oil*
*Cayenne pepper (optional)*
*Sprigs of watercress, to garnish*

Preheat oven to fairly hot (220°C, 425°F, Gas Mark 7). Wipe birds carefully both inside and out with a damp cloth or absorbent paper. Reserve livers.

In a small bowl or cup, blend 2 level tablespoons softened butter with lemon juice and a generous seasoning of salt and freshly ground pepper. Rub body cavities of grouse with this flavoured butter. Place sliced apple and onion in cavity of each bird with a piece of raw beefsteak. You'll find that this will moisturise and flavour birds. Cook grouse as in Roast Grouse recipe (page 197).

When ready to serve: spread fried bread *croûtes* with liver mixture. Remove grouse from the oven; discard trussing thread and barding strips; remove sliced apple and onion and beef pieces and place bird on *croûtes*. Skim pan juices of fat if necessary and spoon over bird. Garnish with sprigs of watercress and serve immediately.

*The Robert Carrier Cookery Course*

# Roast Partridge

*Serves 2*

*1 young partridge*
*Butter*
*¼ level teaspoon dried thyme*
*Lemon juice*
*Salt and freshly ground pepper*
*Barding strip of fat pork*
*(or 2 unsmoked bacon slices)*
*Flour*
*Wine, to finish sauce*
*Sprigs of watercress, to garnish*

Preheat oven to fairly hot (220°C, 425°F, Gas Mark 7).

## To prepare Partridge

Wipe bird carefully both inside and out with a damp cloth or absorbent paper. Reserve liver. Blend 2 level tablespoons of softened butter with dried thyme, lemon juice and salt and freshly ground pepper, to taste. Stuff seasoned butter into the cavity of the bird, together with its liver.

Truss partridge. Cover breast with a paper-thin slice of barding pork fat or 2 slices of fat unsmoked bacon, and tie in place with string. Brush bird with a tablespoon of softened butter.

## To cook Partridge

Lay partridge in a roasting tin or casserole – just large enough to hold it so that cooking juices do not spread over too large an area – and roast until tender but still very juicy. The time will depend very much on the age and size of birds: a young and tender one will be ready in 25 to 30 minutes, while an older one will need closer to 45 minutes. Baste frequently with pan juices throughout cooking time, otherwise there is a danger of the flesh being on the dry side.

Ten minutes before the end of cooking time, untie the barding fat and discard it. Dredge breasts of partridge with flour and return to the oven to finish cooking and brown breast.

## To serve

Transfer partridge to a hot serving dish and remove trussing threads or skewers. Keep hot while you make a gravy with the pan juices, a little stock and a splash of wine. Garnish partridge with sprigs of watercress and serve with its own gravy. Bread sauce or browned breadcrumbs are the traditional accompaniments.

*The Sunday Times*

# Pheasant with Green Apples

*Cooking apples — Bramleys of course — Calvados and cream blend together to create the green-tinged, highly flavoured cream sauce that gives this elegant casserole its name. A pleasing variation on the Pheasant Normandy theme.*

*Serves 4*

*1 pheasant (1.2 kg/2¼ lb) dressed*
*100 g/4 oz green bacon, cut into large dice*
*½ Spanish onion, finely chopped*
*1 clove garlic, finely chopped*
*2 tablespoons butter*
*2 tablespoons olive oil*
*4 small cooking apples*
*4 tablespoons Calvados*
*Salt and freshly ground pepper*
*300 ml/10 fl oz double cream*

Preheat oven to slow (160°C, 325°F, Gas Mark 3).

### To prepare Pheasant

Cut pheasant into 4 serving portions. Sauté diced green bacon and finely chopped onion and garlic in butter and olive oil in a heatproof casserole until golden. Remove bacon and vegetables from casserole and reserve. In the same pan brown pheasant portions on all sides. Remove portions from casserole and keep warm.

Peel, core and slice apples thickly and sauté in remaining fat until they start to turn golden. Pour over Calvados. Remove apple slices from casserole and set aside.

Skim fat from pan juices. Return pheasant portions to casserole; surround with apple slices, bacon, onion and garlic, and season with salt and freshly ground pepper, to taste. Simmer, covered, for 10 minutes. Cover casserole and cook in preheated oven for 30 minutes. Add cream, mixing in well, and cook for a further 30 minutes, or until pheasant portions are tender.

### To serve

Remove pheasant portions and bacon to a clean casserole and keep warm. Purée sauce and apples. Correct seasoning; reheat sauce and pour over pheasant portions. Serve immediately.

*Harper's Bazaar*

# Country Fricassée of Rabbit

*Serves 4*

*1 rabbit*
*2 tablespoons olive oil*
*2 tablespoons butter*
*Salt and freshly ground pepper*
*2 tablespoons flour*
*2 tablespoons brandy*
*4 tablespoons white wine*
*4 tablespoons rich beef stock*
*2 cloves garlic, finely chopped*
*Bouquet garni (2 stalks celery, 4 sprigs*
*parsley, 1 sprig thyme, 1 sprig rosemary)*
*100 g/4 oz fat salt pork, diced*
*10 small onions*
*10 button mushrooms*
*2 Italian peeled tomatoes, seeded*
*and cut into thin strips*
*2 tablespoons finely chopped parsley*
*Fried croûtons*

Have the rabbit cut into pieces. Brown lightly in oil and butter in a heavy casserole. Season with salt and freshly ground pepper. Sprinkle lightly with flour and continue to brown, turning constantly with a wooden spoon. Heat the brandy, pour over the pieces of rabbit, and ignite. Mix the white wine and stock together and add to the casserole with finely chopped garlic and a *bouquet garni*. Bring to boil; skim; reduce heat and simmer gently for 30 minutes over a moderate heat.

Add the bacon, onions and mushrooms cut into two. Cook for another 30 minutes. Garnish with tomato strips and chopped parsley. Serve very hot with fried croûtons.

*The Sunday Times*

# Jean-Pierre's Mustard Rabbit

*Dijon mustard – produced by Messrs Grey and Poupon – is the secret of this French country recipe. Rub the rabbit with generous quantities of the mustard; top it with thin slices of fat salt pork and thin rounds of lemon and onion, and bake it in a preheated oven for forty-five to sixty minutes. Rabbit with a real country flavour.*

*Serves 2 to 4*

*1 saddle and legs of rabbit*
*Strong French mustard*
*Salt and freshly ground pepper*
*Slices of fat salt pork*
*2–3 slices lemon*
*1 medium-sized onion (sliced in 4)*
*5 tablespoons butter*
*1 tablespoon thyme*
*Dry white wine, cut with a little water*

Preheat oven to 190°C (375°F, Gas Mark 3). Flatten out saddle and legs in a baking dish. Spread liberally with mustard and salt and freshly ground pepper; cover rabbit with slices of fat salt pork; cover with alternate rounds of lemon and onion. Cover lemon and onion with butter and sprinkle with powdered thyme. Moisten with a little wine and water from time to time and bake in preheated oven for 45 to 60 minutes.

*The Sunday Times*

# Mother's Fried Rabbit

*Serves 4*

*1 tender young rabbit*
*Coarse salt*
*Freshly ground pepper*
*Flour*
*2 egg yolks, well beaten*
*Fresh breadcrumbs*
*Olive oil, butter and lard,*
*in equal quantities*

Cut the rabbit into 8 pieces. Sprinkle the pieces generously with coarse salt and let them stand for 24 hours. When ready to cook: wash rabbit pieces in cold water; pat dry with a clean cloth and season to taste with freshly ground pepper. Sprinkle pieces lightly with flour; dip in beaten egg yolks, and then in breadcrumbs. Place pieces in refrigerator

for 1 hour to firm breadcrumb coating.

Combine olive oil, butter and lard in a deep frying pan or shallow casserole and heat until a cube of bread turns brown in 1 minute. Put rabbit pieces in fat and cook over a low flame, turning the pieces occasionally until they are golden brown on all sides and cooked through.

*Vogue*

# Venison Steaks in the Pan

*Serves 4*

*4 venison steaks, about 2.5 cm/1 in thick*
*2–4 tablespoons butter*
*4–6 tablespoons dry sherry*
*Salt and freshly ground pepper*
*2 tablespoons finely chopped parsley*
*Redcurrant jelly*

Sauté venison steaks in butter, turning them once or twice, until they are sufficiently cooked. Moisten with dry sherry, season with salt and freshly ground pepper, to taste; turn the meat once more and then serve on a heated serving dish garnished with pan juices and finely chopped parsley. Serve with redcurrant jelly.

*Vogue*

# Vegetables

*Over the past two months I have been planning my new vegetable garden in the country for planting this spring. Not an eighteenth-century kitchen garden with parterres and romantic vistas like the one I created at Hintlesham Hall, but an intimate cottage garden – more nineteenth-century in feeling – to go with my red-brick cottage set between its vineyard and ancient wood. Vegetables are of prime importance to us now that science has proved that their anti-oxidant qualities are necessary for our health. We have always known that vegetables were good for us. But few of us realised that vegetarians stand 40% less risk of getting cancer or having heart disease. And now that the supermarkets are full of delicious fresh vegetables, cleaned and sold in portion-controlled packs for us, there is no longer any excuse for sticking to the old 'meat with 2 veg' school of menu-making. It's now meat (or rice or pasta, or even barley or couscous) with 3 to 5 vegetables for our modern, healthy way of living.*

# Orange Beetroot (Harvard Beets)

*Serves 4*

*1 large cooked beetroot*
*1 teaspoon grated orange rind*
*150 ml/5 fl oz orange juice*
*2 tablespoons lemon juice*
*2 tablespoons sugar*
*1 level tablespoon cornflour*
*1–2 tablespoons butter*
*Salt and freshly ground pepper*

Peel and dice beetroot. Heat orange rind with orange and lemon juice. Mix sugar and cornflour, and stir into hot liquid. Cook, stirring constantly until thickened. Add the diced beetroots and butter. Season to taste with salt and freshly ground pepper and heat through.

*The Robert Carrier Cookery Course*

# Brussels Sprouts à la Polonaise

*Serves 4*

*450 g/1 lb small Brussels sprouts*
*Salt and freshly ground pepper*
*4 to 6 tablespoons butter*
*Grated rind and juice of 1 lemon*
*2 tablespoons finely chopped parsley*
*Whites of 2 hard-boiled eggs, finely chopped*
*Thin lemon slices*

Cut off stem ends and remove any wilted or damaged outer leaves from small Brussels sprouts. (If Brussels sprouts are older, remove tough outer leaves entirely.) Soak sprouts in cold water with a little salt or lemon juice for 15 minutes.

Add sprouts to boiling, salted water and simmer, uncovered, for 5 minutes. Cover pan and continue to cook for 7 (if very young) to 15 minutes longer, or until just tender. Drain well and season generously with salt and freshly ground pepper.

Place seasoned Brussels sprouts in a heated serving dish. Brown butter lightly in a frying pan, add lemon juice to taste, and pour over sprouts; then sprinkle with grated lemon rind, finely chopped parsley and egg whites. Garnish with lemon slices.

*The Weekend Telegraph*

# Brussels Sprouts with Buttered Breadcrumbs

*Breadcrumbs – both toasted and fresh – add crisp, crunch and flavour to Brussels sprouts in the following two recipes. If you haven't tried the 'breadcrumb touch', you don't know what you are missing. It makes a party dish out of an old winter standby.*

## Serves 4

450 g/1 lb small Brussels sprouts
Salt and freshly ground pepper
4–6 tablespoons toasted breadcrumbs
½ clove garlic, finely chopped
4 tablespoons butter
Lemon juice

Prepare Brussels sprouts. Add sprouts to boiling salted water and simmer uncovered for 5 minutes. Cover pan and continue to cook for 7 (if very young) to 15 minutes longer, or until just tender. Drain well and season generously with salt and freshly ground pepper.

Combine hot seasoned sprouts in a frying pan with toasted breadcrumbs and finely chopped garlic, and sauté in butter until breadcrumbs are golden. Sprinkle with lemon juice, to taste.

*The Robert Carrier Cookery Course*

# Breadcrumb Browned Brussels Sprouts au Gratin

## Serves 4

450g/1 lb small Brussels sprouts
Salt and freshly ground pepper
Crushed dried chillies
Butter
600 ml/1 pint Rich Cheese Sauce (see page 206)
8 walnuts, finely chopped
4 tablespoons grated breadcrumbs

Prepare Brussels sprouts. Add sprouts to boiling salted water and simmer uncovered for 5 minutes. Cover pan and continue to cook for 7 (if very young) to 15 minutes longer, or until just tender. Drain well and season generously with salt, freshly ground pepper and crushed dried chillies. Place hot seasoned sprouts in a buttered ovenproof dish. Pour over Rich Cheese Sauce.

Melt 4 tablespoons butter in a small saucepan; add finely chopped nuts and freshly grated breadcrumbs; simmer for a minute or two, then spoon over cheese sauce. Bake in a moderately hot oven (190°C, 375°F, Gas Mark 5) for 10 minutes.

# Rich Cheese Sauce

*Makes 450 ml/15 fl oz*

*3 tablespoons butter*
*3 tablespoons flour*
*450 ml/15 fl oz hot chicken stock*
*300 ml/10 fl oz double cream*
*3 tablespoons freshly grated Gruyère*
*3 tablespoons freshly grated Parmesan*
*Salt and freshly ground pepper*
*Crushed dried chillies*
*Freshly grated nutmeg*

Melt butter in a thick-bottomed saucepan or in the top of a double saucepan; stir in flour and cook for 2 to 3 minutes, stirring constantly, until smooth. Blend in hot chicken stock and then double cream, stirring vigorously.

Stir in grated Gruyère and Parmesan cheeses and season with salt, freshly ground pepper and crushed dried chillies, to taste, and add a little freshly grated nutmeg.

Reduce heat and simmer for about 20 minutes, stirring from time to time, to keep skin from forming. When sauce is reduced to two-thirds of original quantity, strain through a fine sieve.

*Great Dishes of the World*

# French Fried Cauliflower

*This recipe is too simple to be true. Just dip lightly poached, drained cauliflower florets in a simple batter and deep-fry until crisp and golden. Serve with a well-flavoured tomato sauce (try one of the chilled pasta sauces on sale in your local supermarket) and you will have a first course, a vegetarian lunch or a supper dish of which you can be proud.*

*Serves 4*

*1 cauliflower*
*Salt*
*Oil for deep-frying*
*1 egg*
*150 ml/5 fl oz milk*
*2 tablespoons dry white wine*
*150 g/4 oz flour*
*Tomato sauce*

Discard outer green leaves; wash cauliflower; and leave in cold salted water for 30 minutes. Drain. Heat oil to 190°C (375°F).

### To make Batter

Beat egg in a bowl; add milk and dry white wine and beat. Add flour and salt, to taste, and beat until smooth.

### *To prepare Cauliflower*

Separate cauliflower into small florets and poach in boiling water for 5 minutes. Drain. When ready to cook, dip florets into batter. Deep-fry until golden. Drain and serve immediately with tomato sauce.

*The Robert Carrier Cookery Course*

# Little Broccoli Towers

*Cooked broccoli florets (or diced cooked carrots) achieve party status when cooked in little dariole moulds with a creamy custard sauce. Serve them with grilled or roasted meats, poultry or game . . . or try a colourful trio of towers (broccoli, carrot and cranberry jelly) with your Christmas turkey.*

*Serves 6*

*450 g / 1 lb broccoli*
*Salt*
*Butter for greasing*
*2 shallots, chopped*
*2 teaspoons butter*
*2 tablespoons chicken stock*
*2 eggs*
*125 ml / 4 fl oz milk*
*125 ml / 4 fl oz double cream*
*Freshly ground pepper*

Bring a pan of salted water to the boil. Add the broccoli and blanch for 3 minutes. Drain, refresh under cold running water and drain again on absorbent paper.

Lightly butter six 150 ml (5 fl oz) dariole moulds or soufflé dishes. Break off the best of the tiny florets of broccoli and use them to line the base and sides of the moulds. Preheat the oven to 190°C (375°F, Gas Mark 5). In a frying pan, heat 2 teaspoons butter. Add the chopped shallots and sauté until soft. Chop the remaining broccoli coarsely and add to the shallots with the chicken stock. Simmer for 2 minutes.

In a bowl, beat the eggs and milk together. Stir in the double cream and season with salt and freshly ground pepper to taste. Set aside. Divide the sautéed broccoli-onion mixture between the moulds. Place them in a roasting tin and add boiling water to come halfway up the sides of the moulds (a *bain marie*). Bake in the preheated oven for 10 minutes. Remove the *bain marie* from the oven. Divide the custard between the moulds. Return them to the oven and bake for a further 18 to 20 minutes.

To serve, run a knife round the edge of each mould and turn out the broccoli towers on to a heated serving plate.

*Carrier's*

# Little Carrot Towers

*Serves 4*

*450g/1 lb carrots*
*Butter*
*75 ml/3 fl oz chicken stock*
*Salt*
*2 eggs*
*Freshly ground pepper*
*½ tablespoon finely chopped parsley*

Preheat oven to moderate (180°C, 350°F, Gas Mark 4). Wash and scrape carrots, dice and place in a saucepan; cover with cold water and cook over a high heat until water boils. Drain.

In a clean pan simmer blanched carrots in 2 tablespoons butter, chicken stock and salt, to taste, for about 30 minutes, until carrots have absorbed most of the liquid without burning and are tender. Purée carrot mixture with eggs. Transfer to a bowl and mix with 2 tablespoons softened butter and season with salt and freshly ground pepper, to taste. Press into 4 well-buttered 150 ml (5 fl oz) dariole moulds; place moulds in a roasting pan and add enough boiling water to come halfway up moulds, and cook until set in preheated oven for 30 minutes.

Remove from oven and keep carrot-filled moulds warm in hot water until ready to serve. When ready to serve: turn carrot moulds out on to heated serving dish, placing them alternately with Broccoli Towers (see page 207). Sprinkle tops with finely chopped parsley.

*Carrier's*

# Crisp-fried
# Courgette Coins

*Thinly sliced young courgettes (the smallest you can buy) become little green 'coins' in minutes if you sauté them in butter flavoured with half a vegetable (or chicken) stock cube. A symphony of colourful greens if you don't let them brown while cooking.*

*Serves 4 to 6*

*8–12 courgettes*
*2 tablespoons butter*
*2 tablespoons olive oil*
*½ chicken stock cube, crumbled*
*Salt and freshly ground pepper*

Trim tops and tails of courgettes. Slice courgettes very thinly. Heat butter and olive oil in a frying pan. Stir in crumbled chicken stock cube. Add sliced courgettes and sauté in combined fats over a medium heat until just tender, stirring from time to time to keep courgettes from browning. Season generously with salt and freshly ground pepper. Serve immediately.

*Carrier's*

# Courgette Soufflés

*Medium-sized courgettes cut in half, lightly poached and hollowed out, form attractive containers for light golden soufflés. An elegant accompaniment to grills of all kinds.*

### Serves 4

*4 medium courgettes*
*Butter for greasing*
*1½ tablespoons butter*
*½ tablespoon flour*
*100 ml/3 fl oz milk*
*3 tablespoons freshly grated Parmesan*
*Salt and freshly ground pepper*
*1 egg, separated*

Wipe courgettes with a damp cloth. Trim off the ends and cut the courgettes in half lengthways. In the top of a steamer, over simmering water, steam the courgette halves in batches for 4 minutes or until just tender. Cool slightly.

With a teaspoon, scoop out the pulp from each courgette half, chop into small dice and reserve.

Preheat the oven to 170°C (325°F, Gas Mark 3) and grease an ovenproof dish large enough to take the courgette shells in one layer. Lay them in the dish side by side.

Heat 1 tablespoon of the butter in a small frying pan and sauté the reserved diced courgette pulp for 4 minutes or until tender, stirring occasionally with a wooden spoon.

Heat the remaining ½ tablespoon butter in a heavy-based saucepan and blend in the flour. Cook over a low heat for 2 to 3 minutes to make a pale roux, stirring occasionally with a wooden spoon. Pour in the milk gradually, stirring vigorously with a wire whisk to prevent lumps forming. Bring to the boil and simmer for 1 to 2 minutes, or until thickened. Remove from the heat and stir in the freshly grated Parmesan cheese. Season with salt and freshly ground pepper to taste. Beat in the egg yolk and stir in the sautéed courgette flesh.

In a clean bowl whisk the egg white to stiff peaks. With a large metal spoon, fold it into the courgette mixture and carefully but quickly spoon it into the courgette shells. Cook in the preheated oven for 20 to 25 minutes or until the courgette soufflés are puffed and golden. Transfer to a heated serving plate with a palette knife and serve immediately.

*The Robert Carrier Cookery Course*

## Haricots Verts en Persillade

*Serves 4 to 6*

*1.25 kg /1½ lb baby green beans★*
*Salt*
*50 g/2 oz butter*
*2–3 tablespoons finely chopped parsley*
*Freshly ground pepper*
*Crushed dried chillies*
*Lemon slices, to garnish*

Top and tail the green beans – they should be young enough not to require stringing. Bring a pan of salted water to the boil. Throw in the beans; bring to the simmering point again. Remove the pan from the heat and drain. Run cold water over the beans to refresh them, and if not used immediately, refrigerate the beans.

Pound the butter with finely chopped parsley and season with a little salt, freshly ground pepper and crushed dried chillies. When ready to serve, season the beans generously with salt and ground pepper, and simmer in half the herb butter until heated through. Serve immediately, with the buttery juices poured over them, and garnished with the remaining herb butter and lemon slices.

★ It is essential to use very young baby beans for this dish as they are not cooked, merely brought to the boil. This method can be adapted for small beans – large beans are unsuitable. Simmer small beans for 5 to 8 minutes, until they are cooked but still crisp.

*Carrier's*

## Leeks à la Vinaigrette

*Serves 4*

*12 small leeks or 8 large ones*
*Salt and freshly ground pepper*
*6–8 tablespoons olive oil*
*2 tablespoons wine vinegar*
*Mustard*
*2–3 tablespoons finely chopped parsley*

Clean and trim leeks. Simmer in boiling salted water for 20 minutes, or until tender. Drain thoroughly. Arrange leeks in an hors d'oeuvre dish and allow to cool. Combine olive oil and vinegar with salt, freshly ground pepper and mustard, to taste; pour over leeks and garnish with finely chopped parsley.

*The Robert Carrier Cookery Course*

# Leeks au Gratin

*A rich cheese sauce does a great deal to bring poached young leeks up to party standard. Just poach the leeks for five minutes: drain thoroughly and bake them in a shallow ovenproof baking dish with butter until tender. Just before serving, top with Cheese Sauce and serve immediately.*

*Serves 4*

*12 small leeks or 8 large ones*
*100 g/4 oz butter*
*Salt and freshly ground pepper*
*300–450 ml/10–15 fl oz Rich Cheese Sauce (see page 206)*

Preheat oven to 190°C (375°F, Gas Mark 5). Simmer leeks in boiling salted water for 5 minutes. Drain thoroughly. Place leeks in a shallow ovenproof baking dish; add butter and salt and freshly ground pepper, to taste, and cook in preheated oven for 35 to 40 minutes, or until tender. Drain pan juices; add to Rich Cheese Sauce; pour over leeks and serve immediately.

*Cooking with Carrier*

# Buttered Peas Elysées

*Serves 4*

*450 g/1 lb frozen peas*
*Salt*
*4 tablespoons butter*
*4 tablespoons chicken stock*
*Freshly ground pepper*
*½ teaspoon sugar*
*4 lettuce leaves cut into thin strips*
*1 egg yolk*
*4 tablespoons double cream*

Bring a saucepan of salted water to the boil, add the peas and simmer for 1 minute. Drain, refresh under cold running water, drain again. Replace the peas in the saucepan and add the butter and chicken stock. Season with salt, freshly ground pepper and sugar to taste. Cover with the lettuce strips and simmer over a low heat for 10 minutes, or until peas have absorbed the liquid.

In a small bowl blend the egg yolk and double cream together with a whisk. Stir this liaison into the peas and lettuce. Correct the seasoning, transfer to a heated serving dish and serve immediately.

*The Robert Carrier Cookery Course*

# Purée Saint-Germain

*A delicious purée of peas, lettuce and onions, to serve as a vegetable accompaniment.*

*Serve 4*

*1 kg/2 lb fresh shelled peas*
*1 heart of lettuce, shredded*
*12 tiny spring onions*
*(or ½ Spanish onion, sliced)*
*3 sprigs parsley*
*8 tablespoons butter*
*4 tablespoons chicken stock or water*
*Sugar*
*Salt*
*2 boiled potatoes (optional)*
*Freshly ground pepper*

Put peas in a saucepan with shredded heart of lettuce, spring onions, parsley, half the butter, chicken stock or water, and sugar and salt, to taste. Bring to the boil and cook slowly until peas are tender. When cooked, remove parsley and drain peas, reserving juices. Blend to a fine purée in an electric mixer (or press through a fine sieve) and reheat in the top of a double saucepan, adding a little of the strained juices and the remaining butter. If purée is too thin, add puréed potatoes to lend body. Season with freshly ground pepper.

*The Robert Carrier Cookery Course*

# Roman Peas

*Serves 4*

*2 tablespoons finely chopped Parma ham*
*½ Spanish onion, finely chopped*
*4 tablespoons butter*
*450 g/1 lb shelled peas, fresh or frozen*
*150 ml/5 fl oz beef stock*
*Sugar*
*Salt and freshly ground pepper*
*2 tablespoons butter*
*1 tablespoon finely chopped parsley*

Sauté finely chopped ham and onion in butter until onion begins to take on colour. Add peas and beef stock, and season to taste with sugar, salt and freshly ground pepper. Simmer peas, covered, for 10 to 15 minutes. Just before serving, top with butter and finely chopped parsley.

*Robert Carrier's Kitchen*

# Super Potato Chips

*Serves 4*

*450–700 g/1–1½ lb potatoes*
*Oil for deep-frying*
*Salt and freshly ground pepper*

Peel the potatoes and cut them into sticks about 3 mm (⅛ in) square and 7.5 cm (3 in) long. Rinse in cold water to remove the excess starch and drain thoroughly; dry on absorbent paper. Heat the oil in a deep-fat fryer to 190°C (375°F).

Fill the frying basket half to two-thirds full of potatoes and immerse it gently into the hot oil. Shake the basket from time to time while frying to keep the potatoes from sticking together. Continue to fry until the potatoes are nearly tender. Drain them well and spread on a baking tray lined with absorbent paper to absorb the excess oil while you fry the remaining potatoes in the same way.

Reheat the oil to 190°C (375°F) and fry the potatoes a second time in small quantities until golden brown. Drain on absorbent paper. Spoon into a heated serving dish, sprinkle with salt and freshly ground pepper and serve immediately.

*Robert Carrier's Kitchen*

# Greek Lemon Potatoes

*This is a Middle Eastern version of our own roast potatoes. The difference? – a crumbled vegetable stock cube and the juice and rind of a lemon give this dish its unique flavour.*

*Serves 4*

*1 kg/2 lb potatoes*
*Juice and grated rind of 1 lemon*
*1 vegetable stock cube, crumbled*
*Salt and freshly ground pepper*
*4 tablespoons butter*

Preheat the oven to 190°C (375°F, Gas Mark 5). Peel the potatoes and cut in half lengthways and then cut length into 3. Place the cut potatoes in a *gratin* dish and sprinkle with the grated lemon rind, half the juice and sprinkle with crumbled vegetable stock cube. Season generously with salt and freshly ground pepper. Dot the butter over the surface and bake in the preheated oven for 15 minutes.

Drain the excess fat from the dish and sprinkle the potatoes with the remaining lemon juice, toss the potatoes and bake a further 20 to 25 minutes, or until golden brown and tender. Correct the seasoning and transfer to a heated serving dish using a slotted spoon. Serve immediately.

*Vogue*

# Pommes Fifine

*My lovely old friend Fifine had her own recipes for many things – fish, especially – but her way with potatoes has to be tasted to be believed.*

*Serves 3 to 4*

*3 large new potatoes (450 g / 1 lb)*
*1 medium-sized onion, finely chopped*
*4 level teaspoons butter*
*3 tablespoons olive oil*
*Salt and freshly ground pepper*
*2 level tablespoons finely chopped parsley*

Scrub potatoes clean and boil them in their jackets in salted water for 15 minutes only, so that they remain undercooked.

Meanwhile, sauté onion in 1 level table-spoon butter until golden: 4 to 5 minutes. Put aside. Cool potatoes by plunging them into cold water. Then peel and cut them into 6mm (¼ in) dice. In a large, heavy frying pan, heat oil with remaining butter. Add diced potatoes and sauté over a high heat for 5 to 6 minutes, until crisp and golden on all sides.

Season to taste with salt and freshly ground pepper. Return sautéed onion to the pan; toss lightly to mix it thoroughly with the potatoes and sauté them for 1 minute longer. Drain well and serve immediately, garnished with finely chopped parsley.

*The Robert Carrier Cookery Course*

# Gratin Dauphinois

*Here it is – my favourite potato dish. Not light, not cholesterol-free, but utterly and scrumptiously delicious. For eighteen years we served it twice daily at both my restaurants . . . and customers were asking for more. I even eat it cold (just try and stop me) on the morning after a dinner party.*

*Serves 4*

*450 g / 1 lb new potatoes*
*150 ml / 5 fl oz double cream*
*8 tablespoons freshly grated Gruyère cheese*
*4 tablespoons freshly grated Parmesan*
*Butter*
*Salt and freshly ground pepper*

Preheat oven to 180°C (350°F, Gas Mark 4). Butter a fireproof shallow casserole or deep *gratin* dish. Peel and slice potatoes thinly and soak in cold water for a few minutes. Drain and dry thoroughly with a clean tea towel.

Place layer of sliced potatoes on bottom of dish in overlapping rows; pour over a quarter of the cream, sprinkle with 2 tablespoons grated cheese (mixed Gruyère and Parmesan), dot with butter, and season to taste with salt and freshly ground pepper. Continue this process until dish is full, finishing with layer of grated cheese. Dot with butter and cook in preheated oven for 1 to 1¼ hours, or until

potatoes are cooked through. If top becomes too brown, cover with aluminium foil. Serve very hot.

*Vogue*

## Pommes Sarladaises

*Serves 4*

*2–4 tablespoons goose fat*
*450 g / 1 lb new potatoes*
*Salt and freshly ground pepper*
*Thinly sliced black truffles*

Grease a a frying pan with goose fat. Peel and slice potatoes thinly and soak in cold water for a few minutes. Drain and dry thoroughly with clean tea towel.

Place a layer of sliced potatoes on bottom of frying pan in overlapping rows; sprinkle with salt and freshly ground pepper, to taste, and a few thin slices of truffle. Repeat until pan is filled, or potatoes are used up, finishing with a layer of potatoes. Cover potatoes with a plate to weight them and to keep moisture in, and sauté them over a gentle heat until bottom layer is crisp and golden, adding a little more butter from time to time if necessary. Turn potatoes like a pancake and cook again (without the plate) until potatoes are cooked through and nicely browned. Turn out potato 'cake' and serve immediately.

*The Sunday Times*

## Pommes de Terre Duchesse

*Serves 4*

*1 kg / 2 lb potatoes*
*2–4 tablespoons butter*
*2 eggs*
*2 egg yolks*
*Salt and freshly ground pepper*
*Fresh nutmeg*

Peel and slice potatoes thickly; cook them, covered, in simmering salted water until they are soft, but not mushy. Drain well; return potatoes to pan and remove all moisture by shaking pan over the heat until they are dry.

Rub the potatoes through a fine sieve; add 2 to 4 tablespoons butter, beating with a wooden spoon until mixture is very smooth. Combine eggs and egg yolks and beat gradually into potato mixture. Season to taste with salt, freshly ground pepper and freshly grated nutmeg, and beat until mixture is very fluffy.

If potatoes are to be used as a garnish, pipe mixture through a pastry tube to make a border for any meat, fish or vegetable dish; brush with butter and brown under grill. Or shape them into individual shapes with a pastry tube, brush with butter and brown under the grill.

*The Sunday Times*

# Pommes Soufflées

*I cannot pretend that these crisp, puffed little pillows are easy to make. Luck plays a part in it as well as the type of potato used, and even professional chefs admit to a high failure rate. The secret is in starting the cooking at a low temperature, so that the potatoes do not brown, leaving them to cool and then cooking at a higher temperature; it is the shock of the change in temperature that causes them to puff up. Console yourself that any pillows that have not puffed up will make excellent potato crisps.*

*Serves 4*

*700 g / 1½ lb potatoes*
*Oil for deep-frying*
*Salt and freshly ground pepper*

Peel the potatoes and cut them into slices 1.5 mm (⅟₁₆ in) thick (paper thin – use a food processor or mandolin cutter if you have one). Trim the slices to an even shape, about 5 cm (2 in) long and 2 cm (¾ in) wide. Don't rinse them, but pat the slices dry with absorbent paper.

Heat the oil in a deep-fat fryer to 130°C (275°F). When the oil is hot add a few of the potato slices. Fry for 4 to 5 minutes, until soft but not at all coloured. Remove the oil, drain them on absorbent paper and leave to cool.

Repeat with the remaining potatoes in small batches. Raise the temperature of the oil to 190°C (375°F). Again, working in small batches, put the part-cooked potatoes in the frying basket and lower it into the oil. Fry, turning the slices about gently with a slotted spoon, until they are puffed and golden.

Drain on absorbent paper and keep hot while you fry the remaining potatoes. Season with salt and freshly ground pepper to taste and serve immediately.

*Robert Carrier's Kitchen*

# Pea, Sweetcorn or Carrot Purée

*Serves 4 to 6*

*700 g / 1½ lb frozen peas or 450 g / 1 lb frozen sweetcorn or 700 g / 1½ lb fresh carrots, thinly sliced*
*4 tablespoons chicken stock*
*4 tablespoons butter*
*1–2 tablespoons instant potato powder*
*1–2 tablespoons double cream*
*Salt and freshly ground pepper*
*Lemon juice and sugar (optional)*

Place frozen peas or sweetcorn, or thinly sliced raw carrots, in a pan. Add chicken stock and butter. Bring to the boil; push a sheet of greaseproof paper down into the pan

on top of vegetables; reduce heat to moderate and simmer until very tender – about 5 minutes for frozen vegetables, 10 to 12 minutes for fresh carrots.

Pour contents of pan into a blender. Add instant potato powder. Turn to maximum speed and blend for 2 minutes, stopping occasionally to scrape down sides of goblet with a spatula. (If blender is not available, put vegetables through a mouli, or rub through a fine sieve. In the case of sweetcorn, return contents of sieve to purée to give it bulk and texture.)

Return purée to pan. Beat vigorously with a wooden spoon over a moderate heat until purée is thoroughly hot again, adding just enough cream so that it still holds its shape. Season purée to taste with salt and freshly ground pepper. In addition, pea purée will be improved by a squeeze of lemon juice, sweetcorn by ½ teaspoon sugar. Serve immediately.

*Note:* if you wish, you can serve a tablespoon or two of the cooked peas or sweetcorn kernels for garnish. Carrot purée looks good with a garnish of finely chopped parsley.

*Food, Wine & Friends*

# Little Vegetable Packets

*Spinach-wrapped celery stalks encase chopped spring onions and mushrooms in this intriguing vegetable accompaniment for grilled or roast meats.*

*Serves 4*

*2 tablespoons butter*
*8 spring onions, finely chopped*
*225 g/8 oz mushrooms, finely chopped*
*Salt and freshly ground pepper*
*1 tablespoon finely chopped fennel leaves*
*8 celery stalks*
*16 spinach leaves, stalks removed*

Melt the butter in a frying pan and sauté the spring onions and mushrooms, seasoned with salt and freshly ground pepper, for 15 minutes, or until the mushrooms have lost their moisture. Add the chopped fennel.

Meanwhile, cut the celery stalks into sixteen 6 cm (2½ in) pieces. Bring a saucepan of salted water to the boil and blanch the celery for 3 minutes. Drain, and then plunge them into cold water. Blanch the spinach leaves, two at a time, for 1 minute and then refresh them in a cold water. Drain the celery and the spinach leaves on absorbent paper.

Place 2 teaspoons of the mushroom stuffing in one of the celery pieces and place another celery piece on top. Wrap the stuffed celery pieces in 2 spinach leaves. When ready to

serve: steam over boiling salted water for 10 minutes to ensure the mushroom stuffing is warm. Serve immediately as an accompaniment to a meat dish, presented on individual plates.

*Robert Carrier's Kitchen*

# Quick Stir-Fried Vegetables

*Serves 4*

*450 g / 1 lb vegetables, of your choice*
*Oil*
*Salt*
*1 tablespoon soy sauce*
*1 tablespoon sake, or dry sherry*

Wash the vegetables of your choice and slice diagonally across the grain.

Blanch sliced vegetables by cooking in boiling salted water (see times below). Drain.

| | |
|---|---|
| Carrots | 5 to 6 minutes |
| Courgettes | 2 to 3 minutes |
| Green beans | 3 minutes |
| Asparagus | 2 to 3 minutes |

Then sauté blanched vegetables in 2 tablespoons oil for 1 to 2 minutes; add ¼ teaspoon salt, 150 ml (5 fl oz) water and finely ground pepper, and cook for 2 to 3 minutes longer. Add soy sauce and *sake* (or dry sherry) and cook for 1 minute longer.

*The Robert Carrier Seminar of Cooking*

## Stir-fried Vegetable Variations

• Equal quantities each sliced shitake mushrooms, red and yellow pepper strips and spring onion segments.

• Equal quantities each sliced yellow and green courgettes, sliced celery and blanched tiny new potatoes

• Equal quantities each poached cauliflower and broccoli florets, tiny button mushrooms and small cherry tomatoes

• Equal quantities each poached asparagus segments, spring onion segments, sliced button mushrooms and bean sprouts.

# Couscous as a Vegetable

*A special pot, known in French-speaking North Africa as a couscousière, is used to make this dish, but you can substitute a saucepan with a steamer which fits snugly over the top. Moisten your couscous, available from specialist food stores, and place in a bowl in the steamer top.*

*Serves 4*

## Steaming Bouillon

*2 tablespoons olive oil*
*1 Spanish onion, quartered*
*4 carrots, scraped and cut into chunks*
*4 stalks celery, cut into chunks*
*2 fat cloves garlic, crushed*
*1 teaspoon ground ginger*
*¼ teaspoon cayenne pepper*
*¼ teaspoon ground cumin*

## Couscous

*450 g/1 lb couscous*
*4 tablespoons butter*
*4 tablespoons olive oil*
*6 tablespoons Steaming Bouillon*
*Pinch each of salt, cayenne pepper, ground cumin, ground ginger, paprika and ground cinnamon*

Heat olive oil in the base of *couscousière* or saucepan, add quartered onion and chunks of carrot and celery. Sauté vegetables for 5 minutes until lightly browned.

### *To prepare Couscous*

Place the grain in a bowl and moisten with 6 tablespoons water, 1 at a time, working it evenly with your fingertips, as though you were rubbing fat into flour. The grain will absorb the water without any trouble, and look and feel almost as it did when it came out of the packet. Line steamer top with a clean tea towel (wrung out in boiling water, just in case any trace of detergent remains), and wrap couscous in this.

Sprinkle the browned vegetables with the crushed garlic and spices. Stir well and pour on 1.2 l (2 pints) water, stir again and bring to the boil. Fit steamer over top of pan containing Steaming Bouillon, allow to simmer for 45 minutes, uncovered – occasionally drawing a fork through the grains to separate them and to prevent any lumps forming.

After 45 minutes cooking time, fluff Couscous with a fork to separate grains and transfer to a bowl that will fit the steamer. Add the butter and fluff it in with a fork and do likewise with the olive oil and 4 tablespoons of the Bouillon from the pan below the steamer. Sprinkle on the spices and

season with salt and fork in. Bring Bouillon back to the boil and place the bowl in the top half of the steamer; and cover. Steam for a further 45 minutes over steaming Bouillon, adding 2 tablespoons Bouillon after 15 minutes and fluffing it in with a fork.

When ready to serve, toss the cooked Couscous with a fork to separate grains and serve on a heated serving platter.

*Robert Carrier's Kitchen*

# Quick Fried Couscous with Diced Vegetables

*Serves 4 to 6*

*450 g/1 lb couscous (see page 219)*
*Couscous steaming bouillon as above*
*4 tablespoons butter*
*½ crumbled vegetable stock cube*
*2 pinches each salt, cayenne pepper, ground cumin, ground ginger, paprika and ground cinnamon*
*2–4 tablespoons freshly grated Parmesan*

Steam couscous as in recipe on page 219. Transfer cooked couscous to a bowl. Cut boiled carrots, celery and onion (from bouillon) into small dice and add to couscous. Season with salt, cayenne pepper, ground cumin, ground ginger, paprika and ground cinnamon, to taste. Mix well.

When ready to cook; heat butter and ½ vegetable stock cube in a large frying pan; add couscous and cook over a medium heat, stirring, until couscous and vegetables are heated through. Stir in freshly grated Parmesan; correct seasoning and serve immediately.

*Carrier's*

# Salads

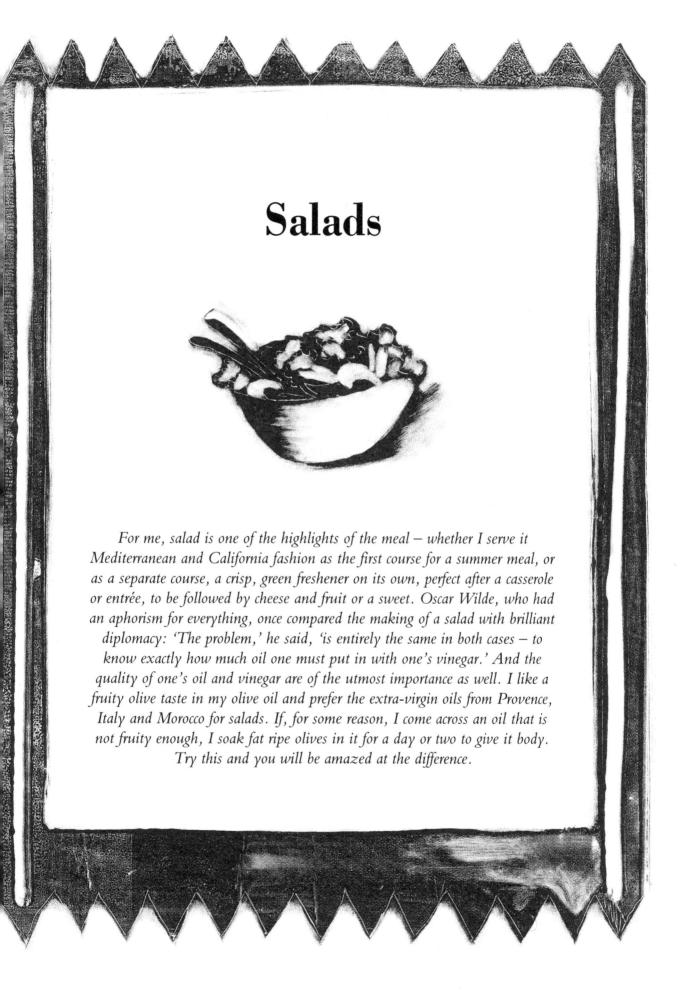

*For me, salad is one of the highlights of the meal – whether I serve it Mediterranean and California fashion as the first course for a summer meal, or as a separate course, a crisp, green freshener on its own, perfect after a casserole or entrée, to be followed by cheese and fruit or a sweet. Oscar Wilde, who had an aphorism for everything, once compared the making of a salad with brilliant diplomacy: 'The problem,' he said, 'is entirely the same in both cases – to know exactly how much oil one must put in with one's vinegar.' And the quality of one's oil and vinegar are of the utmost importance as well. I like a fruity olive taste in my olive oil and prefer the extra-virgin oils from Provence, Italy and Morocco for salads. If, for some reason, I come across an oil that is not fruity enough, I soak fat ripe olives in it for a day or two to give it body. Try this and you will be amazed at the difference.*

## Tossed Green Salad

*Every day I must have my 'fix' of a tossed green salad – at least once per day; sometimes twice. Occasionally I make a mixed green salad – with cooked or raw vegetables (or fish, poultry or game) added – for a colourful and healthy first course. Whatever form it takes, the important things to remember are: dry each chilled leaf of lettuce to make sure your vinaigrette dressing isn't 'watery'; use extra-virgin olive oil and lemon juice, Balsamic vinegar or wine vinegar in a three to one proportion to make the dressing, three portions of oil to one of lemon or vinegar; add finely chopped garlic and/or red onion and fresh green herbs just before tossing the salad; and, most important of all, toss the salad just before serving.*

*Serves 4 to 6*

*1–2 heads lettuce*
*1 recipe Basic French Dressing*

Wash lettuce leaves well in a large quantity of water. Drain well and dry thoroughly in a cloth or a salad basket so that there is no water on them to dilute the dressing.

Pour French Dressing into salad bowl and arrange prepared lettuce leaves on top. At the table, give a final toss to the ingredients to ensure that every leaf is glistening with dressing. Check seasoning and serve.

## Green Salad Variations

• Add other salad greens in season – cos lettuce, endive, chicory, batavia, young spinach leaves, watercress and French mâche (corn salad, or lamb's lettuce).
• Add finely chopped garlic or shallots, or a combination of the two, to salad dressing.
• Add fresh green herbs – finely chopped chervil, basil, tarragon, chives, coriander or eau de colgne mint – to the dressing.
• For crunch appeal, add diced celery, green pepper or fennel.

*The Robert Carrier Cookbook*

## Basic French Dressing – Simple Vinaigrette Sauce

*1 tablespoon lemon juice*
*1–2 tablespoons wine vinegar*
*½ teaspoon dry mustard*
*Coarse sea salt and freshly ground pepper*
*6–8 tablespoons extra-virgin olive oil*

In a small bowl, mix together lemon juice, wine vinegar and dry mustard, and season to taste with sea salt and freshly ground pepper.

Mix well. Then add olive oil, and beat with a fork, until the mixture emulsifies.

*The Robert Carrier Cookbook*

# Tossed Green Salad with Herbs

*Serves 4 to 6*

*2 heads lettuce*
*Choice of salad greens: endive, young*
*spinach, watercress, chicory, dandelion,*
*mâche, etc.*
*1 clove garlic*
*1 teaspoon each: fresh basil, marjoram,*
*chervil, and chives*
*Basic French Dressing*

Wash and prepare lettuce and salad greens of
your choice. Shake dry in a salad basket, or
dry each leaf carefully in a clean tea towel.
Wrap in tea towel and allow to crisp in
refrigerator until ready to use. Make salad as
for Tossed Green Salad, page 222, tossing
leaves in Dressing until glistening.

*The Sunday Times*

# Tossed Green Salad with Avocado

*Serves 4 to 6*

*2 heads lettuce*
*1 bunch watercress*
*1 clove garlic*
*2 teaspoons finely chopped chives*
*Basic French Dressing*
*1 avocado pear, peeled and sliced*
*Lemon juice*

Wash and prepare lettuce and watercress.
Shake dry in a salad basket, or dry each leaf
carefully in a clean tea towel. Wrap in tea
towel and allow to crisp in refrigerator until
ready to use.

Rub wooden salad bowl with cut clove of
garlic. Arrange lettuce and watercress in bowl.
Chop garlic and chives finely; sprinkle over
the salad and dress with Basic French
Dressing.

Garnish with wedges of avocado which
you have marinated in lemon juice to keep
from going brown. Just before serving, toss
salad until each leaf is glistening.

*The Sunday Times*

# Citrus Salad

*Serves 6*

*1 cos lettuce*
*2 bunches watercress*
*3 oranges*
*2 grapefruit*
*1 lime*

## Mustard and Herb Dressing

*½ teaspoon dry mustard*
*½ teaspoon salt*
*¼ teaspoon caster sugar*
*3 tablespoons tarragon vinegar*
*1 teaspoon finely chopped shallot*
*1 teaspoon finely chopped parsley*
*1 teaspoon finely chopped tarragon*
*1 clove garlic, finely chopped*
*9 tablespoons olive oil*
*Pinch or two of crushed dried chillies*

In a bowl blend mustard, salt, caster sugar and tarragon vinegar to a smooth paste. Stir in finely chopped shallot, parsley and tarragon and lightly crushed garlic. Leave for 1 hour. When ready to use: add olive oil, 1 tablespoon at a time, beating with a fork until dressing emulsifies. Season with crushed dried chillies to taste. Wash lettuce and dry each leaf carefully. Cut lettuce coarsely across the grain and arrange in a glass bowl. Wash watercress and cut away stalks. Make a border of the leaves around the outer edge of bowl. With a sharp knife, peel oranges removing all pith and segment. Repeat with grapefruit. Arrange orange and grapefruit segments in centre of bowl of salad greens and sprinkle over prepared dressing.

Slice lime thinly and make a cut to the centre of each slice on one side. Twist slices and arrange around watercress border.

*Robert Carrier's Kitchen*

# Winter Salad

*Serves 4*

*225 g/8 oz white cabbage*
*225 g/8 oz red cabbage*
*150 ml/5 fl oz carton soured cream*
*6 tablespoons chopped walnuts*
*1 small clove garlic, finely chopped*
*Salt and freshly ground pepper*

With a sharp knife finely slice white and red cabbage. Pour soured cream into a large bowl; add chopped walnuts and finely chopped garlic and season with salt and freshly ground pepper, to taste. Add finely sliced cabbage and toss with a fork until evenly coated. Spoon on to a platter and serve.

*Harper's Bazaar*

# Cucumber and Nasturtium Leaf Salad

*Serves 4 to 6*

*2 cucumbers*
*36 small Nasturtium leaves*
*Well-flavoured vinaigrette dressing*

Peel and slice cucumbers thinly. Wash Nasturtium leaves. Drain and pat dry. Pour over vinaigrette dressing and toss well. Garnish with Nasturtium flowers if desired.

*Food, Wine & Friends*

# Nine Herb Salad of Hintlesham

*My restaurant at Hintlesham Hall was famous for its half-acre herb garden. With the home-grown herbs (nine in all) we made our house salad – a forerunner of today's mesclun salads.*

*Serves 4 to 6*

*1 salad bowl lettuce*
*1 Romaine lettuce*
*Mâche (corn salad)*
*12 sprigs of tarragon*
*12 sprigs of basil*

*12 sprigs of purple basil*
*12 sprigs of pourprier (purslane)*
*12 sprigs of roquette (arugula)*
*12 sprigs of flat-leafed Italian parsley*
*Mustard and Herb Dressing (see page 224)*
*Coarsely chopped fennel*
*Coarsely chopped chives*
*Coarsely chopped parsley*

Wash lettuces well. Drain well. Wash mâche (corn salad) carefully in a large quantity of water, snipping off root ends. Drain. Cut fresh herbs into full-leafed sprigs about 2.5 cm (1 in) long. Wash well. Drain. Shake lettuces, mâche and herbs dry in a salad basket. Chop fennel, chives and parsley.

Arrange salad in a salad bowl. Pour over dressing; sprinkle with coarsely chopped fennel, chives and parsley and toss well.

*Hintlesham Hall*

# Chinese Salad

*Serves 4 to 6*

*2 little gem lettuces*
*½ bunch watercress*
*6 radishes, thinly sliced*
*150 g/6 oz fresh bean sprouts*

## Dressing

*4 thin slices root ginger*
*6 tablespoons olive oil*
*2 tablespoons lemon juice*
*1 teaspoon soy sauce*
*Salt and freshly ground pepper*

Wash and dry the lettuces and watercress and remove any yellow or damaged leaves. Wash and trim the bean sprouts. Dry well with a clean tea towel.

Peel the root ginger and chop finely. In a bowl combine the olive oil, the lemon juice and soy sauce. Season with salt and freshly ground pepper to taste, and beat with a fork until the dressing emulsifies. Stir in the chopped ginger. In a salad bowl combine the lettuce, watercress, thinly sliced radishes and the bean sprouts. Pour over the dressing and toss the salad until every leaf glistens. Serve immediately.

*Robert Carrier's Kitchen*

# Raw Spinach Salad

*This fresh tasting salad of young raw spinach leaves, quartered hard-boiled eggs and sliced avocado and onion, is tossed in a mustard-and-parsley-flavoured dressing just before serving. Excellent as a first course for grilled fish or hamburger. Try it, too, with a little chopped grilled bacon added, as a light lunch or supper dish.*

*Serves 4 to 6*

*450 g/1 lb young raw spinach leaves*
*6–8 tablespoons olive oil*
*2–3 tablespoons wine vinegar*
*1 clove garlic, finely chopped*
*1 tablespoon finely chopped parsley*
*½ teaspoon dry mustard*
*Salt and freshly ground pepper*
*2 hard-boiled eggs, cut in quarters*
*1 ripe avocado, peeled and diced*
*½ small onion, thinly sliced*

Wash spinach several times in cold water (spinach should be young and tender). Tear off stems; drain and chill until ready to use. Combine next five ingredients in a bowl to make a dressing and season to taste with salt and freshly ground pepper. Arrange spinach leaves in a salad bowl. Pour dressing over them; toss salad well and garnish with quartered hard-boiled eggs, diced avocado and onion rings.

*The Robert Carrier Cookbook*

# St Tropez Salad

*Serves 4 to 6*

*½ head curly endive*
*2 little gem lettuces*
*French bread*
*2 cloves garlic*
*Coarse salt*
*Olive oil*
*8 anchovy fillets*

## Well-flavoured French Dressing

*Mustard*
*6-8 tablespoons olive oil*
*2–3 tablespoons wine vinegar*
*Salt and freshly ground pepper*

## Garnish

*4 hard-boiled eggs, cut in half*
*Black olives*

Wash and dry curly endive and lettuces, removing any yellowed or damaged leaves. Slice French bread into 8 thin rounds. Dry rounds in oven and then rub each lightly with garlic; sprinkle with coarse salt and olive oil, using about 4 tablespoons olive oil. Place 1 anchovy fillet on each round.

Mix together mustard, 6 to 8 tablespoons olive oil, 2 to 3 tablespoons wine vinegar and salt and freshly ground pepper, to taste.

Add prepared endive and lettuce and toss until each leaf glistens with dressing. Garnish salad with garlic-rubbed bread and halved hard-boiled eggs. Sprinkle with black olives.

*Daily Telegraph Magazine*

# Salade Paysanne I

*Serves 4 to 6*

*2 heads lettuce, washed and chilled*
*100 g/4 oz fat salt pork, diced*
*2 tablespoons olive oil*
*2 hard-boiled eggs, chopped*
*Salt and freshly ground pepper*
*1–2 tablespoons finely chopped chervil,*
*tarragon or basil*
*Wine vinegar*

Wash and dry lettuce leaves thoroughly and chill. Sauté finely diced fat salt pork in olive oil until it is golden brown. Place lettuce in salad bowl; sprinkle with diced pork and hot fat. Add chopped eggs, salt, freshly ground pepper, herbs and vinegar, to taste. Mix well and serve immediately.

*Great Dishes of the World*

# Salade Paysanne II

*Looking for a light salad first course that is easy to make and yet never fails to please? Try this country salad of endive, radicchio and Belgian chicory (or whatever leaf you choose) and topped for the occasion with chopped walnuts, crumbled Roquefort cheese and thin strips of sautéed bacon. We used to serve it at Carrier's.*

*Serves 4 to 6*

## Salad

*50 g/2 oz Roquefort cheese*
*75 g/3 oz  bacon, sliced*
*1 tablespoon butter*
*1 tablespoon olive oil*
*175–225 g/6–8 oz walnuts*
*1 head curly endive*
*1 head radicchio*
*1 head Belgian chicory*

## Dressing

*6 tablespoons olive oil*
*2 tablespoons wine vinegar*
*Salt and freshly ground pepper*
*1 tablespoon finely chopped parsley*

Crumble Roquefort and leave in an airy place on absorbent paper to dry out. Cut bacon slices in a fine *julienne* and sauté in butter until cooked. Drain off butter; add olive oil and sauté *julienne* of bacon again until golden and crisp. Remove from pan and dry on absorbent paper.

Coarsely chop walnuts. Remove outer leaves from curly endive and discard. Pluck sprigs from remainder of curly endive and soak in cold water. Remove outer leaves of radicchio and discard. Separate remaining leaves and soak in cold water. Remove any brown leaves from chicory and discard. Cut chicory across the grain into 12 mm (¹/₂ in) slices. Soak in cold water.

### *To make Dressing*

Stir olive oil into wine vinegar and season to taste with salt and freshly ground pepper, and chopped parsley. Drain and dry radicchio leaves, toss in one-quarter of the dressing and arrange on the bottom of a salad bowl. Drain and dry curly endive and Belgian chicory and mix together with remaining dressing. Pile into salad bowl.

Sprinkle salad with bacon, chopped walnuts and crumbled Roquefort, and serve.

*Carrier's*

# Green Bean Salad

*There is one simple secret to this salad, but it is a vital one which will stand you in good stead throughout the entire world of vegetable cooking: for maximum flavour, cook the beans until they are just tender but still distinctly crisp to the bite. Toss with vinaigrette dressing while the beans are still a little warm.*

*Serves 4*

*700 g/1½ lb fresh young green beans
Salt*

## Vinaigrette Dressing

*6–8 tablespoons olive oil
2–3 teaspoons tarragon vinegar
Freshly ground pepper
2–3 tablespoons very finely chopped onion
2–3 tablespoons very finely chopped parsley
1 teaspoon finely chopped fresh tarragon
Pinch of finely chopped garlic*

Top and tail young green beans. Bring a pan of salted water to a brisk boil. Drop in beans (this immersion in boiling water helps to 'set' the brilliant colour of all green vegetables); bring to the boil again and simmer until just tender.

In a small bowl, combine olive oil with tarragon vinegar, and salt and freshly ground pepper, to taste, and beat with a fork until they form an emulsion. Stir in very finely chopped onion, herbs and a pinch of finely chopped garlic, to taste.

As soon as beans are cooked, drain them thoroughly in a colander and put them in a serving bowl. Pour dressing over warm beans. Toss thoroughly and taste for seasoning, adding more salt or freshly ground pepper if necessary. Serve cold.

*Great Dishes of the World*

# Salades Composées

*French 'composition salads' – salades composées – make wonderful first course or luncheon salads for spring and summer meals. The procedure is simple: just toss the elements of your choice – raw or cooked – in a Vinaigrette Dressing, sprinkle with chopped fresh herbs or flavour with finely chopped onion, shallot, garlic, or crumbled cooked bacon.*

## Salade Italienne

*Lettuce leaves, crisp rings of fennel, sprigs of fresh fennel and stuffed green olives.
Vinaigrette Dressing*

## Salade Mexicaine

*Cos lettuce leaves, canned corn kernels and red pepper strips. Vinaigrette Dressing flavoured with mustard and finely chopped parsley or chives.*

## Salade Japonaise

*Lettuce leaves and sprigs of watercress, garnished with crisp radishes cut into flower shapes. Vinaigrette Dressing flavoured with finely chopped garlic and soy sauce.*

## Salade Fermière

*Lettuce leaves and sprigs of watercress, garnished with tomato wedges and quartered hard-boiled eggs. Vinaigrette Dressing flavoured with mustard and chopped onion.*

## Salade Provençale

*Lettuce leaves and barely cooked cauliflowerets, garnished with black olives and anchovy strips. Vinaigrette Dressing flavoured with mustard and finely chopped garlic.*

## Salade Gitane

*Chick peas, lentils and haricots blancs, soaked overnight and then cooked separately in water until just tender; each tossed, separately while still warm, in a Vinaigrette Sauce, flavoured with chopped onion and anchovies. Garnish with tomato wedges and black olives.*

## Salade Tricolore

*Lettuce leaves and thin strips of barely cooked carrot and celery tossed in a Mustard Vinaigrette with strips of raw green and red cabbage.*

## Salade Paysanne

*Lettuce leaves, sliced mushroom and diced Swiss cheese, tossed in a Mustard Vinaigrette. Garnished with walnut halves and crumbled cooked bacon.*

## Salade Jardinière

*Lettuce leaves (Salad Bowl), cooked green beans and carrot strips and raw cucumber strips. Vinaigrette dressing. Garnish, if desired, with nasturtiums.*

*Homes and Gardens*

# Sweets and Puddings

*If, like me, you enjoy ending your meal with a delicious sweet or pudding, this is the chapter for you – from the simplest and freshest – Sangria Fruit Salad, Summer Pudding, Pears in Chablis – to the more exotic – Oeufs à la Neige, Diplomat au Kirsch, Raymond Olivier's Poire Vefour and Alain Senderens' Soupe aux Fruits Exotiques. I particularly like the gala (but easy to make) Peaches in Champagne, shiny Little Green Apples in their Crème de Menthe flavoured syrup and Mrs Moxon's unbeatable Lemon Posset (as long as your lemons are tart and juicy enough). Ginger ice cream is a treat, as is Barry Wine's Hot Chocolate Soufflé topped (at the table) with the tingling cold freshness of coffee granita or ice cream. And if you prefer to end the meal on a savoury note, there's a spectacular 'pineapple' savoury set-piece, moulded from a highly flavoured cheese mousse and topped with fresh green pineapple fronds.*

# Little Green Apples

*Small Granny Smiths are great for this –
peeled and cored, but left whole, then
simmered in a green Crème de Menthe
syrup and filled with raisins or sultanas
and chopped blanched almonds.*

*Serves 3 to 6*

*4 tablespoons raisins or sultanas
Crème de Menthe
8 tart dessert apples
225 g/8 oz sugar
Juice of 2 lemons
Green food colouring (optional)
6 tablespoons chopped blanched almonds*

Sprinkle raisins or sultanas with 1 tablespoon Crème de Menthe in a cup and leave to soak until needed. Peel and core apples, leaving them whole.

Combine sugar and lemon juice with 450 ml (15 fl oz) water in a wide, heavy pan. Stir over a moderate heat until sugar has dissolved; then flavour syrup with 2 to 3 tablespoons Crème de Menthe and deepen colour slightly if necessary with a drop or two of green food colouring.

Poach apples in the syrup for 5 to 7 minutes, or until just tender, turning them once or twice.

Transfer apples to a serving dish with a slotted spoon. Combine soaked raisins or sultanas with chopped almonds. Fill centre of each apple with this mixture. Allow to cool. Boil poaching liquid until reduced to a light syrup (110°C/225°F on a sugar thermometer). Cool slightly.

Spoon syrup over each apple to cover it with a delicate green glaze. Chill.

Just before serving: stir 1 teaspoon Crème de Menthe into syrup to give added flavour, and then spoon glaze over apples again to give high gloss.

Serve 1 to 2 apples per person.

*Vogue*

# Peaches in Champagne

*Serves 6*

*6 large, ripe peaches
6 tablespoons cognac
2 tablespoons caster sugar
12 blanched almond halves, cut into 3
spikes each
½ bottle champagne
Mint leaves, to garnish*

Put the peaches in a large bowl, pour over boiling water to cover and leave for 30 seconds. Drain and peel carefully. Put the peaches in a shallow dish and sprinkle over the brandy and sugar. Cover and refrigerate for at least 2 hours, turning the peaches 2 or 3 times in the brandy and sugar marinade.

Just before serving, stick 6 almond spikes

into each peach and place in a wide champagne glass or a wine glass. Top up with champagne and decorate with mint leaves. Serve immediately.

*Hintlesham Hall*

# Fresh Peaches Romanoff

*Serves 4 to 6*

*4 to 6 ripe peaches*
*Lemon juice*
*6 tablespoons icing sugar*
*3 tablespoons Cointreau*
*3 tablespoons rum*
*300 ml/10 fl oz double cream*
*3 tablespoons Kirsch*
*Coarsely grated rind of 1 orange*

### To prepare Peaches

Put peaches in a sieve and pour enough boiling water over them to loosen their skins. Peel peaches, holding them in a soft cloth to protect your fingers and avoid bruising the fruit. Cut them in half; remove stones and slice peaches lengthways into lemon juice.

*Note:* they must be coated with lemon juice as quickly as possible or they will start to turn brown.

Drain peach segments and toss in a bowl with tablespoons of the icing sugar. Pour over them a mixture of Cointreau and rum. Cover bowl and put in the refrigerator to chill. One hour before serving, whip double cream until soft peaks form. Sweeten with remaining icing sugar and flavour with Kirsch. Spoon whipped cream into macerated peaches, tossing until every slice is coated with creamy liqueur mixture.

### To serve

Pile into individual dishes and dust with coarsely grated orange rind. Keep cold until time to serve.

*Robert Carrier's Kitchen*

# Champagne Fruit Salad

*One quarter bottle of champagne and 2 tablespoons cognac or brandy – nothing more – makes the simplest fruit salad of diced or sliced pears, apples, bananas and grapes seem extravagant fare.*

*Serves 6 to 8*

1 medium-sized pineapple
4 pears, peeled, cored and sliced
4 Cox's Orange Pippins, peeled, cored and sliced
4 plums, sliced
4 bananas, peeled and sliced
1 bunch grapes, halved and seeded
1 tin apricot halves
Icing sugar
2 tablespoons brandy
2 tablespoons lemon juice
¼ bottle champagne

Peel, core and slice pineapple into rings. Reserve top. Slice each ring in half and combine with pears and apples, plums, bananas, halved, seeded grapes and tinned apricot halves in a mixing bowl. Dust with icing sugar to taste; moisten with brandy and lemon juice; toss well and chill. Just before serving, transfer to serving bowl; pour over champagne and decorate with pineapple top.

*The Sunday Times*

# Sangria Fruit Salad

*This fruit salad recipe, marinated in spiced red wine, makes the most out of Sangria. I far prefer it to the refreshing Spanish drink of the same name.*

*Serves 6 to 8*

1 orange, peeled and diced
1 lemon, peeled and diced
½ grapefruit, peeled and diced
Peels of the above, studded with cloves
2 peaches, peeled and sliced
2 bananas, peeled and sliced
1 bunch grapes, halved
2 pears, peeled and diced
2 apples, peeled and diced
Red wine
1 cinnamon stick
Cognac
Sugar
Sprigs of fresh mint

Combine orange, lemon, grapefruit, together with their peels studded with cloves, peaches, bananas, grapes, pears and apples in a glass bowl. Add red wine to just cover, with cinnamon stick and cognac and sugar to taste. Toss fruit well and chill for at least 2 hours. Just before serving, garnish with sprigs of mint.

*Vogue*

# Fruit in a Blanket

*Chunky dice of fresh pineapple (or ripe strawberries, raspberries or sliced peaches), tossed in Kirsch, covered with whipped unsweetened double cream and then topped with a layer of Barbados sugar, is a fabulously easy sweet. It started out to be a fruit-layered version of Crème Brûlée, but in the excitement of the dinner party conversation, I found I had forgotten to put it under the grill.*
*I've never looked back.*

*Serves 4 to 6*

*3 slices fresh pineapple, peeled and cored*
*4 tablespoons Kirsch*
*3 large, juicy oranges*
*450 ml/15 fl oz double cream*
*100–150 g/4–6 oz Barbados sugar*

Cut the pineapple slices into eighths. Sprinkle with Kirsch and leave to soak while you prepare the oranges. Using a sharp knife, and working over a dish to catch the juices, peel the oranges right down to the flesh, taking all the white pith and membrane away with the peel. On a plate, to catch the juices, slice the oranges horizontally, removing any pips, then cut the slices into quarters.

In a glass serving bowl, toss the pineapple and orange pieces together with their juices. Whip the cream until just stiff enough to hold

its shape. Spread it thickly over the fruit, smoothing out the top with the back of a spoon. Chill until ready to serve.

*The Robert Carrier Cookery Course*

# Summer Pudding

*A traditional English pudding which seems to have been devised specially to show off to best advantage the splendid variety of soft fruits which grow in this country. It should be chilled overnight to be firm enough to cut. Serve very cold with cream, either in a jug or whipped.*

*Serves 4 to 6*

*100 g/4 oz red currants*
*100 g/4 oz blackcurrants*
*450 g/1 lb cherries*
*100–150 g/4–6 oz sugar*
*225 g/8 oz raspberries*
*8–10 large slices, white bread,*
*about 6 mm/¼ in thick*
*Whipped cream*

Remove stalks from currants. Pit cherries. Wash currants and cherries quickly under the cold tap, shaking off excess moisture. In a heavy saucepan, dissolve sugar in 150 ml (5 fl oz) water. Add fruit, stir very gently and simmer over a low heat for 5 minutes. Remove from heat and allow to cool. Drain and reserve syrup.

Trim crusts from bread. Sprinkle a 900 ml (1½ pint) pudding basin with water. Cut an 8 cm (3 in) round from one slice of bread to fit the base of the basin; lay this in place. Cut about 5 of the slices in half lengthways and use to line the sides, trimming them if necessary. Press the bread lightly in place to completely cover the basin.

Fill basin with fruit, packing it down well. Reserve any juice that remains. Cut 2 slices of bread in half to form 4 triangles and use these to cover the top of the fruit, trimming the bread if necessary. Press a flat plate of the same diameter on top of the pudding and weigh it down well. Chill pudding and sauces overnight in the refrigerator. The following day, turn the pudding out carefully on to a flat serving dish; ladle over remaining juices, taking care not to leave any white patches where the bread has not absorbed the sauces from the fruit. Serve very cold.

*Note:* should the pudding collapse, pour off the juice to serve separately and serve the pudding entirely covered with whipped cream to resemble a *bombe*.

*Great Dishes of the World*

# Pears in Chablis

*Serves 4 to 6*

*1 kg/2 lb small pears*
*225 g/8 oz sugar*
*150 ml/5fl oz water*
*Cinnamon*
*150 ml/5fl oz Chablis, or other dry white wine*
*Whipped cream*

Peel pears but do not core them. Put them in a saucepan with the sugar, water and cinnamon. Simmer, covered, for about 15 minutes. Add Chablis and continue to cook over a low heat, uncovered, for 15 minutes.

Put pears in a deep serving dish. Reduce liquid to the consistency of a light syrup. Pour syrup over the pears and chill. Serve very cold with whipped cream

*Homes and Gardens*

# Pears 'Belle Hélène'

*Serves 4 to 8*

*8 firm, ripe dessert pears*
*225 g/8 oz sugar*
*Thinly pared strip of lemon peel*
*Vanilla essence*
*Vanilla ice cream*

## Chocolate Sauce

*150 g/6 oz bitter chocolate, broken*
*4 tablespoons butter*
*6 tablespoons double cream*
*6 tablespoons single cream*
*Vanilla essence (optional)*

### *To prepare Pears*

Preheat oven to moderate (180°C, 350°F, Gas Mark 4). Combine sugar and lemon peel with 600 ml (1 pint) water in a heavy saucepan. Bring to the boil, stirring until sugar has melted, and flavour to taste with vanilla essence. Peel, halve and core pears, and arrange them in one layer in a large baking dish, flat side down.

Pour vanilla-flavoured syrup over pears; cover dish tightly with foil and bake in preheated oven for 15 to 20 minutes, or until pears are tender but not disintegrating. Place pears in a container so they are completely immersed in the syrup to prevent discoloration, if necessary adding a little extra water. Cool and chill until ready to serve.

### *To prepare Chocolate Sauce*

In a double saucepan, stir broken chocolate with butter until smoothly melted. Gradually beat in double and single cream; then bring to the boil and simmer over direct heat for 2 to 3 minutes, stirring constantly. Flavour to taste with a few drops of vanilla essence if desired.

*Note:* this simple sauce may be cooled and reheated just before serving. If it should curdle, you can restore the emulsion by beating in a tablespoon of cold water.

Just before serving: place a scoop of ice cream in each of 8 individual cups. Press a pear half gently to either side of each scoop and coat with hot Chocolate Sauce.

*The Robert Carrier Cookery Course*

# Poire Vefour

*An exquisite sweet from the Grand Vefour in Paris, at the time of the famous Raymond Oliver, once one of France's most famous chefs. It's not difficult to make, providing you take it carefully stage by stage.*

*Serves 6*

*6 large firm dessert pears*
*150 g/6 oz sugar*
*Vanilla pod, split*
*1–2 tablespoons lemon juice*
*¼ –½ teaspoon vanilla essence*

## Crème Pâtissière

*450 ml/15 fl oz milk*
*1 5 cm/2 in piece of vanilla pod, split*
*5 egg yolks*
*100 g/4 oz caster sugar*
*2 tablespoons plain flour*
*1 tablespoon cornflour*
*2 tablespoons butter*
*3–4 tablespoons Grand Marnier*
*150 ml/5 fl oz double cream whipped*

## Decoration

*18 almond macaroons*
*450 ml/15 fl oz double cream*
*1 tablespoon caster sugar*
*12–18 crystallised violets*

### To prepare Pears

In a wide saucepan, combine sugar and vanilla pod with 900 ml to 1.2 l (1½ to 2 pints) water. Stir over a low heat until sugar has dissolved, then bring to the boil. Peel pears; cut them in half lengthways and remove cores. Brush each pear liberally with lemon juice as soon as you have prepared it, to prevent discoloration.

Lower pear halves into syrup, bring to the boil again and cover surface with a piece of greaseproof paper. Poach very gently, for 5 to 10 minutes, until pears are tender without a trace of mushiness. Remove saucepan from heat. Taste syrup and intensify vanilla flavour with a little essence (the restaurant describes it as *un sirop très vanille*). Allow pears to cool in their syrup.

### To prepare Crème Pâtissière

Pour milk into a medium-sized saucepan and add vanilla pod, split to produce maximum flavour. Bring to boiling point over a low heat. Cover pan and put aside to infuse until needed. In a bowl, whisk egg yolks with sugar until thick and light. Gradually whisk in flour and cornflour. Fish out vanilla pod. Pour milk into egg yolk mixture, beating with the whisk until well blended. Pour mixture back into the pan. Bring to the boil over a moderate heat, stirring constantly. Then simmer for 3 minutes longer, beating vigorously with a wooden spoon to disperse

lumps. (These lumps invariably form, but they are easy to beat out as the cream thickens.)

Remove pan from heat. Beat in butter and continue to beat for a minute or two longer to cool the Crème Pâtissière slightly before adding the Grand Marnier.

Pass the cream through a sieve if necessary. Put it in a bowl and cover with a sheet of lightly buttered greaseproof paper to prevent a skin forming on top. Allow to become quite cold; fold in whipped double cream.

### To serve

Select 6 deep tulip-shaped bowls large enough to take a whole pear standing up. Cover the bottom of each individual bowl with 3 tablespoons Crème Pâtissière, smoothing it out evenly with a spatula. Cut macaroons in half; scatter evenly over Crème Pâtissière – use the crumbs as well. Spread remaining Crème Pâtissière evenly over the macaroons. Drain poached pears thoroughly and place one pear in each dish. Whisk double cream lightly with the caster sugar, and use to decorate the top of each dish. Dot with a few crystallised violets, and chill lightly until ready to serve.

*Note:* you can fish out the vanilla pod when you have finished, dry it carefully and store it in a screwtop jar for future use.

*The Robert Carrier Cookbook*

# Cherries Jubilee

*Serves 4*

*600 g/1¼ lb dark red cherries*
*100 g/4 oz sugar*
*150 ml/5 fl oz water*
*1 stick cinnamon*
*Juice and grated rind of ½ orange*
*1 teaspoon cornflour*
*Lemon juice*
*4 tablespoons cognac*
*4 tablespoons cherry brandy*
*Vanilla ice cream*

In a medium-sized saucepan, combine sugar, water, cinnamon, orange juice, grated orange rind, cornflour (dissolved in 4 tablespoons lemon juice) and bring slowly to boil. Allow to bubble for 5 minutes, stirring from time to time, until sauce is reduced to desired consistency.

Add cherries and heat through.

At the table, reheat cherries and syrup in a chafing dish. Pour cognac and cherry brandy with a ladle, heat over a high heat and pour over cherries. Ignite, and when flames die down, pour hot mixture over individual portions of vanilla ice cream.

*Homes and Gardens*

# Cake Balls with Hot Fudge Sauce

*This is the nursery sweet par excellence –
vanilla ice cream formed into scoop-sized
balls, coated with amaretti crumbs and
served with a rich dark hot fudge sauce.*

*Serves 6*

*Vanilla ice cream
Amaretti biscuits, crushed*

### Hot Fudge Sauce

*150 ml/6 fl oz double cream
4 tablespoons unsalted butter
1 tablespoon granulated sugar
4 tablespoons soft dark brown sugar*

About 1 hour before serving transfer the vanilla ice cream to the main cabinet of your refrigerator to soften slightly. Crumble amaretti biscuits finely on to a large plate. Half an hour before serving, with an ice cream scoop shape 12 even-sized balls of vanilla ice cream. Roll the balls in crumbled amaretti biscuits to coat, shaking off the excess. Place the balls on a tray and put in the freezing compartment of your refrigerator.

### To make Hot Fudge Sauce

In a large, heavy-bottomed saucepan combine the double cream and unsalted butter. Set the pan over a moderate heat and simmer, stirring constantly with a wooden spoon, until the butter has melted and the cream just comes to a low boil. Add the sugars to the pan and continue cooking over a low heat until the sugars have dissolved. Bring to the boil and boil for 2 minutes, or until thick and glossy.

### To serve

Arrange 2 cake balls on each of 6 individual serving plates and pour a little Hot Fudge Sauce over the top of each cake ball. Serve remaining sauce separately.

*Robert Carrier's Kitchen*

# Cold Sabayon with Kummel

*We all know Italian Zabaglione (hot whipped egg sauce with Marsala). This Frenchified, lighter version whisks egg yolks, sugar and white wine over hot, but not boiling, water until thickened. Dissolved gelatine is added while the mixture is still warm and then kummel, vanilla essence and whipped cream are added to finish the sweet. Delicious.*

*Serves 4*

*4 egg yolks*
*3 tablespoons granulated sugar*
*4 tablespoons white wine*
*1 ½ teaspoons gelatine*
*3–4 tablespoons kummel*
*¼ teaspoon vanilla essence*
*190 ml/7 ½ fl oz double cream, whipped*

## Decoration

*1 lemon*
*1 tablespoon toasted flaked almonds*

In the top of a double saucepan combine egg yolks, sugar and wine and whisk mixture over hot, but not boiling, water until it thickens (approximately 10 to 15 minutes). Remove from heat.

In a small bowl sprinkle gelatine over 2 tablespoons cold water and leave gelatine to absorb. Place bowl in a saucepan of simmering water until gelatine dissolves. Allow to cool slightly. Stir gelatine into egg yolk mixture. Place top of double saucepan in a bowl of ice and stir Sabayon continually until it begins to set. Remove pan from ice.

With a large metal spoon fold kummel, vanilla essence and whipped cream into Sabayon. Pour into individual champagne glasses and chill. Pare rind of lemon with a vegetable peeler. Remove any pith carefully with a knife. Cut peel into very fine shreds (the length of a matchstick) 3.75 cm x 3 mm (1½ x ⅛ in). Bring a small saucepan of water to the boil; reduce heat and simmer *julienne* of lemon for 5 to 6 minutes. Drain and refresh under cold running water. Drain and dry on absorbent paper. Sprinkle flaked almonds on each Sabayon and sprinkle with *julienne* of lemon.

*Carrier's*

# Mrs Moxon's Lemon Posset

*One day when looking through the book stalls along the Seine in Paris, I came upon a nineteenth-century English cookbook written by a Mrs Elizabeth Moxon. It was here that I first discovered the delicious lemon pudding that I call Mrs Moxon's Lemon Posset. I served it in both my restaurants and I look upon it as one of my favourite winter puddings. When feeling low, it is the best 'pick-me-upper' I know.*

*Serves 6*

*Finely grated rind and juice of 2–3 tart, juicy lemons*
*600 ml/1 pint double cream*
*150 ml/5 fl oz dry white wine*
*Sugar*
*Whites of 3 eggs*

Add finely grated lemon rind to double cream and whisk until stiff. Stir in dry white wine (to get whipped cream 'ready' for the acidity of the lemon juice) and then the lemon juice. Add sugar, to taste, and then whip again until smooth.

In another bowl, whisk egg whites until they form peaks and fold into whipped cream and lemon mixture. Chill until ready to serve.

When ready to serve, whisk mixture again (you will find that it has separated in the refrigerator) and transfer to a glass serving dish, or 6 individual glasses.

Decorate each serving with a few berries, a small shiny green leaf, a sprig of fresh mint, or a small biscuit.

*Note:* a tart lemon flavour is absolutely essential for this recipe. So, if your lemons are not juicy enough, add more. Once, I found it necessary to use 4 large lemons to give the optimum lemony flavour to this simple but delicious pudding.

*Great Dishes of the World*

# Oeufs à la Neige

*A marvellously delicate sweet, equally at home in the nursery and as a finale to the most sophisticated dinner party.*

*Serves 6*

*450 ml/15 fl oz milk*
*300 ml/10 fl oz single cream*
*2 tablespoons sugar*
*1 strip orange peel*
*1 vanilla pod, split*
*2 teaspoons cornflour*
*4 egg yolks*
*Salt*
*4 egg whites*
*75–100 g/3–4 oz caster sugar*

## To prepare Sauce

In a heavy saucepan, combine 300 ml (10 fl oz) milk with the cream, 2 tablespoons sugar, orange peel, and a vanilla pod which you have split lengthways. Bring to the boil slowly; remove from heat and leave, covered, to infuse for 30 minutes. Remove orange peel and vanilla pod; rinse and dry vanilla pod thoroughly, and store in a stoppered jar for future use.

Blend cornflour smoothly with a little of the cream mixture. Stir back into the pan and bring to the boil slowly, stirring constantly. Simmer for 2 or 3 minutes until cornflour no longer tastes raw,

Beat egg yolks lightly in a bowl. Add cornflour cream in a very thin stream, beating vigorously. Return to the pan and cook over a low heat, stirring constantly, until sauce coats back of spoon. Take great care not to let it boil, or egg yolks will curdle. Put Sauce aside to cool while you prepare 'Islands', giving it an occasional stir to prevent a skin forming on top.

## To prepare 'Islands'

Combine remaining milk with 600 ml (1 pint) water in a wide, deep frying pan. Add a pinch of salt to the egg whites in a spotlessly clean and dry bowl, and whisk until soft peaks form. Gradually whisk in caster sugar and continue to whisk to a stiffer, glossy meringue.

Bring milky water to the boil and reduce heat to a bare simmer.

Take up a twelfth of the meringue mixture on a large spoon, shape it into a mound and drop on to the surface of the simmering milk.

Cook 3 or 4 'Islands' at a time for just 4 minutes, flipping them over carefully with a fork halfway through. Do not overcook them, or they will start disintegrating. As soon as it is ready, lift each island out with a slotted spoon and lay it on a wire rack to drain thoroughly. This is very important; otherwise, islands will continue draining on to the custard sauce.

## To serve

Pour Sauce into a glass serving dish and pile 'Islands' gently on top. Sauce should be about 2 cm (¾ in) deep. Chill until ready to serve.

*The Robert Carrier Cookery Course*

# Zuppa Inglese

*Serves 8*

*1 sponge cake (in 2 layers)*
*900 ml/1½ pints milk*
*½ teaspoon vanilla essence*
*¼ level teaspoon powdered cinnamon*
*1 strip lemon peel*
*Pinch of salt*
*4 tablespoons sugar*
*1 tablespoon cornflour*
*8 egg yolks*
*6–8 tablespoons rum*
*Juice and grated rind of ½ orange*
*4 tablespoons Kirsch*
*Finely grated chocolate*

Combine milk, vanilla essence, cinnamon, lemon peel and salt in a saucepan and bring to boiling point. Remove from heat. Mix sugar and cornflour together in the top of a double saucepan. Add egg yolks and blend well. Gradually stir in scalded milk and cook over hot water, stirring constantly, until mixture is smooth and thick. Remove from heat. Cool. Remove lemon peel.

At least 2 hours before serving: place one cake layer on serving dish; sprinkle with rum and orange juice and cover with about two-thirds of the cooled custard mixture. Top with second layer; sprinkle with Kirsch and pour on remaining sauce. Chill. Just before serving, remove from refrigerator and sprinkle with finely grated chocolate and orange peel.

*Vogue*

# English Trifle

*The Box Tree is a Manhattan restaurant in the grand tradition. It serves new cuisine starters and main courses and finishes with a series of new old-fashioned puddings. My favourite, English Trifle, is garnished with a wheel of raw and poached fruits.*

*Serves 4 to 6*

*375g/15 oz can whole peeled apricots*
*1 sponge cake, about 20 cm (8 in)*
*in diameter*
*8–10 tablespoons sweet Marsala*
*2 tablespoons cornflour*
*Sugar*
*300 ml/10 fl oz hot milk*
*3 eggs*
*100 g/4 oz crumbled macaroons*
*600 ml/1 pint double cream, whipped*
*½ teaspoon vanilla essence*
*2 red skinned apples, cut into paper-thin slices and dipped in lemon juice*
*to preserve colour*
*Fresh fruits (strawberries, raspberries, blueberries)*
*1 pear, poached in port*
*Chopped almonds (optional)*

Drain syrup from canned whole peeled apricots. Remove pits from apricots. In an electric blender or food processor, purée apricots until smooth.

Cut sponge cake into 2 layers and spread half of the apricot purée between layers. Assemble cake again and cut into 5 x 2.5 cm (2 x 1 in) strips. Arrange strips in bottom of a glass serving bowl. Pour over sweet Marsala and spread remaining apricot purée on top.

Combine cornflour, 2 tablespoons sugar and a little warm milk and mix to a smooth paste. Combine with remaining hot milk in the top of a double saucepan and bring to the boil. Cook over water, stirring constantly, until mixture thickens. Remove pan from heat. Beat in eggs, 1 at a time. Return pan to heat and simmer over hot but not boiling water for 10 minutes, stirring occasionally. (Do not allow mixture to come to the boil, or custard will curdle.)

Stir macaroons into custard and leave to soak. Beat custard well to dissolve macaroons and leave to cool. Pour custard over sponge strips. Chill for at least 2 hours.

Before serving, whisk together whipped double cream, vanilla essence and sugar, to taste, until mixture thickens. Cover custard with whipped cream and decorate with apple slices, which you have dipped in lemon juice to preserve colour, and fresh fruits. Top trifle with poached pear and decorate rim with chopped almonds, if desired.

*Sunday Express Magazine*

# Bread and Butter Pudding à l'Orange

*A creamy filling, fragrant with orange, enclosed in a crisp, caramelised casing of golden bread slices. Serve hot or lukewarm.*

*Serves 6*

*100–150 g/4–6 oz softened butter*
*10–12 slices thick-cut white bread*
*4 level tablespoons marmalade*
*Juice and finely grated rind of 2 large oranges*
*Juice and finely grated rind of 1 lemon*
*75 g/3 oz caster sugar*

## Custard

*450 ml/15 fl oz milk*
*2 eggs*
*2 level tablespoons caster sugar*
*25 g/1 oz seedless raisins (optional)*
*4 level tablespoons lightly whipped cream*

Preheat oven to moderately hot (200°C, 400°F, Gas Mark 6). Generously grease a shallow, 1.8 l (3 pint) baking dish with some of the butter.

### *To prepare Cases*

Remove crusts from bread. Spread slices with butter and marmalade, and cut into triangles

(4 to each slice). Combine juice and finely grated rinds of oranges and lemon in a bowl. Add caster sugar and stir until dissolved.

Line bottom and sides of prepared baking dish completely with bread triangles, soaking them in orange syrup as you use them, and arranging them buttered side up. Fill lined dish with some of remaining bread triangles, reserving a few to decorate top of pudding.

### To make Custard

Heat milk to just below boiling point. Beat eggs lightly in a bowl and pour hot milk on to them gradually, beating constantly. Return mixture to pan; add sugar, and raisins, if used, and stir over a low heat until custard thickens enough to coat back of spoon. (Take great care not to let custard boil, or eggs will curdle. Use a double saucepan for this operation if you have one.) Remove custard from heat; cool slightly and stir in cream.

### To assemble Pudding

Pour custard over bread in the baking dish. Cut remaining bread triangles in half; soak each one in remaining orange syrup and arrange them on top of the pudding in an attractive pattern. Sprinkle pudding with any leftover orange syrup. Bake pudding for 30 minutes, or until crisp and golden on the outside, with a soft, creamy centre.

*The Robert Carrier Cookery Course*

# Diplomat au Kirsch

*Serves 8*

*225 g/8 oz candied fruits*
*Kirsch*
*8 dry sponge or boudoir biscuits*
*750 ml/1¼ pints double cream*
*100 g/4 oz icing sugar*
*½ teaspoon vanilla essence*

## Crème Pâtissière

*2 egg yolks, beaten*
*4 tablespoons icing sugar*
*1 teaspoon cornflour*
*300 ml/10 fl oz milk*
*Kirsch*

Dice candied fruits; each piece should be 6 mm (¼ in). Soak in Kirsch to cover for 30 minutes. Drain, reserving Kirsch. Place sponge biscuits cut into 12 mm (½ in) cubes in a bowl; pour over reserved Kirsch. Drain.

Whip double cream until thick and smooth; flavour lightly with icing sugar and vanilla essence, to taste. Fold in diced fruits and sponge biscuits and spoon into a mould. Cover the mould with aluminium foil and seal with its cover. Put mould in freezer for two hours. Turn out just before serving. Top with Crème Pâtissière.

### *To make Crème Pâtissière*

Combine beaten egg yolks, icing sugar and cornflour in the top of a double saucepan and mix well; stir in milk and cook over water, stirring constantly, until sauce is smooth and thick. Do not let sauce come to the boil or eggs will curdle. Remove from heat and flavour generously with Kirsch. Chill.

*Robert Carrier's Kitchen*

# Denys Gentes' Raspberry Charlotte

*Denys Gentes, handsome young chef/proprietor of Clodenis restaurant in Montmartre, loves the old-fashioned sweets of his Nîmois childhood. His rich, fresh Raspberry Charlotte reflects this passion. A classic French Charlotte mould is made of metal with plain, slightly-sloping sides and two little heart-shaped handles. You can also use a large fluted brioche mould or soufflé dish, or, for that matter, any other mould with tall sides and a flat bottom.*

*Serves 4 to 6*

*15–18 sponge finger biscuits*
*2 tablespoons (2 sachets) powdered gelatine*
*1 kg/2 lb fresh or frozen raspberries*

*4–6 tablespoons caster sugar*
*450 ml/15 fl oz double cream*
*5 tablespoons milk*
*2 tablespoons Framboise (optional)*
*Lightly sweetened whipped cream*
*Fresh raspberries, or mandarin orange segments*

Line base of a 1.8 l (3 pint) charlotte mould with a circle of dampened greaseproof paper. Line sides (not bottom) of mould with a tight layer of sponge finger biscuits★. Put powdered gelatine in a bowl with 6 tablespoons warm water. Leave to soften.

In an electric blender or food processor, purée raspberries until smooth. Strain three-quarters of the raspberry purée through a fine sieve into a bowl. Add caster sugar and stir well. Chill remaining unsweetened raspberry purée.

Meanwhile, stand bowl containing softened gelatine, to which you have added a glass of sweetened raspberry purée, in a saucepan containing 2.5 cm (1 in) hot water and stir over a low heat until gelatine is dissolved. Combine raspberry gelatine mixture with remaining sweetened raspberry purée and leave until cold, but not set, whisking occasionally.

Lightly whisk double cream and milk until thick enough to hold a trail. Fold in raspberry mixture and flavour, if desired, with Framboise.

Pour raspberry mixture into lined mould and chill for at least 5 hours. To unmould charlotte, use a pair of scissors and snip off tips of sponge finger biscuits until they are level with top of filling. If charlotte has stuck to mould, dip mould briefly in and out of very hot water. Turn out onto a flat serving plate. Remove lining paper.

Decorate charlotte with a little lightly sweetened whipped cream. Pour a little chilled unsweetened raspberry purée around charlotte and decorate with fresh raspberries, or mandarin orange segments.

★When it comes to lining the mould, you can choose between sponge finger biscuits and strips of sponge cake. If you use sponge finger biscuits, they will fit better; the finished result is more attractive if you alternate brown and white sides on the outside. If you have difficulty making them stand up around the sides of the mould, try brushing them with a little sugar syrup to hold them in place.

*Homes & Gardens*

# Little Summer Fruit Towers

*Serves 6*

## Sponge

*Butter*
*3 eggs*
*75 g/3 oz caster sugar*
*75 g/3 oz plain flour, sifted*

## Strawberry Bavaroise Filling

*24–30 strawberries, mashed*
*Finely grated rind of 1 orange*
*150 ml/5 fl oz pint milk*
*1 egg yolk*
*2 level tablespoons sugar*
*1 teaspoon powdered gelatine*
*150 ml/5 fl oz double cream*
*2 tablespoons Grand Marnier, or Cointreau*
*Red food colouring*
*2 egg whites*

## Raspberry Cream

*300 ml/10 fl oz cream*
*¼ teaspoon vanilla essence*
*1 punnet raspberries*
*Powdered sugar*
*Lemon juice (or Raspberry liqueur)*

# Garnish

*Whipped cream and ripe raspberries or strawberries*

Preheat oven to 180°C (350°F, Gas Mark 4). Grease a jelly roll pan (30 x 20 cm/12 x 8 inches) and line with buttered waxed paper.

## To make Cake

Beat eggs and sugar over hot water until mixture leaves a ribbon on the surface. Remove from heat and fold in flour. Put cake mixture into pan and level off with a spatula. Bake in preheated oven for 15 to 20 minutes or until cake is golden and springy. Turn out onto a wire rack and peel off waxed paper. Cool.

## To make Fruit Filling

In a small bowl, combine mashed strawberries and grated orange rind. Mix well.

Put the milk, egg yolk and sugar into the top of a double saucepan. Set over boiling water and whisk until light and fluffy. Lower heat until water just simmers; and cook, over simmering watter, stirring continuously, until the custard is thick enough to coat the back of a spoon, about 10 minutes. Remove from the heat and leave to cool.

In a small bowl, sprinkle the gelatine over 3 tablespoons cold water and leave to soften. Place the bowl in the pan of simmering water until the gelatine dissolves. Remove from the heat and pour into the mashed strawberry and orange rind mixture. Stir into the thickened custard. Place the pan of strawberry custard in a bowl of crushed ice, stirring constantly until the custard is on the point of setting.

Whip the cream until soft peaks form. Then fold into the strawberry custard.

To line six 150 ml (5 fl oz) turret moulds with sponge: carefully slice sponge cake into 2 thin layers 6 mm (1/4 in) thick, using a serrated knife. From one layer, cut a circle to fit the bottom of each mould. Then cut a strip to fit completely round inside of each mould, trimming ends so that there is no overlap. Fill sponge-lined moulds with strawberry mixture and chill until firmly set.

## To make Raspberry Cream

Whip cream until stiff. Beat in vanilla essence. Purée raspberries with a little powdered sugar and lemon juice or raspberry liqueur, to taste. Add to whipped cream and whisk until thoroughly blended.

## To serve

Turn towers out on to a wire rack over a flat dish. Mask each tower completely with raspberry cream and transfer to individual serving dishes. Top each tower with a swirl of whipped cream and garnish with a ripe raspberry or strawberry.

*Food, Wine & Friends*

249

# Barry Wine's Hot Chocolate Soufflé with Coffee Ice Cream

*Barry and Karen Wine's restaurant in New York, the Quilted Giraffe, is the hottest ticket in town, according to food buffs in the know. Wonderful clear soups are served in square Japanese dishes with attractive mosaics of seafood and artfully cut vegetables; pan-seared (almost raw) cubes of tuna fish are set on a delicate bed of Chinese vegetables; the finest slices of lightly grilled polenta are coupled with black truffles. But perhaps the most deliciously startling dish is the Hot Chocolate Soufflé into which an icy-cold bitter espresso ice cream is tossed, in front of the diner. The rich, hot chocolate soufflé contrasts to perfection with the cold, bitter ice cream.*

### Serves 4 to 6

*225 g/8 oz bitter-sweet chocolate, broken into pieces*
*125 g/5 oz butter, diced*
*150 ml/5 fl oz lukewarm water*
*5 egg yolks*
*About 9 egg whites, at room temperature*
*4 oz sugar*
*Icing sugar*
*4–6 scoops coffee ice cream*
*Whipped cream*

Preheat oven to fairly hot (220°C, 425°F, Gas Mark 7). Combine chocolate pieces and diced butter in a bowl. Place bowl in a saucepan containing 5 cm (2 in) boiling water until chocolate and butter have melted. Brush insides of four to six 240 ml (8 fl oz) soufflé dishes (Barry Wine uses tin charlotte moulds) with a thin coating of softened butter. Coat bowls with sugar simply by filling the first one with sugar, turning it to coat sides entirely, then pouring sugar into next bowl.

In an electric mixer, combine lukewarm water and egg yolks and beat together at high speed for 10 minutes. In clean bowl of electric mixer, start beating egg whites and sugar at high speed. While they are beating, fold beaten egg yolks into chocolate mixture. Beat egg whites until quite glossy and moderately stiff. Fold egg whites into chocolate mixture, one-third at a time. Ladle soufflé mixture into prepared soufflé dishes and bake in preheated oven for 5 to 7 minutes, depending on their size.

Immediately upon removing from oven, sprinkle each soufflé with icing sugar; drop a scoop of coffee ice cream into centres and cover holes with a dollop of whipped cream.

*Sunday Express Magazine*

# Soupe Exotique

*Serves 12*

*2 small pineapples*
*2 ripe pawpaws*
*2 ripe mangoes*
*4 kiwi fruit*
*16 strawberries, hulled and sliced (optional)*
*4 passion fruits, halved and seeded, seeds reserved*
*20 mint leaves*
*Juice of 6 oranges*
*Juice of 2 lemons*
*Icing sugar (optional)*

Cut off both ends of the pineapples and remove the skins with a sharp knife. Cut the pineapple into quarters and remove the cores. Cut approximately 20 slices from each pineapple and reserve the rest for the dressing. Peel the pawpaws, cut in half and remove the pips. Reserve 2 tablespoons of the pips. Cut half the pawpaw flesh in 8 mm (⅓ in) dice.

Peel the mangoes and cut each one lengthways into 3 slices. Dice half the mango into 8 mm (⅓ in) pieces, and reserve. Peel the kiwi fruit and slice thinly.

Put the prepared fruit in a large bowl, the sliced pineapple and kiwi at the bottom, the diced pawpaw and mango and sliced strawberries (optional) on top. Set aside.

## To make Dressing

Put the reserved pineapple, the passion fruit and reserved seeds and 10 mint leaves in a blender and blend to a pulp. Add orange juice and lemon juice to taste. Pass the soup through a fine sieve into a bowl. If the soup is too thick, thin it with a little more orange juice; orange juice will also reduce excess acidity, or you may add a little icing sugar to taste if you wish.

Pour the dressing over the prepared fruit, cover the bowl and chill.

## To serve

About 30 minutes before serving, remove the fruit salad from the refrigerator. Mix it lightly with a large spoon and divide it between 12 individual glass serving dishes. Cut the remaining 10 mint leaves into a fine *julienne*. Decorate each serving with a few strips of mint *julienne* and sprinkle with pawpaw pips. Leave to come to room temperature before serving.

*Robert Carrier's Kitchen*

# Ginger Ice Cream

*The richest, most scrumptious ice cream I know is this version of ginger ice cream, lavishly flavoured with ginger and topped with ginger syrup and thin slices of preserved ginger.*

*Serves 4 to 6*

*225 g/8 oz sugar*
*600 ml/1 pint milk*
*300 ml/10 fl oz double cream*
*1 teaspoon ground ginger*
*Finely grated zest of 1 large orange*
*8 medium-sized egg yolks*
*Cracked ice*
*350g/12 oz jar stem ginger in syrup*
*½ teaspoon vanilla essence*
*1 tablespoon strips of orange peel*

Make a rich ginger custard: in a thick-bottomed saucepan, combine sugar, milk, double cream, ground ginger and orange zest and bring to the boil. Remove pan from heat. Cover and leave to infuse for 5 to 10 minutes. Lightly beat egg yolks. Pour into ginger cream and mix gradually until custard is light and foamy. Return pan to heat and cook over a low heat, stirring constantly, until custard is thick enough to coat the back of a spoon. Pour custard into a bowl and cover. Set in a bowl filled with cracked ice and leave to cool completely.

Drain syrup from stem ginger. Reserve syrup. Thinly slice 4 pieces of stem ginger. Finely chop remaining stem ginger. Stir finely chopped stem ginger and vanilla essence into cooled custard. Cover and chill for at least 2 hours. Cover custard and freeze until it begins to harden about 2.5 cm (1 in) around sides of container. Beat to break up ice particles. Replace cover and continue to freeze for 5 hours, or overnight.

About 1 hour before serving: transfer ice cream to a refrigerator to soften slightly. To serve, pile ice cream in a glass serving dish. Scatter stem ginger and orange strips on top and dribble over a little reserved ginger syrup.

*Robert Carrier's Kitchen*

| **Vanilla Parfait** | **Chocolate Ice Cream** |
|---|---|

*Serves 4*

75 g / 3 oz sugar
100 ml / 4 fl oz water
6 egg yolks
550 ml / 18 fl oz whipping cream
½ vanilla pod

Put water and sugar in a large saucepan and bring to boil and cook until mixture becomes a syrup. Whisk egg yolks very hard, slowly adding hot sugar syrup. Continue to whisk till mixture is light and fluffy.

Scrape seeds from vanilla pod and add to whipping cream. Whisk until soft peaks are formed. Fold cream into egg and syrup mixture and pour into a chilled mould or *Bombe* mould and freeze for 2 to 3 hours before serving.

*The Robert Carrier Seminar of Cooking*

*Serves 4*

100 g / 4 oz sugar
600 ml / 1 pint whipping cream
100 g / 4 oz bitter chocolate, chopped
5 egg yolks

If using the freezing compartment of your refrigerator, turn it down to its lowest setting. In a pan, bring sugar, whipping cream and chopped chocolate to the boil, stirring occasionally until chocolate melts. Pour chocolate cream mixture over egg yolks, whisking constantly. Return to the pan and heat to just below boiling point, but do not let mixture boil.

Strain chocolate cream mixture into a clean bowl over ice. Place mixture into the freezing compartment of your refrigerator and freeze, covered, until mixture begins to harden 2.5 cm (1 in) around the sides of the container. This takes about 1 to 2 hours.

Remove from fridge and whisk until the ice particles are broken down. Return to freezer. Twenty minutes before serving, transfer mixture to the main compartment of your refrigerator to defrost lightly. Use as desired.

*The Robert Carrier Seminar of Cooking*

# Roman Ice Punch

*This high-profile Roman iced pudding uses a meringue mixture to give the rum-and-citrus-flavoured 'punch' its special texture.*

Serves 4 to 6

125 g/1 oz sugar
300 ml/10 fl oz water
3 oranges
2 lemons
100 ml/3½ fl oz white rum
½ tablespoon dry white wine
1 egg white
50 g/2 oz icing sugar
Rum to sprinkle over finished dish

Put water and sugar in a saucepan and bring to the boil; remove from heat.

Grate the rinds of the oranges and lemons and add grated rind to hot syrup; infuse for 30 minutes. Add rum and juice from oranges and lemons to the syrup; flavour with white wine to taste. Strain mixture through fine sieve.

Put mixture in a bowl set in a container in which you have put a mixture of water, ice cubes and salt. Place in freezer, scraping down sides from time to time, until nearly set. Make a meringue: beat egg white till it forms soft peaks, add icing sugar and continue to beat until very stiff. Stir meringue into punch mixture and return to freezer to set.

When ready to serve, scoop into serving dish and sprinkle with white rum.

*The Robert Carrier Seminar of Cooking*

# Burnt Honey Ice Cream

*A golden 'egg custard' ice cream with the rich, true flavour of burnt honey to give it added lustre. One of my top favourites.*

Serves 4

225 g/8 oz granulated sugar
600 ml/1 pint milk
300 ml/10 fl oz double cream
8 egg yolks

## Burnt Honey Sauce

Water
225 g/8 oz granulated sugar
8 tablespoons clear honey

### *To make Rich Custard*

Combine sugar, milk and double cream in a saucepan and bring to the boil. Remove pan from heat; cover and leave for 5 to 10 minutes. In a large bowl beat egg yolks lightly. Pour cream mixture into lightly beaten egg yolks and mix gradually, stirring, until custard is light and foamy. Transfer custard to a clean saucepan and cook over a

low heat, stirring with a wooden spoon, until custard coats the back of spoon. Do not let custard come to the boil or it will curdle. Pour rich custard into a large bowl and set in a large bowl filled with cracked ice; cover smaller bowl with a plate and let custard cool completely.

### To make Burnt Honey Sauce

In a small saucepan, bring granulated sugar and 4 tablespoons water to the boil. Boil for 5 minutes, or until sugar turns to a deep brown. Add another 4 tablespoons of water (covering your hand with a cloth to avoid being splashed); blend with a wooden spoon and cook for a further 1 to 2 minutes to the soft ball stage. Stir in clear honey; remove from heat and allow to cool.

### To make ice Cream

Stir half the cooled Burnt Honey Sauce into the cooled custard and chill, covered, for 2 hours. Then freeze in an ice cream freezer (according to manufacturer's instructions), or freezing compartment of your refrigerator in the following manner: pour custard into a container that will fit your freezing compartment and freeze until mixture begins to harden about 2.5 cm (1 in) around the sides of the container. When mixture starts to harden, beat with a whisk or a fork, then leave until firmly frozen, 2 to 3 hours.

About 1 hour before serving, transfer ice cream to the main cabinet of your refrigerator to soften.

### To serve

Pile ice cream high in a glass serving dish and dribble over a little Burnt Honey Sauce. Serve immediately.

*Robert Carrier's Kitchen*

# Cheese 'Pineapple' Dessert

*A flamboyant cheese-flavoured finale to a buffet meal: the 'pineapple' is formed from a ball of chilled mixed cheeses, spiked with cognac, Worcestershire sauce and lemon juice, smoothed into a pineapple shape with a spatula dipped in hot water. For maximum effect, top with pineapple leaves and assorted sliced fruits.*

*Serves 6*

*225 g/8 oz Cheddar cheese, grated*
*100 g/4 oz Roquefort cheese, sieved*
*100 g/4 oz cream cheese*
*Juice of ½ lemon*
*1–2 tablespoons cognac*
*1–2 tablespoons Worcestershire sauce*
*2 tablespoons warm milk*

2 tablespoons mayonnaise
1 tablespoon chopped parsley
Cayenne pepper to taste
Paprika
6 stuffed olives, sliced

## Garnish

*Pineapple top (use the fruit of the pineapple
for a sweet at another meal)
Eating apples (cored and sliced with a cutter
to make apple 'flowers' and sliced into
rounds and wedges) topped with cheese balls
or spread with cheese*

Mix first ten ingredients together until smooth; roll into a ball and then gently shape into form of a pineapple with a spatula dipped in hot water. Chill in refrigerator.

When ready to serve: dust pineapple with paprika, score with a knife, and stud with sliced olives. Top with pineapple leaves, if available. Surround 'pineapple' with cored and sliced, red and green eating apples soaked in lemon juice; cored apple slices topped with cream cheese balls dusted with parsley; and apple wedges spread with Roquefort cheese and dusted with parsley.

*Robert Carrier's Kitchen*

# Cakes

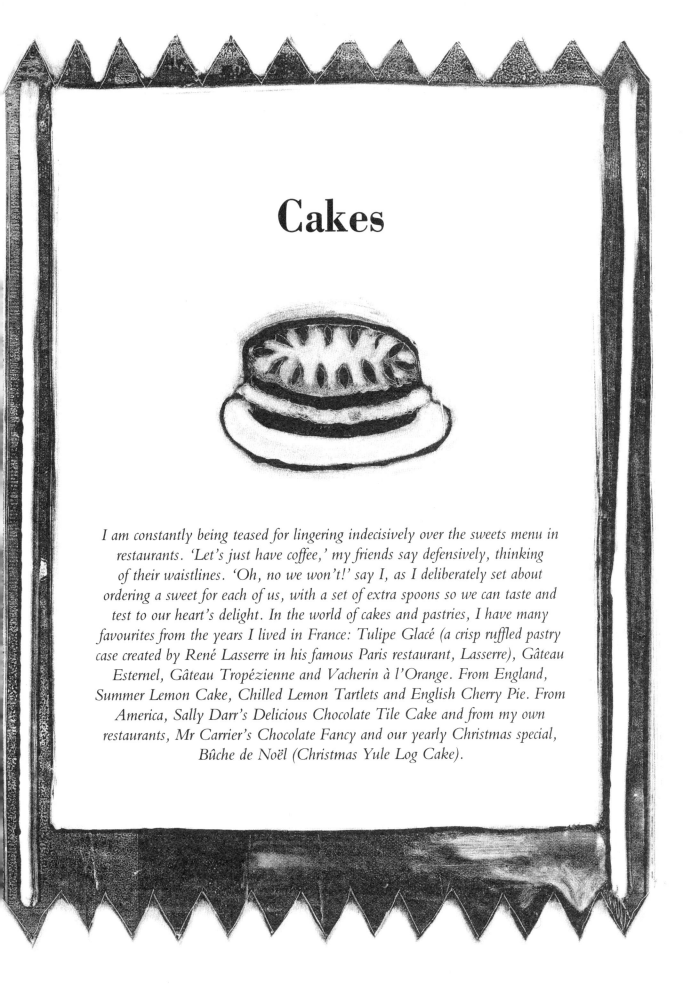

*I am constantly being teased for lingering indecisively over the sweets menu in restaurants. 'Let's just have coffee,' my friends say defensively, thinking of their waistlines. 'Oh, no we won't!' say I, as I deliberately set about ordering a sweet for each of us, with a set of extra spoons so we can taste and test to our heart's delight. In the world of cakes and pastries, I have many favourites from the years I lived in France: Tulipe Glacé (a crisp ruffled pastry case created by René Lasserre in his famous Paris restaurant, Lasserre), Gâteau Esternel, Gâteau Tropézienne and Vacherin à l'Orange. From England, Summer Lemon Cake, Chilled Lemon Tartlets and English Cherry Pie. From America, Sally Darr's Delicious Chocolate Tile Cake and from my own restaurants, Mr Carrier's Chocolate Fancy and our yearly Christmas special, Bûche de Noël (Christmas Yule Log Cake).*

# American Strawberry Shortcake

*This is in the book because it reminds me of my childhood, and I must admit that is a year or two ago. Dad used to make it — it was his favourite pudding. And now that I stop and think about it, it's one of mine.*

*Don't serve it at a formal dinner party, though. It's more of a summer family sweet — to serve at a family supper when berries are at their best.*

*Serves 4 to 6*

## Shortcake Mixture

*225 g/8 oz flour*
*2 teaspoons baking powder*
*½ level teaspoon salt*
*2–4 tablespoons sugar*
*4 tablespoons softened butter*
*150 ml/5 fl oz milk*
*2 egg yolks, lightly beaten*

## Berry Mixture

*1 kg/2 lb fresh strawberries, sliced*
*Sugar*
*Lemon juice*
*Softened butter*

*300 ml/10 fl oz double cream*

## To make American Shortcake (a sort of soft scone mixture)

Sift flour with baking powder, salt and sugar. Work in softened butter with a fork. Add milk and eggs, little by little, stirring continuously, until mixture holds together but is still soft. Turn out on floured board. Roll out or pat into 4 rounds; place on a greased baking sheet and bake for 10 to 15 minutes in a hot oven (220°C, 425°F, Gas Mark 7) or until pale gold.

## To serve

Split warm shortcakes in half crossways. Place bottom halves, cut sides up, on serving platter and spread with softened butter. Spoon half the sliced berries (to which you have added sugar and lemon juice, to taste) over buttered shortcakes and top with other halves, cut sides down. Spoon on rest of sliced berries and whipped cream.

*The Sunday Times*

# Tulipe Glacé aux Fraises des Bois

*These delicate 'tulip' pastry cases – made of an American 'cookie' dough and filled with fruits and ice cream – are perhaps one of the most copied restaurant 'dessert menu' recipes I know since I first published René Lasserre's original version in my regular cookery column in The Sunday Times more than thirty years ago. Hats off, René . . . for a wonderful recipe.*

Serves 4 to 6

125 g/5 oz flour
125 g/5 oz icing sugar
2 egg yolks
3 egg whites
1 large orange, greased, to form
pastry shapes
French strawberries
Fresh wild strawberries
1 fresh pineapple, peeled, cored and diced
Kirsch
Vanilla ice cream
Double cream, whipped

Sift flour and icing sugar into a mixing bowl; add egg yolks and whites and mix well. Grease a cold baking sheet and make four circles on it with a large saucer or side plate. Spread 1 dessertspoon of mixture over each circle using back of teaspoon. Bake in a moderate oven (180°C, 350°F, Gas Mark 4) for 5 to 6 minutes, or until just turning brown at edges.

Remove each round from baking sheet; turn over and, working quickly, place each circle over top of greased orange. Place tea towel gently over pastry to prevent burning hands and mould pastry to fit orange. Remove and continue as above, baking two to four circles as you go.

### To serve

Fill four to six cases with strawberries, wild strawberries and diced fresh pineapple which you have marinated in Kirsch; add a scoop of vanilla ice cream and decorate with whipped cream and more berries.

This recipe makes 12 tulips. Cases will keep for days in a biscuit box.

*Great Dishes of the World*

# Gâteau Esternel

*Serves 6*

*1 tablespoon dried yeast*
*4 tablespoons lukewarm water*
*150 g/6 oz butter*
*Flour*
*4 eggs*
*225 g/8 oz caster sugar*
*Pinch of salt*
*8 tablespoons orange marmalade*
*225 g/8 oz plain chocolate*
*1 tablespoon Cointreau*

## Syrup

*200 ml/8 fl oz water*
*100 g/4 oz granulated sugar*
*3 tablespoons Cointreau*

Preheat oven to moderately hot (200°C, 400°F, Gas Mark 6).

### To prepare Cake

In a small bowl sprinkle yeast into lukewarm water. Wait 6 minutes then stir until dissolved.

Melt butter in the top of a double saucepan. Lightly grease a 21 cm (8 in) savarin mould with a little of the melted butter and dust out with flour.

In a small bowl whisk eggs and sugar until light and fluffy. Sift 225 g (8 oz) flour with salt and fold into egg and sugar mixture with a large metal spoon, followed by remaining melted butter and dissolved yeast mixture. Pour into prepared savarin mould and bake in preheated oven for 10 minutes.

Lower oven temperature to moderate (180°C, 350°F, Gas Mark 4) and cook cake for a further 25 minutes, or until golden brown. Unmould on to a wire rack and leave to cool.

### To make Syrup

In a small saucepan dissolve sugar in water over a low heat; bring to the boil and boil until temperature reaches 100°C (220°F), or about 10 minutes. Take off heat; flavour with Cointreau and leave to cool.

Cut cake in half and moisten both halves (cut sides) with syrup, reserving 3 tablespoons. Spread with orange marmalade and reform cake.

Melt chocolate in the top of a double saucepan; add reserved syrup and Cointreau, beating with a wooden spoon until smooth. Place cake on a serving platter; cover with chocolate mixture, using a palette knife to give a smooth finish, and serve.

*Robert Carrier's Kitchen*

# Gâteau Tropézienne

## Cake

*4 eggs*
*225 g/8 oz caster sugar*
*½ teaspoon vanilla essence*
*or grated rind of ½ lemon*
*75 g/3 oz flour*
*25 g/1 oz cornflour*
*100 g/4 oz butter*

## Almond Crumb Topping

*2 tablespoons softened butter*
*25 g/1 oz flour*
*100 g/4 oz sugar*
*½ teaspoon powdered cinnamon*
*100 g/4 oz chopped almonds*

## Crème Pâtissière

*5 egg yolks*
*225 g/8 oz sugar*
*3 level tablespoons cornflour*
*450 ml/15 fl oz warm milk*
*¼ teaspoon vanilla essence*

## Decoration

*Icing sugar*

### *To make Cake*

Combine eggs, sugar and vanilla essence or grated lemon rind and whisk mixture in the top of a double saucepan, over simmering water, until it is very light, thick and lukewarm. Transfer mixture to an electric mixer and beat at high speed for 3 to 5 minutes, or until mixture holds shape.

Sift the flour and cornflour and fold carefully into the mixture a little at a time until thoroughly blended. Melt butter in the top of a double saucepan, taking care that it does not bubble or separate; add it immediately to mixture and pour into a buttered and floured cake tin. Bake for 20 minutes in a moderate oven (180°C, 350°F, Gas Mark 3).

### *To make Almond Crumb Topping*

Combine softened butter, flour, sugar, powdered cinnamon and chopped almonds in a bowl and work together with your fingers to a crumbly mixture. Sprinkle topping thickly over cake and continue baking for about 25 minutes more.

## To make Crème Pâtissière

Beat egg yolks and sugar together until mixture is lemon-coloured. Mix in flour, then add milk and vanilla essence and mix thoroughly. Place mixture in top of a double saucepan and cook over simmering water, stirring constantly, until smooth and very thick; remove from heat, put through sieve and allow to cool.

*Note:* do not allow mixture to come to the boil or eggs will curdle.

## To assemble Gâteau

Allow cake to cool. Then turn out of tin. Slice into two layers; place bottom layer, cut side up, on a flat cake plate and spread with a thick layer of chilled Crème Pâtissière. Top with other layer and chill until time to serve. Sprinkle top of cake with a little sieved icing sugar just before serving.

*Daily Telegraph Magazine*

# Mr Carrier's Chocolate Fancy

*This round-domed creation covered in leaves of chocolate with curls of chocolate caraque was one of the first cakes I created when I first opened Carrier's restaurant in 1968. And it was one that reappeared on the menu time and time again during the eighteen years that I ran the restaurant. It was given its name 'because it was chocolate . . . and because Mr Carrier always fancied it'. I still do.*

*Butter and flour for the cake tin*
*150 g/6 oz softened butter*
*135 g/5½ oz caster sugar*
*150 g/6 oz chocolate, melted and cooled*
*6 egg yolks*
*8 egg whites*
*75 g/3 oz flour*
*Pinch of salt*
*25 g/1 oz cocoa powder*
*Icing sugar for dusting*

## Cream Filling

*450 ml/15 fl oz double cream*
*1 tablespoon caster sugar*
*2 drops vanilla essence*

# Apricot Glaze

*3 tablespoons apricot jam*
*1 tablespoon lemon juice*

# Decoration

*225 g/8 oz plain chocolate*
*1 tablespoon olive oil*

Preheat the oven to 150°C (300°F, Gas Mark 2). Cut a disc of greaseproof paper to fit a 21 cm (8 in) cake tin with a depth of 6 cm (2 ½ in). Lightly grease and flour the disc and cake tin.

## *To make Cake*

In a large bowl, cream the butter with a wooden spoon, gradually adding 75 g (3 oz) of the caster sugar and beat until the mixture is light and fluffy. Stir in the cooled, melted chocolate and beat in the egg yolks, one at a time. In a clean, dry bowl whisk the egg whites to soft peaks. Whisk in the remaining sugar 1 tablespoon at a time and whisk until the mixture becomes glossy and stands in soft peaks again.

Sift the flour, pinch of salt and the cocoa on to a sheet of greaseproof paper. With a large metal spoon fold one-third of the egg white mixture, alternately with one-third of the flour mixture, into the butter and chocolate mixture, until all the ingredients are incorporated; finally, give a light beating to blend, with a wooden spoon.

Spoon into the prepared cake tin and bake in the preheated oven for 1 to 1 ¼ hours, or until cooked. Test with a skewer, which should come out clean when inserted. Leave to cool in the cake tin for 5 minutes then run a sharp knife around the inside of the cake tin. Turn out on to a wire rack and leave to become quite cold. When cold, horizontally cut the cake into 3.

## *To prepare Filling*

In a bowl whisk the double cream with the caster sugar and vanilla essence to soft peaks.

## *To assemble Cake*

Place the bottom layer of the cake on a serving dish and spread evenly with half the sweetened cream. Place the second layer on top and repeat. Place the top layer in position; scrape away any cream that has oozed out of the cake.

## *To make Glaze*

In a small saucepan, combine the apricot jam and lemon juice and bring to the boil, stirring with a wooden spoon to blend. Brush to coat the cake.

## To decorate

In a bowl over a saucepan of simmering water, melt the chocolate with the olive oil, stirring occasionally with a wooden spoon. Pour immediately on to a marble slab or baking tray and with a palette knife work the chocolate until evenly spread and beginning to dry. With a long, thin-bladed sharp knife, using it at a right angle to the chocolate, shave off flat wafers about 5 cm (2 in) wide and the depth of the cake.

Use the remaining chocolate for caraque curls: holding the knife at a steeper angle, shave the chocolate off in long curls. With a palette knife, carefully arrange the wafered chocolate around the outside of the cake, overlapping the pieces slightly. Then lay the caraque on top to cover the cake in neat rows. Dredge with icing sugar and serve immediately.

*Robert Carrier's Kitchen*

# Chocolate 'Tile' Cake

*Sally Darr was a self-taught cook who, with her husband, insurance broker John Darr, ran one of New York's most enchanting restaurants. This is her cake. Not easy to do if you are a cake-baking beginner, but more than worth the trouble for a very special occasion when you want to pull out 'all the stops'.*

*Serves 14 to 16*

## Chocolate Cake

*150 g/6 oz semi-sweet chocolate
3 tablespoons strong coffee
5 large eggs, separated
110 g/4½ oz sugar
Pinch of salt*

## Ganache Cream

*375 g/13 oz semi-sweet chocolate
500 ml/18 fl oz double cream*

## Chocolate 'Tiles'

*150 g/6 oz semi-sweet chocolate
Unsweetened cocoa powder
Icing sugar*

Preheat oven to moderate (180°C, 350°F, Gas Mark 4).

## To make Chocolate Cake

Butter a 32 x 22 cm (13 x 9 in) Swiss roll tin and line with waxed paper, leaving a 5 cm (2 in) overhang on each end. Butter paper.

Melt chocolate with coffee in the top of a double saucepan over hot water.

Stir occasionally. Leave to cool. Beat egg yolks until smooth. Gradually add sugar, beating constantly until mixture is very pale and forms a ribbon when whisk is raised. Stir in chocolate mixture.

In a clean bowl, and with a clean whisk, beat together egg whites and salt until stiff peaks form. Stir about one-quarter of egg whites in chocolate mixture, then gently fold this into remaining egg whites. Pour cake mixture into prepared tin, spreading evenly, and bake in centre of preheated oven for 14 minutes, or until puffed and just beginning to pull away from sides of tin. Leave to cool for at least 1 hour.

## To make Ganache Cream

Lower oven to slow (170°C, 325°F, Gas Mark 3). Place semi-sweet chocolate in a single layer in a deep baking tin and leave in oven until chocolate just melts. While chocolate is melting, heat double cream until hot, but not simmering. Pour hot double cream on to melted chocolate little by little, working and stirring mixture with a rubber spatula until smooth and shiny. Transfer mixture to a bowl, straining if necessary, to remove lumps, and leave, covered, until mixture reaches room temperature, stirring occasionally to keep smooth. Chill Ganache Cream, the bowl and beaters of an electric mixer for 1 hour.

## To make Chocolate 'Tiles'

Place a 37 cm (15 in) length of waxed paper down centre of a baking sheet, securing each end with a dab of softened butter. Place semi-sweet chocolate in a single layer in another baking tin and leave in slow oven until chocolate just melts. Stir and pour on to lined baking sheet, spreading evenly over length of baking sheet to about 22 cm (9 in) wide. (It should be about 3 mm/ ⅛ in thick.) Chill for at least 1 hour. Remove from refrigerator and leave at room temperature for 5 minutes before cutting.

Using a ruler and a knife, carefully cut chocolate lengthways into two 7 cm (2 ½ in) wide strips with one 8 cm (3 in) wide strip in the middle, being careful not to cut through waxed paper. Then cut strips at right angles into 2 cm (¾ in) sections to make 'tiles'. Chill until needed.

## To assemble Cake

Over top, sift a light coating of unsweetened cocoa powder. Cover cake in its tin with a sheet of waxed paper and a baking sheet and invert cake onto them. Remove Swiss roll tin and waxed paper from cake. Slip out baking sheet. Trim edges of cake. Divide cake lengthways into 3 equal strips. Using 2 wide metal spatulas, transfer 1 cake strip to baking sheet; separate other 2 strips by pushing them several inches apart.

Remove Ganache Cream, bowl and beaters from refrigerator. Transfer 450 ml (15 fl oz) of Ganache Cream to chilled bowl, returning remainder to refrigerator. Beat until soft swirls form. Do not overbeat or cream will harden. Spread half of the beaten cream evenly on cake strip on baking sheet, and top with a second cake strip. Spread remaining beaten cream evenly over second layer and top with final strip. Smooth sides and trim rough edges. Chill for 30 minutes.

Chill another bowl and beaters. Beat remaining Ganache Cream in chilled bowl as before. Do not overbeat. Remove cake from refrigerator. Spread beaten cream evenly over top and sides. Remove chocolate 'tiles' from refrigerator. Measure height of cake and if it is less than 7 cm (2½ in), trim the 7 cm (2½ in) wide strips of 'tiles' to fit height of cake. Using a sharp knife, cut through waxed paper lengthways to separate 3 strips of 'tiles'. Put an 8 cm (3 in) wide strip of 'tiles' on to top of cake, leaving waxed paper on top. Place 2 remaining strips along sides of cake, aligning side 'tiles' with those on top so a knife can later pass between 'tiles' for easy cutting. Cover top and sides of cake tightly with aluminium foil. Press gently so that 'tiles' will adhere to Ganache Cream. Put cake in freezer for 1 hour.

## To serve

Remove cake from freezer and remove foil. Trim ends of cake with a knife dipped in hot water. To release cake from baking sheet, draw a taut string carefully under cake. Tip cake on its side; place a long serving dish against bottom and turn cake upright. Peel off top and side strips of waxed paper, taking care to leave 'tiles' in proper alignment. To create a pattern on top of cake, place 2 strips of foil diagonally over top of cake, sift over icing sugar, then lift off foil.

*Note:* make this delicious gâteau on the day you serve it. Otherwise cake may subside and Ganache thicken.

*Sunday Express Magazine*

# Vacherin à l'Orange

*Vacherin à l'Orange is an unusual and sophisticated dessert. The piquancy of the lemon and orange flavouring contrasts superbly with the sweetness of the meringue.*

*Serves 6 to 8*

## Meringue

*5 egg whites*
*250 g/10 oz caster sugar*
*Grated rind of 1 orange*

## Filling

*50 g/2 oz unsalted butter*
*250 g/10 oz icing sugar*
*2 egg yolks*
*4 drops orange food colouring*
*2 tablespoons lemon juice*
*Grated rind of 1 orange*
*2 tablespoons orange-flavoured liqueur (optional)*
*2 tablespoons double cream*
*4 oranges, peeled, white pith removed and thinly sliced*

Preheat the oven to cool 160°C (300°F, Gas Mark 2). With a pencil, draw a 23 cm (9 in) circle (use a plate as a guide) on a piece of non-stick silicone paper. Place the paper on a baking sheet. Set aside.

### To make Meringue

In a large mixing bowl, beat egg whites with a wire whisk, or rotary beater until they form stiff peaks. Beat in 50 g (2 oz) of the sugar and continue beating for 1 minute or until the mixture is very stiff and glossy. (You should be able to turn the bowl upside-down without the mixture falling out.) Using a metal spoon fold in the remaining sugar and the grated orange rind.

Spread one-third of the mixture on to the circle of paper to make a layer about 6 mm (¼ in) thick. Fill a large forcing bag, fitted with a 2.5 cm (1 in) star nozzle, with the remaining mixture and pipe it around the edge of the circle in decorative swirls, to form a case. Place baking sheet in preheated oven and bake the meringue for 1 hour. Turn off the oven and leave the meringue in the oven for a further 10 to 15 minutes, or until it is crisp on the outside but still soft in the centre.

Remove the baking sheet from the oven and leave the meringue to cool completely. When it is cold, lift it off the baking sheet carefully and discard the paper from the bottom. Set aside.

### *To make Filling*

In a medium-sized mixing bowl, beat the butter until it is soft and creamy. Sift in the icing sugar bit by bit and cream it with the butter until the mixture is thoroughly blended. Add the egg yolks and beat well. Combine orange food colouring with lemon juice, grated orange rind and liqueur if you are using it, and add to egg yolk mixture. Beat until mixture is well blended, then beat in double cream.

### *To serve*

Spoon the mixture into the meringue case, smoothing it with the back of the spoon. Arrange thin orange slices on top and serve the Vacherin immediately.

*Robert Carrier's Kitchen*

# French Walnut Roll

*Oil for baking tin*
*2 tablespoons plain flour*
*Pinch of salt*
*½ teaspoon baking powder*
*100 g/4 oz walnuts*
*6 eggs, separated*
*100 g/4 oz caster sugar*
*Sifted icing sugar, to decorate*

## Filling

*150 ml/5 fl oz double cream*
*75–100 g/3–4 oz caster sugar*

Select a Swiss roll tin measuring 23 cm x 35 cm (9 x 14 in) and brush bottom and sides lightly with oil; line tin with greaseproof paper, and oil the paper lightly as well. Preheat oven to moderate 180°C (350°F, Gas Mark 4).

### *To make Cake*

Sift flour, salt and baking powder into a small bowl. Grind walnuts coarsely in a small mouli (nuts must not be ground too finely, or they will release too much oil and make the cake heavy). Whisk egg yolks with 100 g (4 oz) sugar over hot water until mixture leaves a trail on the surface when beaters are lifted. Remove bowl from heat and continue whisking until cool. Fold in ground walnuts with a metal spoon.

Whisk egg whites until stiff but not dry (wash and dry your whisk carefully so that no trace of the egg yolk mixture remains). Fold into walnut mixture gently but thoroughly. Finally, fold in sifted flour mixture. Pour batter into prepared tin and level it off with a spatula.

Bake for 20 to 25 minutes, or until well risen and springy to the touch.

While cake is in the oven, prepare a surface

for rolling it: lay a damp cloth on the table; cover with a sheet of greaseproof paper and sprinkle with 1 teaspoon caster sugar. Turn cake out on to sugared paper and carefully peel off lining. Lay a fresh sheet of greaseproof paper in its place and carefully roll cake up together with paper and cloth, starting at one of the longer sides. Leave to cool.

### To make Filling

When roll is cool, whip cream until it forms soft peaks and sweeten to taste with caster sugar.

### To assemble Walnut Roll

Carefully unroll cake and remove top paper. Spread cake evenly with whipped cream and roll it up again, this time without the aid of the cloth and paper underneath. Lay on a long, flat serving dish, seam side down, and dust liberally with sifted icing sugar.

*Note:* do not fill roll too far in advance. If icing sugar begins to dissolve, dust again just before serving.

*Entertaining*

# Bûche de Noël

*As far as I am concerned, every Christmas party must have its Bûche de Noël (a Christmas Yule Log cake, covered with chocolate icing 'wood-bark' and 'mushrooms'). This rich buttercream-filled sponge roll has always spelled Christmas for me ever since I first lived in Paris aged twenty-two . . . all those years ago.*

*Serves 8*

*Butter*
*Flour*
*3 eggs*
*75 g/3 oz granulated sugar*
*10 g/½ oz cocoa powder*
*3 tablespoons apricot jam*
*1 tablespoon Kirsch*
*2–3 tablespoons powdered coffee, or chocolate*
*Angelica leaves*
*Glacé cherries*

## Vanilla Butter Icing

*150 g/6 oz softened butter*
*¾ teaspoon vanilla essence*
*1½ tablespoons Grand Marnier*
*350 g/12 oz icing sugar, sifted*

# Chocolate Butter Icing

*225 g/8 oz unsweetened chocolate*
*350 g/12 oz icing sugar, sifted*
*150 g/6 oz softened butter*

Preheat oven to moderate (180°C, 350°F. Gas Mark 4). Butter a Swiss roll tin measuring 15 x 22 cm (6 x 8½ in) and line with greaseproof paper. Lightly butter and flour paper. Take the bowl in which you intend to whisk up the cake and select a large saucepan over which it will fit firmly. Pour 5 cm (2 in) water into pan and bring to the boil. Reduce heat.

## To make Cake

Combine eggs and granulated sugar in the selected bowl. Set over barely simmering water and whisk until very thick, light and lukewarm (10 minutes if using an electric blender at high speed). Remove bowl from heat, stand it on a cool surface and continue to whisk until mixture leaves a distinct trail on the surface when beaters are lifted and mixture has cooled (5 minutes if using an electric blender at high speed).

Sift 60 g (2½ oz) flour and the cocoa powder 3 times and fold lightly but thoroughly into mixture with a large metal spoon. Pour batter into prepared tin and bake in preheated oven for 25 minutes, or until

surface springs back when gently pressed with your fingertip. Lay a damp cloth on a table; cover with a sheet of greaseproof paper and turn cake out on to paper; carefully peel off lining paper. Trim edges. Lay a fresh sheet of greaseproof paper in its place and carefully roll cake up together with paper and cloth, starting at one of the short sides. Leave cake to cool.

## To make Vanilla Butter Icing

Cream softened butter, vanilla essence and Grand Marnier with an electric mixer. Gradually beat in sifted icing sugar until smooth.

## To make Chocolate Butter Icing

Melt unsweetened chocolate in the top of a double saucepan; add sifted icing sugar and mix with an electric mixer. Add softened butter a little at a time, whisking until smooth. Continue whisking until thick enough to spread.

*Note:* if the icings are too soft to pipe, allow to harden a little in your refrigerator.

## To assemble Bûche de Noël

Unroll cake; remove greaseproof paper and spread with Vanilla Butter Icing. Roll up cake

wrapped in clingfilm and chill until icing becomes firm.

When ready to decorate cake remove clingfilm. Cut off a thin slice at one end diagonally and trim slice to an approximate circle.

Heat apricot jam and Kirsch until runny. Brush both ends of cake with this apricot glaze. Ice cake generously with Chocolate Butter Icing, using a pastry bag with a flattened notched nozzle, running strips of icing along cake to look like bark. Ice outside of branch (the cut slice of cake) with chocolate icing. Ice both ends of cake with Vanilla Butter Icing; then top of sawn-off branch. Smooth these with a spatula dipped in hot water and, using a No. 2 nozzle, decorate white parts with thinly piped rings of chocolate.

Dust bark with a little powdered coffee, or chocolate, and decorate with angelica leaves and glacé cherries. Store cake in a cool place until ready to serve.

*Carrier's*

# Rum Baba

*King Stanislas of Poland, father-in-law of Louis XV of France, Duke of Lorraine and Bar, was an ardent cook. Among the many creations credited to this noble cuisinier is that of the Baba au Rhum, one of the world's most delicious sweets. History tells us that Stanislas dunked his favourite kugelhof in a rum-flavoured syrup and declared the result a triumph! Later generations of cooks added a scattering of raisins to the dough, and the Baba as we know it today was born. Based on a savarin recipe (see below) the Rum Baba is a featherlight concoction of flour, sugar and eggs made airy with powdered or granulated yeast, and moistened with syrup and with rum.*

*Serves 8*

## Savarin

*90 ml/3 fl oz milk*
*25 g/1 oz fresh yeast*
*50 g/2 oz sugar*
*25 g/1 oz softened butter*
*2 eggs, beaten*
*225 g/8 oz strong flour*
*3 egg yolks*
*Butter for greasing*
*150 ml/5 fl oz double cream, whipped*

## Syrup

*225 g/8 oz sugar*
*3 tablespoons brandy*
*3 tablespoons Cointreau*
*150 ml/5 fl oz dark rum*

## Glaze

*6–8 tablespoons apricot jam*
*1 tablespoon lemon juice*

## Filling

*1 banana, sliced*
*2 oranges, peeled and segmented*
*2 kiwis, peeled and sliced*
*10 strawberries, hulled*
*10 white grapes, seeded*
*10 black grapes, seeded*

### To make Savarin Dough

Warm the milk slightly and dissolve the yeast in it. Add the sugar, softened butter, the beaten eggs and sift in the flour. Mix well with one hand then add the egg yolks and mix well again to a soft dough. Cover with clingfilm and leave in a warm place to rise until doubled in size.

In the bowl, knead the Savarin Dough until it has returned to its original volume.

Butter a 1.6 l (2¾ pint) savarin mould and fill with dough, to about one-third full.

Cover with clingfilm and leave in a warm place to rise until the dough has filled the mould. Meanwhile, preheat the oven to 170°C (325°F, Gas Mark 3). Bake in the preheated oven for 30 to 40 minutes, or until golden brown. Remove from the oven, allow to cool for 5 minutes in the tin then turn out on a wire rack.

### To make Syrup

Put the sugar in a saucepan with 300 ml (10 fl oz) water, stir over gentle heat until the sugar is dissolved, then bring to the boil and boil for 5 minutes. Remove from the heat and add the brandy and Cointreau.

### To prepare Savarin

Place the warm Savarin on a flat serving dish and prick all over with a fork. Spoon three-quarters of the warm syrup evenly over the Savarin, pour over rum, and leave to soak for 2 to 3 hours. Let the remaining syrup cool. Put the prepared fruit in a bowl and pour over the reserved cold syrup. Leave to marinate.

### To make Glaze

Combine the apricot jam with 2 tablespoons water and the lemon juice in a saucepan and heat until the jam is melted. Bring to the boil

and sieve to remove any lumps from the jam. Brush the glaze evenly over the Savarin.

### To serve

Spoon the marinated fruits into the centre of the Savarin. Pipe 8 rosettes of whipped cream round the top of the Savarin and the remaining cream in a scroll round the base.

*Great Dishes of the World*

# Profiteroles with Chocolate Sauce

*Serves 4*

*60 g/2½ oz flour*
*50 g/2 oz butter, diced*
*1 teaspoon sugar*
*2 eggs, beaten*
*Few drops of vanilla essence*
*Crème St Honoré (see below)*

## Chocolate Sauce

*75 g/3 oz unsweetened chocolate*
*2 teaspoons cocoa powder*
*4 tablespoons sugar*
*¼ teaspoon vanilla essence*
*2 egg yolks*

Heat the oven to 220°C (425°F, Gas Mark 7).

Sift the flour on to a sheet of greaseproof paper. Put the diced butter and sugar in a small heavy saucepan, with 150 ml (5 fl oz) water. Bring to the boil slowly. When the liquid boils briskly, remove the pan from the heat. Quickly pour in the flour all at once and beat vigorously with a wooden spoon. Return the pan to a low heat and continue to beat the paste for about 2 minutes until it forms itself around the spoon into a smooth ball, leaving the bottom and sides of the pan clean. Remove from heat.

Add the beaten eggs a little at a time, beating vigorously. Continue to beat until the paste is glossy. Beat in a few drops of vanilla essence. Stand a piping bag fitted with an éclair nozzle in a tall tumbler and fold back the bag top; like this the bag is easy to fill with choux paste. Pipe walnut-sized profiteroles on to a greased baking sheet, allowing plenty of space between each one.

Bake in the oven for 10 minutes. Remove the tray from the oven and reduce the heat to 190°C (375°, Gas Mark 5). Pierce each profiterole in the side with a knife, return them to the oven and bake for a further 10 minutes or until firm and dry. Leave to cool on a wire rack.

### To make Chocolate Sauce

Break the chocolate into a saucepan; blend the cocoa powder with 2 tablespoons water taken from a measured 300 ml (10 fl oz) and add it to the chocolate with the sugar and the rest of the water. Bring to the boil, stirring until well blended. Boil for 15 minutes until syrupy. Remove from the heat and leave to cool slightly. Whisk in the vanilla essence and egg yolks. Chill.

### To serve

Split the profiteroles in half. Pipe the cream into them. Arrange on top of each other in a glass bowl and pour some of the Chocolate Sauce over top. Serve the remaining sauce separately. Serve immediately.

*Robert Carrier's Kitchen*

# Crème Saint Honoré

*This orange-flavoured egg-rich cream – the raison d'être of Gâteau St Honoré – is also used to fill choux pastry and, of course, profiteroles.*

*Serves 4*

*1 strip thinly pared orange zest*
*300 ml/10 fl oz milk*
*4 egg yolks*

*100 g/4 oz sugar*
*25 g/1 oz flour*
*2 teaspoons powdered gelatine, softened in*
*3 tablespoons water*
*½–1 teaspoon vanilla essence*

In a small saucepan, combine milk and orange zest and bring to the boil. Remove from heat.

In a mixing bowl, over hot but not quite simmering water, beat egg yolks until thick and pale in colour. Gradually beat in the sugar and continue beating until the mixture is thick enough to form a ribbon trail when the spoon is lifted.

Discard the zest, then gradually pour the milk on to the egg yolk mixture, beating constantly. Beat in the flour. Strain mixture into a saucepan.

Place the pan over a moderate heat and cook, stirring constantly with a wooden spoon for 2 to 3 minutes, or until the custard thickens enough to coat the back of the spoon. Remove from the heat and stir in the softened gelatine until gelatine is completely dissolved into the sauce. Then stir in vanilla essence, to taste. Cool. In another bowl, and with a clean whisk, whisk egg white until stiff peaks form. Fold carefully into the Crème St Honoré. Pipe into profiteroles.

*Note:* for an easier filling, use whipped cream flavoured with Kirsch, or even more simply, softened vanilla or chocolate ice cream.

*Robert Carrier's Kitchen*

# Provençal Apple Tart

*Thin rounds of flaky pastry (bought, of course) topped with sliced apples, sprinkled with sugar and grated orange rind and dotted with softened butter just before baking, is simple cooking at its best.*

*Serves 4*

*225 g/8 oz flaky pastry*
*4 large tart eating apples*
*225 g/8 oz sugar*
*4 pinches finely grated orange rind*
*4 teaspoons butter*
*Flour for rolling*

On a lightly floured board, roll out the pastry as thin as possible. Cut out four 18 cm (7 in) pastry circles and place them on baking sheets. Prick the pastry and leave in the refrigerator for 30 minutes. Meanwhile, preheat the oven to 220°C (425°F, Gas Mark 7).

Peel and core the apples and slice them very thinly (less than 3 mm/⅛ in). Place overlapping slices on the pastry circles. Sprinkle with sugar and dot each tart with a teaspoon of butter. Cook in the preheated oven for 15 to 20 minutes, or until the pastry is cooked. Serve immediately on individual flat plates.

*Feasts of Provence*

# Chilled Lemon Tartlets

*Tart is just the word for custard-filled lemon tartlets . . . when the custard mixture is flavoured with lemon juice, dry white wine and grated lemon rind. Chilled to perfection.*

*Serves 4*

*225 g/8 oz sweet shortcrust pastry*
*150 ml/5 fl oz milk*
*50 g/2 oz sugar*
*2 egg yolks*
*1½ teaspoons gelatine*
*60 ml/2 fl oz lemon juice*
*30 ml/1 fl oz dry white wine*
*Grated rind of ½ lemon*
*150 ml/5 fl oz double cream*
*1 egg white*

## Decoration

*1 lime*
*1 egg white*
*caster sugar*

### To cook Pastry

Roll out the pastry and use to line 4 individual tartlet tins, 7.5 cm (3 in) in diameter and 2.5 cm (1 in) deep. Blind bake until fully cooked. Cool.

## To prepare Decoration

Thinly pare the rind from the lime and cut it into fine *julienne* strips. Blanch the rind in boiling water for 5 minutes, or until soft and curled. Drain on absorbent paper. When dry, dip in egg white and coat with caster sugar. Leave to dry.

## To make Filling

In a saucepan, heat the milk and 25 g (1 oz) sugar until the sugar has dissolved; bring just to boiling point then remove from the heat. In a bowl, whisk the egg yolks with the remaining sugar until the mixture leaves a ribbon trail when the beaters are lifted. Gradually pour in the scalded milk, whisking constantly, and return the mixture to the saucepan. Heat slowly, stirring constantly with a wooden spoon, until the custard is thick enough to coat the back of the spoon. Leave to cool.

In a small bowl, sprinkle with gelatine over 1½ tablespoons cold water and leave to soften. Put the bowl in a saucepan of hot water and leave until the gelatine has dissolved and the liquid is clear. Leave to cool slightly.

Stir the cooled gelatine into the cooled custard together with the lemon juice, dry white wine and grated lemon rind. Place over a bowl of ice and stir until the mixture is on the point of setting. In a bowl, whip the double cream to soft peaks. With a large metal spoon, fold it into the custard mixture.

## To assemble Tartlets

Brush the pastry case with egg white, then pour in the cream mixture. Leave to set in the refrigerator. When the lemon cream has set, place a bunch of the sugared rind in the centre of each tartlet.

*Robert Carrier's Kitchen*

# Pears in Pastry Sabayon

*Pears poached in apricot-flavoured syrup, encased in a 'cage' of special pastry, and baked until the pastry is crisp and golden, is a highly decorative fruit pastry pudding. Serve with a Marsala- and cognac-flavoured Sabayon Sauce.*

*Serves 6*

*6 pears*
*150 ml/5 fl oz syrup (100 g/4 oz each sugar and water)*
*450 ml/15 fl oz apricot jam*

## Pastry

*250 g/9 oz plain flour*
*1 level teaspoon salt*
*50 g/2 oz lard*
*100 g/4 oz softened butter*
*Water to mix*

## Sabayon Sauce

*4 egg yolks*
*100 g/4 oz sugar*
*6 fl oz Marsala*
*1 tablespoon cognac*

### To prepare Pastry

Sift flour and salt together; rub in lard and half the amount of butter until mixture resembles fine breadcrumbs. Add sufficient water to form into a ball which will just hold together; knead firmly but quickly until smooth. Allow to rest in a cool place for 15 minutes. Roll out into an oblong and spread remaining butter over surface. Fold in half, seal edges, rest for 5 minutes and roll out to 3 mm (⅛ in) thickness. Cut 6 pastry rounds large enough for pears to sit upon and cut remainder of pastry into thin strips.

### To cook Pears

Poach pears in syrup and apricot jam; cool and place 1 pear on each pastry round.

### To make 'Cage' of Pastry Strips

For each pear, cross 2 strips at right angles; seal well with water and place cross at top of each pear. Snip strips at base and seal well

with water. Place pears in pastry on baking sheet and bake in a moderately hot to hot oven (200-230°C, 400–450°F, Gas Mark 6–7) for 20 minutes, or until pastry is golden. Remove and brush with reduced glaze. Serve with cream or Sabayon Sauce.

### To make Sabayon Sauce

Beat egg yolks and sugar until yellow and frothy in the top of a double saucepan. Add the Marsala; place over hot water and cook, stirring constantly, until thick and foamy. Stir in cognac and chill.

*The Sunday Times*

# French Pear Tart

*One of the most famous French pear and custard tarts is called Poires Bourdaloue, named after, it seems, a famous French doctor of the late nineteenth century. My version of this famous sweet slices the poached pear halves horizontally almost through to the base of each pear. Then the halves are set on the custard cream and the tart is baked, until the custard is set. Outstanding . . . the pears, I mean.*

*Serves 4*

*150 g/6 oz sweet shortcrust pastry*
*100 g/4 oz granulated sugar*

*3 small, round ripe dessert pears*
*2 tablespoons brandy*
*175 ml/7 fl oz double cream*
*50 g/2 oz caster sugar*
*1 tablespoon cornflour*
*1 tablespoon lemon juice*
*1 egg, separated*
*3 tablespoons apricot jam (optional)*

Roll out the pastry and use it to line a 18 cm (7 in) tart tin. Part-bake the pastry case and leave to cool.

Combine the granulated sugar and 900 ml (1½ pints) water in a saucepan. Heat gently, stirring, until the sugar is dissolved then bring to the boil and let it simmer gently while you prepare the pears.

Peel the pears and cut them in half lengthways. With a teaspoon, scoop out the central core and seeds; then take a small sharp knife and make a V-shaped incision to remove the fibres leading from the core to the stem.

As soon as the pears are ready, lower them into the simmering syrup and poach them gently until very soft but not disintegrating. This will take 5 to 10 minutes, according to the ripeness of the pears. Lift the pears out of the syrup with a slotted spoon, draining them thoroughly, and put them into a bowl. Pour over the brandy and leave them to soak in it as they cool. Preheat the oven to 160°C (300°F, Gas Mark 2).

## To make Sauce

In a saucepan, gently heat the double cream and 25 g (1 oz) caster sugar. In a small bowl, blend the cornflour with the lemon juice to a smooth paste. Pour a few tablespoons of the warmed cream on to the cornflour and add it to the remaining warm cream. Bring to a boil and simmer gently for 3 minutes, or until thickened, stirring constantly. Remove from the heat.

In a small bowl, lightly beat the egg yolk. Stir it into the warm cream. Pour off the brandy syrup from the pears and add it to the custard cream. Drain the pears of any remaining syrup on absorbent paper, and slice them thinly. Brush the pastry case with egg white and pour in the custard. Arrange the pears in an overlapping circle to cover the entire surface. Sprinkle with the remaining caster sugar and cook in the preheated oven for 30 minutes or until the custard is set.

Serve lukewarm or cold. If serving cold, the pears can be coated with a very thin apricot glaze.

## To make Glaze

Sieve the apricot jam into a saucepan, add 1 tablespoon water and heat gently until melted. Brush carefully over the pears.

*Robert Carrier's Kitchen*

# English Cherry Pie

*Serves 4*

*250 g/10 oz cherries*
*6 tablespoons caster sugar*
*1 tablespoon flour*
*1½ tablespoons butter*
*1 tablespoon Kirsch*
*225 g/8 oz shortcrust pastry*
*1 egg yolk*

Preheat the oven to 200°C (400°F, Gas Mark 6).

## To prepare Filling

Wash the cherries and remove the stalks and stones. Put them into a small, heavy saucepan, add 4 tablespoons caster sugar and 100 ml (4 fl oz) water. Cook over a low heat for 10 to 15 minutes, until the fruit is very soft. Drain the cherries and put to one side. Make the cherry juice up to 150 ml (5 fl oz) with water.

Put 2 tablespoons caster sugar and the flour in a small saucepan, blend with a little of the cherry juice and mix to a smooth paste, then add the remaining juice. Cook over a low flame for 2 to 3 minutes to thicken it, stirring with a wooden spoon. Add the butter and flavour with Kirsch; leave to cool.

## To assemble Pie

Roll out two-thirds of the pastry and use it to line a 21 cm (8 in) flat tin. Place the drained cherries in the pastry case, and pour over the sauce. Roll out the remaining pastry to cover the pie, sealing the edges with a little egg yolk. Using a pastry brush, glaze the top of the pie with egg yolk. Bake the pie in the preheated oven for 10 minutes. Reduce the temperature to 180°C (350°F, Gas Mark 4), and bake for a further 20 to 25 minutes, or until lightly browned. Leave the pie to cool then turn it out onto a serving platter.

*The Robert Carrier Seminar of Cooking*

# Timbale of Glazed Fruit

*Serves 4*

*1 large baked brioche (1 day old)*
*300 ml/10 fl oz apricot jam*
*2–4 tablespoons Kirsch*
*Juice of 1 lemon*
*25 g/1 oz diced mixed peel*
*1–50 g/2 oz split almonds*
*1 ripe pear, peeled and diced*
*12–18 ripe strawberries*
*24–30 raspberries*
*100–150 g/4–6 oz seedless white grapes*
*1 (225 g/8 oz ) can pineapple chunks*
*Whipped cream*

### To make Timbale

Cut off the top of brioche and reserve lid. Then, with a sharp knife, cut around the inside of the brioche 12 mm (½ in) from outside crust and 2.5 cm (1 in) from the bottom. Pass the knife round once or twice to make sure that the inside is free from the crust. Then insert the knife through the crust 2.5 cm (1 in) from the bottom of the brioche and move it gently from right to left to sever the centre, making the hole as small as possible. Lift out the soft centre part, leaving a case or crust of brioche.

### To glaze Timbale

Heat apricot jam with 2 to 4 tablespoons of Kirsch in a saucepan. Pour through a nylon sieve into a clean pan, bring quickly to the boil and add the lemon juice. Brush the brioche case and cover both inside and outside with the syrup to glaze it well. Combine the mixed peel and split almonds and coat the case and lid.

### To prepare Fruits for Filling

In a bowl combine diced pear, strawberries, raspberries, grapes and pineapple chunks, and add remaining apricot glaze.

Just before serving: fill glazed brioche with fruit. Brioche should look well filled and almost overflowing with fruits. Replace the lid and serve immediately with whipped cream.

*Robert Carrier's Kitchen*

# Acknowledgments

*Recipes in this book were originally published in the books and magazines listed in italic at the end of each recipe. Others were premièred at Robert Carrier's restaurants, in his television series or in his cookery courses.*

– Carrier's
– Hintlesham Hall
– The Robert Carrier Seminar of Cooking
– W. H. Allen: publishers of *The Robert Carrier Cookery Course*, 1974.
– Sidgwick & Jackson: publishers of *Entertaining*, 1977; *Food, Wine & Friends*, 1986.
– Book Club Associates: publishers of *Robert Carrier's Kitchen Cookbook*, 1987.
– Boxtree: publishers of *The Vegetarian Gourmet*, 1994.
– Century Hutchinson: publishers of *Taste of Morocco*, 1987.
– Hamlyn: publishers of *Cooking for You*, 1973; *Quick Cook*, 1983; *A Million Menus*, 1984.
– Marshall Cavendish: publishers of *Robert Carrier's Kitchen*, 1980–1 and *Great Dishes of the World*, new ed. 1982
– Thomas Nelson: publishers of *The Robert Carrier Cookbook*, 1965; and *Robert Carrier Cookery Cards*.

– Weidenfeld & Nicolson: publishers of *Feasts of Provence*, 1992.
– *Daily Mirror*
– *Daily Telegraph*
– *Daily Telegraph Magazine*
– *Entertaining*
– *Harper's Bazaar*
– *Homes & Gardens*
– *Sunday Express Magazine*
– *The Sunday Times*
– *Taste*
– *Vogue*
– *Woman's Own*

Thanks to all the chefs, my friends, who have been so generous with their recipes: Sally Darr, Georgette Descats, Fifine, Georges Garin, Denys Gentes, Fredy Girardet, Vernon Jarratt, René Lasserre, Alain Senderens, Albert Stockli, Raymond Oliver, Rolf Widner and Barry Wine.

# Index

Aïoli Fifine, 84-5
Aïoli Sauce, 84-5
Alain Senderens' Rognons de Veau aux Echalotes Rôties, 132-4
Almonds:
  Fingers of Turbot Amandine, 66-7
  Gâteau Tropézienne, 261-2
  German Veal with, 125
  Tagine of Beef with Prunes and Almonds, 114
  Trout with Almonds (*Truite Amandine*), 77
American Planked Steak, 97
American Strawberry Shortcake, 258
Anchovies:
  Egg and Anchovy Barrels, 39
Apples:
  Duck with Sauerkraut and Apple Stuffing, 186-7
  Little Green, 232
  Magret de Canard au Cassis, 184-5
  Green, with Pheasant, 200
  Provençal Tart, 274
Arancini (Little Rice Balls), 64
Argentinian Pumpkin Soup, 16-7
Aromatic Stuffing, 168-70
Artichokes:
  Hearts à la Grecque, 30
  in White Wine with Coriander, 27
  Carciofi alla Romana, 27-8
  Fonds d'Artichauts au Foie Gras, 26-7
  aux Foies de Volaille, 40-1
Asparagus:
  Fresh Asparagus Hollandaise, 23-4
  Sole Soufflés with, 75
Aspic:
  Cold Duck with Orange Jelly, 189-90
  Fish, 72-4
  Fruits de Mer in, 35-6
Aubergines:
  Fredy Girardet's Charlottes d'Aubergines et de Courgettes aux Foies de Volaille, 40-1
Avocado:
  Calf's Liver with Sage and, 130
  Saffron Rice with, 59
  Tossed Green Salad with, 223

Bacon:
  Baked English Trout with, 78
Baked English Trout with Bacon, 78
Baked Fish Spanish Style, 83
Barry Wine's Hot Chocolate Soufflé with Coffee Ice Cream, 250
Barry Wine's Marinated Chicken, 172-3
Basic Chicken Velouté, 182
Basic Fish Velouté, 182
Basic Velouté, 182
Batterfried Scallops, Prawns and Vegetables, 91
Bauernschmaus, 159

Beans:
  Green Bean Salad, 229
  Haricots Blancs en Salade, 25-6
  Haricots Verts en Persillade, 210
  Pasta e Fagioli, 56-7
  Green, Persillade of, 17
  Zuppa di Fagioli, 15
Béarnaise Sauce, 42-3
Beef:
  American Planked Steak, 97
  Steak and Kidney Pudding, 110-1
  with 'Pappardelle' and Orange Gremolata, 121-2
  Boeuf à la Bourguignonne, 117-8
  Boeuf à la Ficelle, 105-6
  Carbonnade of Beef, 111
  Châteaubriand, 100-2
  Chile Con Carne, 118-9
  Corned Beef Hash with Poached Eggs, 109
  Fillet of, en Cochonailles, 108-9
  Flemish Carbonnade, 113-14
  Glazed Fillet of, with Soy, 106-7
  Grilled Steaks with Roquefort Butter, 96
  Japanese, with Fresh Ginger, 115
  Lasagne Bolognese, 54-6
  Minute Sauté of, with Burgundy Garnish, 115-7
  No-Roast Roast, 102-3
  Old English Roast, with Yorkshire Pudding, 103-5
  Porterhouse Steak with Pizzaiola Sauce, 98
  Potted Tournedoes, 105
  Roast Fillet of, 107-8
  Spaghetti with Meat Balls, 50-1
  Steak au Tapis Vert, 99
  Tagine of, with Prunes and Almonds, 114
  Tournedos with Corncakes, 99-100
  Yankee Pot Roast, 119-20
Beef Steak and Kidney Pudding, 110-1
Beef with 'Pappardelle' and Orange Gremolata, 121-2
Beer:
  Cod in Beer Batter, 69-70
Blanquette de Veau, 134-5
Boeuf à la Bourguignonne, 117-8
Boeuf à la Ficelle, 105-6
Boiled Chicken and Rice, 176-7
Bread and Butter Pudding à l'Orange, 245-6
Breadcrumb Browned Brussels Sprouts au Gratin, 205
Broccoli:
  Little Broccoli Towers, 207
Brochette de Moules, 42-3
Brussels Sprouts:
  à la Polonaise, 204
  Breadcrumb Browned, au Gratin, 205
  with Buttered Breadcrumbs, 205
Bûche de Noël, 269-71
Burgundy (Bourguignonne) Sauce, 115-6
Burnt Honey Ice Cream, 254-5

Butter:
  Green, 81, 140
  Lemon, 80
  Maitre d'hôtel, 100
  Roquefort, 95
  Seasoned, 167-8
  Snail, 88
Buttered Peas Elysées, 211

Cabbage:
  Winter Salad, 224
Cakes:
  American Strawberry Shortcake, 258
  Bûche de Noël, 269-71
  Chilled Lemon Tartlets, 275-6
  Chocolate Tile, 264-6
  English Cherry Pie, 278-9
  French Pear Tart, 277-8
  French Walnut Roll, 268-9
  Gâteau Esternel, 260
  Gâteau Tropezienne, 261-2
  Mr Carrier's Chocolate Fancy, 262-4
  Pears in Pastry Sabayon, 276-7
  Profiteroles with Chocolate Sauce, 273-4
  Provençal Apple Tart, 274
  Rum Baba, 271-3
  Timbale of Glazed Fruit, 279-80
  Tulipe Glacé aux Fraises des Bois, 259
  Vacherin à l'Orange, 267-8
Cake Balls with Hot Fudge Sauce, 240
Calf's Liver with Sage and Avocado, 132
Carbonnade of Beef, 111
Carciofi alla Romana, 27-8
Carrots:
  Glazed, 111-2
  Little Carrot Towers, 208
  Pea, Sweetcorn or Carrot Purée, 216-7
Cauliflower:
  French Fried, 206-7
  Ceylonese Chicken Curry, 179-80
Chablis, Pears in, 236
Champagne:
  Fruit Salad, 234
  Peaches in, 232
  Turbot au, 82
Châteaubriand, 100-2
Cheese:
  Breadcrumb Browned Brussels Sprouts au Gratin, 205-6
  and Spring Onion Quiche, 45-6
  Pineapple Dessert, 255-6
  Délices au Gruyère, 41-2
  Gratin Dauphinois, 214-5
  Grilled Pork Chops with Mozzarella, 161-2
  Leeks au Gratin, 211
  Sauce, Rich, 206
  Roquefort Butter, 96
  Salade Paysanne II, 228
  Veal Escalopes Parmigiana, 124
  Veal Parmesan 'Four Seasons', 124

Cherries:
English Cherry Pie, 278-9
Jubilee, 239
Chicken:
à la Kiev, 167-8
Arancini, 63
Barry Wine's Marinated, 170-1
Boiled, and Rice, 176-7
Chopped Chicken Livers with Chicken Fat, 39
Consommé with Lemon Dumplings, 14-5
Country Fried, 166-7
Curried Chicken Liver Crescents, 38
Curry, Ceylonese, 179-80
Curry, Jamaican, 178
Grilled Spring, 171
Lemon Barbecued, 171
Old English Devilled, 166
Old Fashioned Roast, with Aromatic Stuffing, 168-70
Pie, Old English, 181-2
Pot Pie, 183-4
Poulet au Blanc, 174
Poulet aux Poivrons, 175
Roast, with Watercress Stuffing, 170
Singapore Rice Noodles, 62-3
with 40 Cloves of Garlic (*Poulet à l'Ail*), 174-5
Chicken livers:
and Pea Risotto, 61
Arancini, 63
Chopped, with Chicken Fat, 39
Crescents, Curried, 38
Chilled Lemon Tartlets, 275-6
Chile Con Carne, 118-9
Chinese Fried Rice with Prawns and Peppers, 61-2
Chinese Salad, 226
Chinese Steamed Scallops, 89
Chive Sauce, 92
Chocolate:
Barry Wine's Hot Chocolate Soufflé with Coffee Ice Cream, 250
Bûche de Noël, 269-71
Chocolate Butter Icing, 269-71
Chocolate Tile Cake, 264-6
Ice Cream, 253
Mr Carrier's Chocolate Fancy, 262-4
Profiteroles with Chocolate Sauce, 273-4
Sauce, 237, 273-4
Chopped Chicken Livers with Chicken Fat, 39
Citrus Salad, 224
Cod:
Aïoli Fifine, 84-5
Chowder, New England, 68-9
in Beer Batter 69-70
Steaks with Potato Balls, 70-1
Cold Duck with Orange Jelly, 189-90
Cold Parsleyed Ham, 37
Cold Sabayon with Kummel, 241
Coquilles St Jacques aux Herbes de Provence, 90
Corned Beef Hash with Poached Eggs, 109

Coriander:
Artichokes in White Wine with, 27
Corncakes, 99-100
Cotelettes 'Pojarsky', 129
Country Fricassée of Rabbit, 201
Country Fried Chicken, 166-7
Courgettes:
Coins, Crisp-fried, 208
Fredy Girardet's Charlottes d'Aubergines et de Courgettes aux Foies de Volaille, 40-1
Soufflés, 209
Couscous,
as a Vegetable, 219-20
Quick Fried, with Diced Vegetables, 220
Crab,
Dressed, 34
Crème Patissière, 238, 246-7, 261-2
Crème Saint Honoré, 274
Creole Jambalaya, 164
Crisp-fried Courgette Coins, 208
Cucumber,
and Nasturtium Leaf Salad, 225
Salad, Danish, 22
Scales, with Poached Salmon, 72-4
Thai Pork Satays with Peanut Sauce and Cucumber Relish, 154-5
Curried Chicken Liver Crescents, 38
Curry,
Ceylonese Chicken, 178-9
Chicken Liver Crescents, 38
Jamaican Chicken, 176-7
Side Dishes, 180

Danish Cucumber Salad, 22
Daube de Mouton, 151-2
Délices au Gruyère, 41-2
Denys Gentes' Duck with Fresh Figs and Wild Strawberries, 187-8
Denys Gentes' Raspberry Charlotte, 247-8
Diplomat au Kirsch, 246-7
Dressed Crab, 34
Duck:
Cold, with Orange Jelly, 189-90
Denys Gentes', with Fresh Figs and Wild Strawberries, 187-8
and Orange Salad, 191
with Sauerkraut and Apple Stuffing, 186-7
Grilled Magrets de Canards with Soy and Honey, 186
Magret de Canard au Cassis, 184-5
Dumplings:
Lemon, 14-5
with Bauernschmaus, 159

Eggs:
and Anchovy Barrels, 39
Cheese and Spring Onion Quiche, 45-6
Poached, with Corned Beef Hash, 109
Smoked Salmon Quiche, 46
English Cherry Pie, 278-9
English Trifle, 244

Fettucine alla Capricciosa, 52
Fillet of Beef:
en Cochonailles, 108-9

Glazed, with Soy, 106-7
Minute Sauté, with Burgundy Garnish, 115-7
Roast, 107-8
Figs:
Denys Gentes' Duck with Fresh Figs and Wild Strawberries, 187-8
Fingers of Turbot Amandine, 66-7
Fish and Shellfish:
Aïoli Fifine, 84-5
Baked English Trout with Bacon, 78
Baked Fish Spanish Style, 83
Batter-fried Scallops, Prawns and Vegetables, 91
Brochette de Moules, 42-3
Chinese Steamed Scallops, 89
Cod in Beer Batter, 69-70
Cod Steaks with Potato Balls, 70-1
Coquilles St Jacques aux Herbes de Provence, 90
Dressed Crab, 34
Egg and Anchovy Barrels, 39
Fingers of Turbot Amandine, 66-7
Fish Souvlakia, 71
Fruits de Mer in Aspic, Sauce Verte, 35-6
Lobster a l'Americaine, 93-4
Medallions of Lobster with Chive Sauce, 92
Moroccan Grilled Fish with Chermoula, 66
Mussels Cooked Like Snails, 88
New England Cod Chowder, 68-9
Peppered Salmon Steaks, 74
Poached Salmon with Cucumber Scales, 72-4
Pot-au-Feu de Poissons, 85
Potted Shrimps or Prawns, 31
Quick Lobster Newburg, 93
Rich Lobster Soup, 19
Rillettes of Smoked Trout with Diced Vegetables, 31-2
Salade de Moules, 34-5
Smoked Fish Platter, 32-3
Smoked Salmon à la Russe, 33
Smoked Salmon Quiche, 46
Sole Soufflés with Asparagus, 75
Soupe de Poissons Fifine, 18-9
Spinach and Oyster Soup, 20
Tortillons of Sole, 76
Trout Père Louis, 77
Trout with Almonds (*Truite Amandine*), 77
Truite Fourrée au Fumet de Meursault, 78-9
Tuna Fish Sauce, 129
Turbot au Champagne, 82
Turbot en Brochettes, 80
Turbot with Green Butter, 81
Waterzoi of Seafood with the Zest and Juice of an Orange, 86-7
Fish Souvlakia, 71
Flemish Carbonnade of Beef, 113-4
Foie Gras:
Fonds d'Artichauts au, 26-7
Fondant de Volailles, 47-8
Fonds d'Artichauts au Foie Gras, 26-7

Fredy Girardet's Charlottes d'Aubergines et
de Courgettes aux Foies de Volaille, 40-1
French Dressing, 222
French Fried Cauliflower, 206-7
French Pear Tart, 277-8
French Pea Soup with Vegetable Mosaic,
12-3
French Walnut Roll, 268-9
Fresh Asparagus Hollandaise, 23-4
Fresh Lettuce Soup, 14
Fresh Peaches Romanoff, 233
Fruit:
Bread and Butter Pudding a l'Orange,
245-6
Champagne Fruit Salad, 234
Cheese Pineapple Dessert, 255-6
Chilled Lemon Tartlets, 275-7
Citrus Salad, 224
Cold Duck with Orange Jelly, 189-90
Denys Gentes' Duck with Fresh Figs and
Wild Strawberries, 187-8
Denys Gentes' Raspberry Charlotte, 247-8
Duck and Orange Salad, 191
Duck with Sauerkraut and Apple Stuffing,
186-7
English Trifle, 244
Fresh Peaches Romanoff, 233
Glazed Pigeons with Grapes, 194
Greek Orange and Black Olive Salad, 22
Grilled Gammon Steaks with Grapefruit,
163
Guinea Fowl with Exotic Fruits, 194
Guinea Fowl with Pears, 196
in a Blanket, 235
Little Green Apples, 232
Little Summer Fruit Towers, 248-9
Magret de Canard au Cassis, 184-5
Mrs Moxon's Lemon Posset, 242
Orange Beetroot, 204
Orange Gravy, 190-2
Osso Buco à l'Orange, 136
Peaches in Champagne, 232-3
Pears Belle Hélène, 237
Pears in Chablis, 236
Poire Vefour, 238
Pot Roast of Pork with Grapes, 156-7
Provençal Apple Tart, 274
Roast Turkey and Orange Gravy, 190-2
Sangria Fruit Salad, 234
Soupe Exotique, 251
Summer Pudding, 236
Vacherin a l'Orange, 267-8
Waterzoi of Seafood with the Zest and
Juice of an Orange, 86-7
Fruits de Mer in Aspic, Sauce Verte, 35-6

Game:
Country Fricassée of Rabbit, 201
Gilbert Harding's Roast Grouse, 198
Glazed Pigeons with Grapes, 194
Jean-Pierre's Mustard Rabbit, 201-2
Mother's Fried Rabbit, 202
Pheasant with Green Apples, 200
Pigeon Prince Rainier III, 193-4
Roast Grouse, 197

Roast Partridge, 199
Venison Steaks in the Pan, 202
Garlic:
Aïoli Fifine, 84-5
Barry Wine's Marinated Chicken, 172-3
Chicken with 40 Cloves of (*Poulet à l'Ail*),
174-5
Spaghetti with Oil and, 50
Gâteau Esternel, 260
Gâteau Tropézienne, 261-2
Gazpacho (Cold Vegetable) Soup, 12
Gazpacho Salad, 28
German Veal with Almonds, 125
Gilbert Harding's Roast Grouse, 198
Ginger:
Fresh, with Japanese Beef, 115
Ice Cream, 252
Glace de Viande, 100-1
Glazed Fillet of Beef with Soy, 106-7
Glazed Pigeons with Grapes, 194
Gnocchi alla Romana, 58-9
Grapefruit:
Grilled Gammon Steaks with, 163
Grapes:
Pot Roast of Pork with, 156-7
Glazed Pigeons with, 194
Gratin Dauphinois, 214-15
Greek Lemon Potatoes, 213
Greek Orange and Black Olive Salad, 22
Green Bean Dressing, 229
Green Butter, 81
Grilled Gammon Steaks with Grapefruit, 163
Grilled Magrets de Canards with Soy and
Honey, 186
Grilled Marinated Lamb Chops with Green
Butter, 140-1
Grilled Pork Chops with Mozzarella, 161-2
Grilled Spring Chicken, 171
Grilled Steaks with Roquefort Butter, 96
Grouse:
Gilbert Harding's Roast Grouse, 198
Roast Grouse, 197
Gruyère:
Cheese and Spring Onion Quiche, 45-6
Délices au, 41-2
Guinea Fowl:
Guinea Fowl with Exotic Fruits, 194
Guinea Fowl with Pears, 196

Halibut:
Fish Souvlakia, 71-2
Ham:
Cold Parsleyed, 37
Creole Jambalaya, 164
Grilled Gammon Steaks with Grapefruit,
163
Haricots Blancs en Salade, 25-6
Haricots Verts en Persillade, 210
Homemade Sausage Patties, 163
Honey:
Grilled Magrets de Canard with Soy and,
186
Burnt Honey Ice Cream, 254-5
Horseradish Chantilly, 33
Hungarian Veal Gulyas, 136-7

Ice Cream:
Barry Wine's Hot Chocolate Soufflé with
Coffee Ice Cream, 250
Burnt Honey Ice Cream, 254-5
Cake Balls with Hot Fudge Sauce, 240
Chocolate, 253
Ginger, 252
Roman Ice Punch, 254
Vanilla Parfait, 252
Icing:
Chocolate Butter, 269-71
Vanilla Butter, 269-71
Indonesian Lamb Roast, 145-6
Irish Stew, 148
Italian Green Rice, 60
Italian Mushroom Sauce, 57-8
Italian Pork Roast, 156
Italian Stuffed Pepper Appetiser, 29-30

Jamaican Chicken Curry, 178
Japanese Beef with Fresh Ginger, 115
Javanese Satay Sauce, 145
Jean-Pierre's Mustard Rabbit, 201-2
Juniper Berries, Guinea Fowl with, 195-6

Lamb:
Daube de Mouton, 151-2
Fettucine alla Capricciosa, 52
Chops, Grilled Marinated, with Green
Butter, 140-1
Indonesian Roast, 145-6
Irish Stew, 148
in Greek Pastry, 142-3
Lancashire Hot Pot, 148-9
Moroccan Skewered, 140
Quick Sauté of, 141-2
Rack of, in Pastry with Walnuts, 144-5
Rack of Persillé, 144
Ragout of, 150
Roast Leg of, Boulangère, 146
Roast Saddle of Lamb à l'Arlesienne,
146-7
Scots Hotch Potch, 149
Lasagne Bolognese, 54-6
La Soupe au Pistou, 17
Leeks:
à la Vinaigrette, 210
au Gratin, 211
Vernon Jarratt's Leek and Pumpkin Soup,
16
Lemon:
Barbecue Sauce, 171
Barbecued Chicken, 171
Butter, 80
Posset, Mrs Moxon's, 242
Potatoes, Greek, 213
Tartlets, Chilled, 275-7
Lettuce:
Chinese Salad, 226
Fresh Lettuce Soup, 14
Salade Paysanne I, 227
Salade Paysanne II, 228
St Tropez Salad, 227
Tossed Green Salad, 222
Tossed Green Salad with Avocado, 223

Tossed Green Salad with Herbs, 223
Little Broccoli Towers, 207
Little Carrot Towers, 208
Little Green Apples, 232
Little Summer Fruit Towers, 248-9
Little Vegetable Packets, 217-8
Lobster:
  à l'Americaine, 93-4
  Medallions of, with Chive Sauce, 92
  Newburg, Quick, 93
  Soup, Rich, 19
Loin of Pork Boulangère, 160

Maître d'hôtel Butter, 100
Magret de Canard au Cassis, 184-5
Marinades:
  Barry Wine's Chicken, 170-1
  Chermoula, 66
  Cod, 70-71
  Fresh Ginger, 114
  Pot Roast of Pork, 156-7
  Soy, 106-7
  Soy-Honey, 185
Medallions of Lobster with Chive Sauce, 92
Minute Provençal Tarts, 38
Minute Sauté of Beef with Burgundy
    Garnish, 115-17
Moroccan Grilled Fish with Chermoula, 66
Moroccan Skewered Lamb, 140
Mother's Fried Rabbit, 202
Mr Carrier's Chocolate Fancy, 262-4
Mrs Moxon's Lemon Posset, 242
Mushrooms:
  à la Bordelaise, 112
  Cream Sauce, Italian, 54-6
  Duxelles, 143
  Grilled, with Pork Tournedos, 161
  Salad, Raw, 23
  Sauce, Italian, with Polenta, 57-8
Mussels:
  Brochette de Moules, 42-3
  Cooked like Snails, 88
  Salade de Moules, 34-5
Mustard:
  and Herb Dressing, 224
  Rabbit, Jean-Pierre's, 201-2
  Vinaigrette, 31-2

Nasturtium
  Leaf Salad, Cucumber and, 225
New England Cod Chowder, 68
Nine Herb Salad of Hintlesham, 225
No-Roast Roast Beef, 102-3

Oeufs à la Neige, 242-3
Old English Chicken Pie, 181-2
Old English Devilled Chicken, 166
Old English Roast Beef with Yorkshire
    Pudding, 103-5
Old Fashioned Roast Chicken with Aromatic
    Stuffing, 168-70
Olives:
  Greek Orange and Black Olive Salad, 22

Oranges:
  Beetroot, 204
  Bread and Butter Pudding à l', 245-6
  Citrus Salad, 224
  Gravy 190-2
  Greek Orange and Black Olive Salad, 22
  Gremolata, Beef with 'Pappardelle' and,
    121-2
  Jelly, Cold Duck with, 189-90
  Osso Buco l'Orange, 136
  Salad, Duck and, 191
  Vacherin à l'Orange, 267-8
  Waterzoi of Seafood with the Zest and
    Juice of, 86-7
Osso Buco à l'Orange, 136

Pan-Fried Escalopes of Veal Savoyarde,
    123-4
Pan-Fried Veal Chops 'Grandmère', 128
Parsley:
  Ham, Cold, 37
  Italian Green Rice, 60
Partridge:
  Roast, 199
Pasta:
  Fettucine alla Capricciosa, 52
  Gnocchi alla Romana, 58-9
  Lasagne Bolognese, 54-6
  e Fagioli, 56-7
  Penne alla Carbonara, 53-4
  Beef with 'Pappardelle' and Orange
    Gremolata, 121-2
  Spaghetti with Meat Balls (New York
    Style), 50-1
  Spaghetti with Oil and Garlic, 50
  Trenette col Pesto (Noodles with Italian
    Basil Sauce), 53
Pasta e Fagioli, 56-7
Pastry:
  Cheese and Spring Onion Quiche, 45-6
  Chicken Pot Pie, 183-4
  Chilled Lemon Tartlets, 275-6
  Curried Chicken Liver Crescents 38
  English Cherry Pie, 278-9
  French Pear Tart, 277-8
  Fillet of Beef en Cochonailles, 108-9
  Fondant de Volailles, 46-7
  Lamb in Greek Pastry, 142-3
  Minute Provençal Tarts, 38
  Old English Chicken Pie, 181-2
  Pears in Pastry Sabayon, 276-7
  Pissaladière, 44
  Profiteroles with Chocolate Sauce, 273-4
  Provençal Apple Tart, 274
  Rack of Lamb in Pastry with Walnuts,
    144-5
  Smoked Salmon Quiche, 46
  Timbale of Glazed Fruit, 279-80
Peanuts:
  Thai Pork Satays with Peanut Sauce and
    Cucumber Relish, 154-5
Pears:
  Belle Hélène, 237
  Guinea Fowl with, 196
  in Chablis, 236

Poire Vefour, 238-9
Tart, French 277-8
Pea, Sweetcorn or Carrot Purée, 216-7
Peas:
  Elysées, Buttered, 211
  Pea, Sweetcorn or Carrot Puree, 216-7
  Purée Saint-Germain, 212
  Risotto, and Chicken Livers, 61
  Roman, 212
  Soup, French, 12-13
Peaches:
  in Champagne, 232-3
  Romanoff, Fresh, 233
Pears Belle Hélène, 237
Penne alla Carbonara, 53-4
Peppered Salmon Steaks, 74
Peppers:
  Appetiser, Italian Stuffed, 29-30
  Chinese Fried Rice with Prawn and, 61
  Salad, Provençal, 28-9
Persillade of Green Beans, 24-5
Pheasant with Green Apples, 200
Pickled Salmon à la Russe, 33
Pies:
  Chicken Pot, 183-4
  English Cherry Pie, 278-9
  Old English Chicken Pie, 181-2
Pigeon:
  Prince Rainier III, 193-4
  Glazed, with Grapes, 194
Pissaladière, 44
Pistou, La Soupe au, 17
Pizzaiola Sauce, 98
Poached Salmon with Cucumber Scales, 72-
Poire Vefour, 238-9
Polenta with Italian Mushroom Sauce, 57-8
Pommes de Terre Duchesse, 215
Pommes Fifine, 214
Pommes Sarladaises, 215
Pommes Soufflées, 216
Pork:
  Bauernschmaus, 159
  Chops Ardennaise, 160-1
  Cold Parsleyed Ham, 37
  Cooked like Game, 158
  Creole Jamb.alaya, 164
  Grilled Chops with Mozzarella, 161-2
  Grilled Gammon Steaks with Grapefruit,
    163
  Homemade Sausage Patties, 163
  Italian Pork Roast, 156
  Lasagne Bolognese, 54-6
  Loin of, Boulangère, 160
  Pot Roast of, with Grapes, 156-7
  Singapore Rice Noodles, 62-3
  Thai Pork Satays with Peanut Sauce and
    Cucumber Relish, 154-5
  Tournedos with Grilled Mushrooms, 161
Porterhouse Steak with Pizzaiola Sauce, 98
Potatoes:
  Balls, with Cod Steaks, 70-1
  Chips, Super, 213
  Chips, Sweet, 172-3
  Gratin Dauphinois, 214-5
  Greek Lemon, 213

Pommes de Terre Duchesse, 215
Pommes Fifine, 214
Pommes Sarladaises, 215
Pommes Soufflées, 216
Pot Roast of Pork with Grapes, 156-7
Pot-au-Feu de Poissons, 85
Potted Shrimps or Prawns, 31
Potted Tournedoes, 105
Poulet au Blanc, 176
Poulet aux Poivrons, 175
Poultry:
  Barry Wine's Marinated Chicken, 172-3
  Boiled Chicken and Rice, 176-7
  Ceylonese Chicken Curry, 179-80
  Chicken à la Kiev, 167-8
  Chicken Consommé with Lemon
    Dumplings, 14-15
  Chicken Pot Pie, 183-4
  Chicken with 40 Cloves of Garlic
    (*Poulet à l'ail*), 174-5
  Chopped Chicken Livers with Chicken
    Fat, 39
  Country Fried Chicken, 166-7
  Curried Chicken Liver Crescents, 38
  Grilled Spring Chicken, 171
  Guinea Fowl with Exotic Fruits, 194
  Guinea Fowl with Pears, 196
  Jamaican Chicken Curry, 178
  Lemon Barbecued Chicken, 171
  Old English Chicken Pie, 181-2
  Old English Devilled Chicken, 166
  Old Fashioned Roast Chicken with
    Aromatic Stuffing, 168-70
  Poulet au Blanc, 176
  Poulet aux Poivrons, 175
  Roast Chicken with Watercress Stuffing,
    170
  Roast Turkey with Orange Gravy, 191-3
Prawns:
  and Peppers, Chinese Fried Rice and, 61-2
  and Vegetables, with Batter fried Scallops,
    91
  Potted Shrimps or, 31
  Singapore Rice Noodles, 62-3
Profiteroles with Chocolate Sauce, 273-4
Provençal Apple Tart, 274
Provençal Pepper Salad, 28-9
Prunes:
  Tagine of Beef with Prunes and Almonds,
    114
Pumpkin:
  Soup, Argentinian, 16-7
  Soup, Vernon Jarratt's Leek and, 16
Purée Saint-Germain, 212

Quiche:
  Cheese and Spring Onion, 45-6
  Smoked Salmon, 46
Quick Fried Couscous with Diced
  Vegetables, 220
Quick Lobster Newburg, 93
Quick Sauté of Lamb, 141-2
Quick Stir-Fried Vegetables, 218
Quick Tartare Sauce, 67

Rabbit:
  Country Fricassée of, 201
  Jean-Pierre's Mustard, 201-2
  Mother's Fried, 202
Rack of Lamb in Pastry with Walnuts, 144-5
Rack of Lamb Persillé, 144
Ragout of Lamb, 150
Raspberries:
  Charlotte, Denys Gentes', 247-8
  Little Summer Fruit Towers, 248-9
Raw Mushroom Salad, 23
Raw Spinach Salad, 226
Raw Tomato Sauce, 127
Rice:
  Arancini (Little Rice Balls), 64
  Boiled Chicken and, 174-5
  Chicken Liver and Pea Risotto, 61
  Chinese Fried, with Prawns and Peppers,
    61-2
  Italian Green, 60
  Risotto Milanese, 60
  Riz à la Basquaise 62-3
  Saffron, 59
  Saffron, with Avocado, 59
  Singapore Rice Noodles, 62-3
Rich Lobster Soup, 19
Rillettes of Smoked Trout with Diced
  Vegetables, 31-2
Risotto Milanese, 60
Riz à la Basquaise, 63
Roast Chicken with Watercress Stuffing, 170
Roast Fillet of Beef, 107-8
Roast Grouse, 197
Roast Leg of Lamb Boulangère, 146
Roast Partridge, 199
Roast Saddle of Lamb à l'Arlésienne, 146-7
Roast Turkey with Orange Gravy, 191-3
Roman Ice Punch, 254
Roman Peas, 212
Rum Baba, 271-3

Saffron Rice, 59
Saffron Rice with Avocado, 59
Salads:
  Chinese, 226
  Citrus, 224
  Cucumber and Nasturtium Leaf, 225
  Danish Cucumber, 22
  Gazpacho, 28
  Greek Orange and Black Olive, 22
  Green Bean, 229
  Green, Variations, 222
  Haricots Blancs en Salade, 25-6
  Nine Herb Salad of Hintlesham, 225
  Provençal Pepper, 28-9
  Raw Mushroom, 23
  Raw Spinach, 226
  Salade de Moules, 34-5
  Salade de Tomates à la Crème, 25
  Salade Fermière, 230
  Salade Japonaise, 230
  Salade Jardinière, 230
  Salade Mexicaine, 230
  Salade Paysanne I, 227
  Salade Paysanne II, 228

Salade Paysanne, 230
Salade Provençale, 230
Salade Tricolore, 230
Salade, Gitane, 230
Salades Composées, 229-30
Sangria Fruit, 234
St Tropez, 227
Tossed Green, 222
Tossed Green, with Avocado, 223
Tossed Green, with Herbs, 223
Winter, 224
Salad Dressings:
  French, 28, 222, 227
  Herb, 28-9
  Mustard and Herb, 224
  Mustard Vinaigrette, 31-2
  Vinaigrette, for Green Bean Salad, 229
Salade de Moules, 34-5
Salade de Tomates à la Crème, 25
Salade Fermière, 230
Salade Japonaise, 230
Salade Jardinière, 230
Salade Mexicaine, 230
Salade Paysanne I, 227
Salade Paysanne II, 228
Salade Paysanne, 230
Salade Provençale, 230
Salade Tricolore, 230
Salade, Gitane, 230
Salades Composées, 229-30
Salmon,
  (see also Smoked Salmon)
  Poached, with Cucumber Scales, 72-4
  Quiche, Smoked, 46
  Smoked, à la Russe, 33
  Steaks, Peppered, 74
Saltimbocca all'Alfredo, 123
Sangria Fruit Salad, 234
Satays:
  Sauce, Javanese, 145-6
  Thai Pork, with Peanut Sauce and
Cucumber Relish, 154-5
Sauces:
  *Savoury*
  Aïoli, 84-5, 170-1
  Basic Chicken Velouté, 182
  Basic Fish Velouté, 182
  Basic Velouté, 182
  Béarnaise, 42-3
  Burgundy (Bourguignonne), 115-6
  Châteaubriand, 100-1
  Chive, 92
  Cream, 174-5, 177
  Hollandaise, 23-4
  Horseradish Chantilly, 33
  Italian Mushroom, 57-8
  Italian Mushroom Cream, 54-6
  Javanese Satay, 145-6
  Lemon Barbecue Sauce, 171
  Pizzaiola, 98
  Quick Tartare, 67
  Raw Tomato, 127
  Rich Cheese, 206
  Sour Cream Tartare, 67
  Thai Peanut, 154-5

Tomato, 83
Tuna Fish, 120
Verte, 35-6
*Sweet*
  Burnt Honey, 254-5
  Chocolate, 237, 273-4
  Hot Fudge, 240
  Sabayon, 276-7
Sauerkraut:
  and Apple Stuffing, Duck with, 186-7
Sausages:
  Patties, Homemade, 163
Scallops:
  Batter-fried, with Prawns and Vegetables, 91
  Chinese Steamed, 89
  Coquilles St Jacques aux Herbes de Provence, 90
Scots Hotch Potch, 149
Sea bream:
  Moroccan Grilled Fish with Chermoula, 66
Seasoned Butter, 167-8
Shellfish:
  *see* Fish and Shellfish
Shrimp:
  *see* Prawns
Singapore Rice Noodles, 62-3
Smoked Fish Platter, 32-3
Smoked Salmon
  (*see also* Salmon)
  à la Russe, 33
  Quiche, 46
Sole:
  Soufflés with Asparagus, 75
  Tortillons of, 76
Soufflés:
  Barry Wine's Hot Chocolate, with Coffee Ice Cream 250
  Courgette, 209
  Sole, with Asparagus, 75
Soupe de Poissons 'Fifine', 18-9
Soupe Exotique, 251
Soups:
  Argentinian Pumpkin, 16-7
  Chicken Consommé with Lemon Dumplings, 14-5
  French Pea, with Vegetable Mosaic, 12-3
  Fresh Lettuce Soup, 14
  Gazpacho (Cold Vegetable), 12
  La Soupe au Pistou, 17
  New England Cod Chowder, 68
  Rich Lobster, 19
  Soupe de Poissons 'Fifine', 18-9
  Soupe Exotique, 251
  Spinach and Oyster, 20
  Vernon Jarratt's Leek and Pumpkin, 16
  Watercress Vichyssoise, 18
  Zuppa di Fagioli, 15
Sour Cream Tartare Sauce, 67
Spaghetti with Meat Balls (New York Style), 50-1
Spaghetti with Oil and Garlic, 50

Spinach:
  and Oyster Soup, 20
  Salad, Raw 226
Spring Onions:
  Quiche, Cheese and, 45-6
St Tropez Salad, 227
Starters:
  Artichoke Hearts à la Grecque, 30
  Artichokes in White Wine with Coriander, 27
  Brochette de Moules, 42-3
  Carciofi alla Romana, 27-8
  Cheese and Spring Onion Quiche, 45-6
  Chopped Chicken Livers with Chicken Fat, 39
  Cold Parsleyed Ham, 37
  Curried Chicken Liver Crescents, 38
  Danish Cucumber Salad, 22
  Délices au Gruyère, 41-2
  Dressed Crab, 34
  Egg and Anchovy Barrels, 39
  Fondant de Volailles, 47-8
  Fonds d'Artichauts au Foie Gras, 26-7
  Fredy Girardet's Charlottes d'Aubergines et de Courgettes aux Foies de Volaille, 40-1
  Fresh Asparagus Hollandaise, 23-4
  Fruits de Mer in Aspic, Sauce Verte, 35-6
  Gazpacho Salad, 28
  Greek Orange and Black Olive Salad, 22
  Haricots Blancs en Salade, 25-6
  Italian Stuffed Pepper Appetiser, 29-30
  Minute Provençal Tarts, 38
  Pickled Salmon à la Russe, 33
  Pissaladière, 44
  Potted Shrimps or Prawns, 31
  Provençal Pepper Salad, 28-9
  Raw Mushroom Salad, 23
  Rillettes of Smoked Trout with Diced Vegetables, 31-2
  Salade de Moules, 34-5
  Salade de Tomates à la Crème, 25
  Smoked Fish Platter, 32-3
  Smoked Salmon Quiche, 46
Steak:
  American Planked, 97
  and Kidney Pudding, 110-1
  au Tapis Vert, 99
  Bœuf à la Ficelle, 105
  Châteaubriand, 100-1
  Grilled with Roquefort Butter, 96
  Peppered Salmon, 74
  Porterhouse, with Pizzaiola Sauce, 98
  Potted Tournedos, 105
  Tournedos with Corncakes, 99-100
  Venison Steaks in the Pan, 202
Stir-Fried Vegetable Variations, 218
Strawberries:
  Shortcake, American, 258
  Denys Gentes' Duck with Fresh Figs and Wild Strawberries, 187-8
  Little Summer Fruit Towers, 248-9
  Tulipe Glacé aux Fraises des Bois, 259
Stuffed Breast of Veal Provençale, 137-8
Stuffing:
  Aromatic, 168-9

Guinea Fowl, 194
Sauerkraut and Apple, 186-7
Veal, 137-8
Watercress, 170
Summer Pudding, 236
Super Potato Chips, 213
Sweetcorn:
  Corncakes, 99-100
  Pea, Sweetcorn or Carrot Purée, 216-7
Sweet Potato Chips, 172-3
Sweets and Puddings:
  Barry Wine's Hot Chocolate Soufflé with Coffee Ice Cream, 250
  Bread and Butter Pudding à l'Orange, 245-6
  Burnt Honey Ice Cream, 254-5
  Cake Balls with Hot Fudge Sauce, 240
  Champagne Fruit Salad, 234
  Cheese Pineapple Dessert, 255-6
  Cherries Jubilee, 239
  Chocolate Ice Cream, 253
  Cold Sabayon with Kummel, 241
  Denys Gentes' Raspberry Charlotte, 247-8
  Diplomat au Kirsch, 246-7
  English Trifle, 244
  Fresh Peaches Romanoff, 233
  Fruit in a Blanket, 235
  Ginger Ice Cream, 252
  Little Green Apples, 232
  Little Summer Fruit Towers, 248-9
  Mrs Moxon's Lemon Posset, 242
  Oeufs à la Neige, 242-3
  Peaches in Champagne, 232-3
  Pears Belle Hélène, 237
  Pears in Chablis, 236
  Poire Vefour, 238-9
  Roman Ice Punch, 254
  Sangria Fruit Salad, 234
  Soupe Exotique, 251
  Summer Pudding, 236
  Timbale of Glazed Fruit, 279-80
  Tulipe Glacé aux Fraises des Bois, 259
  Vacherin à l'Orange, 267-8
  Vanilla Parfait, 253
  Zuppa Inglese, 244

Tagine of Beef with Prunes and Almonds, 114
Tartare Sauce:
  Quick, 67
  Sour Cream, 67
Thai Peanut Sauce, 154-5
Thai Pork Satays with Peanut Sauce and Cucumber Relish, 154-5
Timbale of Glazed Fruit, 279-80
Tomatoes:
  Pissaladière, 44
  Sauce, Raw, 127
  Salade de Tomates à la Creme, 25
Tortillons of Sole, 76
Tossed Green Salad, 222
Tossed Green Salad with Avocado, 223
Tossed Green Salad with Herbs, 223
Tournedos with Corncakes, 99-100

Trenette col Pesto (Noodles with Italian Basil Sauce), 53
Trifle:
  English, 244
Trout:
  Baked English, with Bacon, 78
  Smoked Rillettes of, with Diced Vegetables, 31-2
  Père Louis, 77
  with Almonds (*Truite Amandine*), 77
  Truite Fourrée au Fumet de Meursault, 78-9
Trout Père Louis, 77
Trout with Almonds (*Truite Amandine*), 77
Truite Fourrée au Fumet de Meursault, 78-9
Tulipe Glacé aux Fraises des Bois, 259
Tuna:
  Sauce, 129
Turbot:
  Amandine, Fingers of, 66-7
  au Champagne, 82
  en Brochettes, 80
  with Green Butter, 81
Turkey:
  Roast, with Orange Gravy, 191-3

Vacherin à l'Orange, 267-8
Vanilla:
  Butter Icing, 269-71
  Parfait, 252
Veal:
  Alain Senderens' Rognons de Veau aux Echalotes Rôties, 132-4
  Avesnoise, 130
  Blanquette de, 134-5
  Calf's Liver with Sage and Avocado, 132
  Cotelettes 'Pojarsky', 129
  Escalopes Parmigiana, 126
  German, with Almonds, 125
  Gulyas, Hungarian, 136-7
  Osso Buco à l'Orange, 136
  Pan-Fried Chops 'Grandmère', 128
  Parmesan 'Four Seasons', 124
  Provençale, Stuffed Breast of, 137-8
  Saltimbocca all'Alfredo, 123
  Savoyarde, Pan-Fried Escalopes of, 123-4

Vitello Tonnato, 130-1
Wiener Schnitzel, 127-8
Vegetables:
  Argentinian Pumpkin Soup, 16-17
  Artichoke Hearts à la Grecque, 30
  Artichokes in White Wine with Coriander, 27
  Batter-fried Scallops, Prawns and Vegetables, 91
  Breadcrumb Browned Brussels Sprouts au Gratin, 205
  Brussels Sprouts à la Polonaise, 204
  Brussels Sprouts with Buttered Breadcrumbs, 205
  Buttered Peas Elysées, 211
  Carciofi alla Romana, 27-8
  Corncakes, 99-100
  Courgette Soufflés, 209
  Couscous as a Vegetable, 219-20
  Crisp-fried Courgette Coins, 208
  Danish Cucumber Salad, 22
  Fonds d'Artichauts au Foie Gras, 26-7
  Fredy Girardet's Charlottes d'Aubergines et de Courgettes aux Foies de Volaille, 40-1
  French Fried Cauliflower, 206-7
  French Pea Soup, 12-13
  Fresh Asparagus Hollandaise, 23-4
  Fresh Lettuce Soup, 14
  Gazpacho Salad, 28
  Gazpacho Soup, 12
  Glazed Carrots, 111-12
  Gratin Dauphinois, 214-15
  Greek Lemon Potatoes, 213
  Greek Orange and Black Olive Salad, 22
  Haricots Blancs en Salade, 25-6
  Haricots Verts en Persillade, 210
  Italian Stuffed Pepper Appetiser, 29-30
  Leeks à la Vinaigrette, 210
  Leeks au Gratin, 211
  Little Broccoli Towers, 207
  Little Carrot Towers, 208
  Little Vegetable Packets, 217-18
  Minute Provençal Tarts, 37
  Orange Beetroot, 204
  Pea, Sweetcorn or Carrot Purée, 216-7
  Persillade of Green Beans, 24-5

Pommes de Terre Duchesse, 215
Pommes Fifine, 214
Pommes Sarladaises, 215
Pommes Soufflées, 216
Provençal Pepper Salad, 28-9
Purée Saint-Germain, 212
Quick Fried Couscous with Diced Vegetables, 220
Quick Stir-Fried Vegetables, 218
Raw Mushroom Salad, 23
Rillettes of Smoked Trout with Diced Vegetables, 31-2
Roman Peas, 212
Salade de Tomates à la Creme, 25
Spinach and Oyster Soup, 20
Super Potato Chips, 213
Sweet Potato Chips, 172-3
Stir-Fried Vegetable Variations, 218
Vernon Jarratt's Leek and Pumpkin Soup, 16
Watercress Vichyssoise, 18
Velouté, Basic, 182
Velouté, Basic Chicken, 182
Velouté, Basic Fish, 182
Venison Steaks in the Pan, 202
Vernon Jarratt's Leek and Pumpkin Soup, 16
Vinaigrette Dressing, for Green Bean Salad, 229
Vitello Tonnato, 130-1

Walnuts:
  Rack of Lamb in Pastry with, 144-5
  Roll, French, 268-9
Watercress:
  Vichyssoise, 18
  Stuffing, Roast Chicken with, 170
Waterzoi of Seafood with the Zest and Juice of an Orange, 86-7
Wiener Schnitzel, 127-8
Winter Salad, 224

Yankee Pot Roast, 119-20
Yorkshire Pudding, 103-4

Zuppa di Fagioli, 15
Zuppa Inglese, 243